ACCOUNTING THOUGHT AND PRACTICE THROUGH THE YEARS

Edited by Richard P. Brief

A Garland Series

KREUGER
GENIUS AND SWINDLER

Robert Shaplen

Garland Publishing, Inc.
New York and London
1986

For a complete list of Garland's publications in accounting,
please see the final pages of this volume.

Library of Congress Cataloging-in-Publication Data

Shaplen, Robert, 1917–
Kreuger, genius and swindler.

(Accounting thought and practice through the years)
Reprint. Originally published: 1st ed. New York :
Knopf, 1960.
Includes index.
1. Kreuger, Ivar, 1880–1932.   2. Svenska
tändsticks AB—History.   3. Kreuger & Toll—History.
4. Sveriges riksbank—History.   5. Commercial criminals—
Sweden—Biography.   6. Swindlers and swindling—
Sweden—Biography.   7. International finance—Corrupt
practices—History.   8. Match industry—History.
I. Title.   II. Series.
HD9999.M22K747   1986   338.7′6625′0924 [B]   86-11958
ISBN 0-8240-7887-X

Design by Bonnie Goldsmith

The volumes in this series are printed on
acid-free, 250-year-life paper.

Printed in the United States of America

BOOKS BY

ROBERT SHAPLEN

Kreuger: GENIUS AND SWINDLER   [1960]

A Forest of Tigers   [1956]

Free Love and Heavenly Sinners   [1954]

A Corner of the World   [1949]

These are BORZOI BOOKS,
published in NEW YORK by ALFRED A. KNOPF

KREUGER

Genius and Swindler

KREUGER

Genius and Swindler

B Y

ROBERT SHAPLEN

WITH AN INTRODUCTION BY

John Kenneth Galbraith

ALFRED · A · KNOPF   NEW YORK

1960

Introduction

John Kenneth Galbraith

I FIRST HEARD of Ivar Kreuger when I went to Harvard as a young instructor in the mid-thirties. Through the agency of Lee, Higginson and Company, an investment banking firm of impeccable reputation, he had taken an astonishing number of the very best people for a cleaning. Thieves, like lawyers, haberdashers, and New York restaurateurs, are concerned about their clientele, and not since John Law had anyone kept larceny on a more aristocratic level. Beacon Street and all the Marquand suburbs, as a result, subscribed heavily to Kreuger and Toll.

My next encounter with Kreuger was five or six years ago when I was working on a history of the 1929 crash. Most of the financial titans who brought, and came to, grief at that time turned out on closer examination to be rather poor types. The speculation and theft of Richard Whitney of the Stock Exchange had a juvenile, rather pathetic quality about it—it was symbolic that his biggest mistake was a company that made applejack. Charles Mitchell the banker, Cutten the speculator, and Meehan the market operator seem to have been inflated mostly by the boom they were riding. When that collapsed, so, more or less, did they. The single exception in this rather commonplace parade was Ivar Kreuger. He was, by all odds, the biggest

thief in the long history of larceny—a man who could
think of embezzlement in terms of hundreds of millions.
This suggested some new and commanding talents. And
not only did he filch from the very top drawer but, somewhat inconsistently, he wanted to be well regarded by the
rich and well-born. The feeling that he was about to lose
the good opinion of his victims had much to do with his
tormented end. A socially less conscious crook would have
gone off to jail and not without some interesting matters to
occupy his mind. As well as being the most interesting man,
Kreuger was also the least known. I resolved to write a
book about him someday.

Such affirmations have been fairly numerous, and this
one I have abandoned with better conscience than most.
For in this admirable volume Robert Shaplen has done the
whole job. He has researched his subject with exemplary
care and, having provided himself with a wealth of material, he has used it with discrimination and restraint. Unlike one or two others who have written about Kreuger, he
has not slighted the story of Kreuger's financial transactions
on the grounds that they were too devious for the average
reader to understand. This, on occasion, may have been so.
But many of these transactions were also too deep for
Kreuger's own partners, his Swedish bankers, and the partners of Lee, Higginson. But they are also the story. It
would be wrong to write about a safecracker and slight his
methods as being too technical.

Mr. Keith Funston, the head of the New York Stock
Exchange, has recently been complaining about the low
state of economic and financial education in the United
States. Even if Mr. Funston is not the best source of this
criticism, I would certainly support him on any mature
effort at improvement. This should include recommending
Mr. Shaplen's study to everyone concerned with financial
matters and certainly to all who are concerned about the

reputation of the financial community. For the study drama-
tizes the three great weaknesses of that community, and no
one should imagine that they were confined in place and
time to New York of the twenties.

First of all, there is the tendency to confuse good man-
ners, good tailoring, and, above all, an impressive bearing
and speech with integrity and intelligence. Kreuger was an
extraordinarily competent actor who had discovered that a
quiet forceful manner plus the ability to remember and recite the latest banality about the international economic situation were sufficient to win him the respect of the very
best men. It cost them millions.

In this community also there is a troublesome and at
times disastrous interdependence. The honest man becomes
committed to the crook before he knows there is anything
wrong. Then he must protect him to protect himself or, in
the more usual case, refuse to believe there is anything
wrong. The Lee, Higginson partners were almost certainly
honest men. And while they were unduly impressionable,
they were, perhaps, not totally gullible. But after a certain
time they could no longer afford to believe that Kreuger
was a fraud. Despite repeated indications that there was
something rotten to the north of Denmark, they denied the
evidence of their eyes and ears. Finally came the pistol shot
in Paris.

Thirdly, there is the dangerous cliché that in the financial world everything depends on confidence. One could
better argue the importance of unremitting suspicion. Kreuger made his career by exploiting the men who had confidence; he was brought down by the men, especially the
relentless Berning, who were trained to take nothing for
granted. They would have got him earlier and with less
damage done if they had not been restrained by those who
thought it a betrayal of the canons of financial confidence
to ask questions.

The most important current lesson of Mr. Shaplen's book is here. Kreuger flourished during the boom years of the twenties; it is the nature of the boom that the men who have confidence and do not ask questions look with uneasiness on the suspicious men who do. And we may lay it down as an absolute rule that, given an excess of confidence, there will be confidence men to take advantage of it. One day we will find out who the current Kreugers are —I confess to doubt that they are on quite the same grand scale—though it would be more interesting and useful to know now.

In drawing this moral, incidentally, I am conscious that I may be doing Mr. Shaplen a disservice. His main aim in writing this book was to develop an important and fascinating piece of financial, economic, and social history. This he has done exceedingly well. While it may save some from the sinners, I hope that the book will not be overlooked by the sinners. Boiler-room operators, peddlers of stocks in the imaginary Canadian mines, mutual-fund managers whose genius and imagination are unconstrained by integrity, as well as all less exotic larcenists, should read about Kreuger. He was the Leonardo of their craft.

Author's Preface

THE STORY of Ivar Kreuger retains its fascination nearly three decades after his death. It will continue to be a subject of study and wonder in decades to come, not only because of the unusual personality of Kreuger himself but also because his rise and fall spanned—in a way, synthesized—the years of boom and depression between 1922 and 1932. The life of no other man more sharply epitomizes that kaleidoscopic period, perhaps because he, like the times, was at once so real and so unreal. The things he was able to do in carrying out his swindle would never again be possible, and in that sense he may also be said to have been the last of a free-wheeling breed.

Kreuger has been the subject of approximately a score of books written by authors in various countries, but almost all these volumes appeared a year or two after his death, before "the dust settled" on what was undoubtedly the greatest financial fraud in history. My purpose in writing this book has been to present a complete new portrait of the man and to tell the story of his life chronologically, from his modest beginnings to the final cataclysmic months in Europe and America when, almost with the inevitability of a Greek drama, disaster overcame him with stark vengeance. In order to obtain fresh material for a definitive account of his career, I spent a number of months in Kreuger's native Sweden and did research in England, France, and

Germany as well as in America. Approximately a hundred
and fifty persons were interviewed, including many who
knew Kreuger well and played important roles in his life
and/or in the lengthy investigation afterward.

It is impossible to list all these sources, but I would like
particularly to thank a number of individuals who were of
outstanding help to me. In Sweden, they include Dr. Hans
Schäffer, of the Swedish Match Company; Jacob Wallenberg and E. Browaldh, bankers; Björn Prytz, Carl Bergman,
J. Sjövall, Eric Lundberg, Gunnar Bergenstråhle, Sune
Schéle, Baron Kurt von Drachenfels, Torsten Kreuger, A.
Gabrielsson, the families of Krister Littorin, Oscar Rydbeck, and Johannes Hellner, and Catherine Djurklou and
Börje Heed. All but the last two, who assisted me in gathering and translating material, were directly involved in one
way or another in the case. Elsewhere in Europe, E. C.
Oakley, Sir Reginald Wilson, and Fred Thompson, who
were among the prominent accountants participating in the
aftermath of the Kreuger scandal, were of great help in in-
terpreting financial facts and theories and in lending me
valuable records. In America I obtained guidance from Edward S. Greenbaum, James N. Rosenberg, Nathan Katz,
and George Hourwich, lawyers prominently engaged in
the case. Others who gave me important material from
their own recollections were Edwin F. Chinlund, Jackson
Martindell, George Murnane, and Anders Jordahl. I wish
also to thank Rudolf J. Klein, economist and broker associated with A. G. Becker & Co., of New York, for having
read the manuscript and given me his expert suggestions,
and Eliot Janeway for his advice. Finally, I must thank
William Shawn, editor of *The New Yorker*, where part of
the book first appeared, and Alfred A. Knopf, Harold
Strauss, and Robert Pick of Alfred A. Knopf, Inc., for their
editorial counsel.

Source material in Europe and America included the

lengthy police records of the investigation conducted in
Stockholm and Paris; the accounting files of Whinney,
Murray & Co. and of Price, Waterhouse & Co.; reports of
the trustees in bankruptcy and of the liquidators of Kreuger
& Toll and of the International Match Corporation; records
of the Swedish Match Company and of a number of Swedish banks; the private files of Krister Littorin and Oscar
Rydbeck, both deceased; court records in proceedings in
the United States under section 21A of the bankruptcy act;
hearings held by Senate committees and by the Securities
and Exchange Commission; files donated by Mr. Greenbaum to the library of Princeton University; the newspaper
files of the New York *Herald Tribune* and of *Dagens
Nyeter*, in Stockholm, and those of *Fortune* and the *Saturday Evening Post*. Virtually all the books written about
Kreuger were read and compared for facts. The best and
most useful of these which appeared in English were: *The
Life and Death of Ivar Kreuger*, by William Stoneman;
Kreuger's Billion Dollar Bubble, by Earl Sparling; *The
Case of Ivar Kreuger*, by Manfred Georg; *The Financier:
The Life of Ivar Kreuger*, by George Soloveytchik; and
The Incredible Ivar Kreuger, by Allen Churchill. A book
distributed in Sweden and privately translated into English,
entitled *The Kreuger Estate*, by Anders Byttner, was of
special help because it presented a pro-Kreuger analysis.
Four books written in Swedish, which I had translated and
which proved of considerable assistance in rounding out the
picture of Kreuger, were: *My Thirteen Years with Kreuger*, by Gunnar Cederschiöld; *The Real Ivar Kreuger*, by
Baron Kurt von Drachenfels; *Ivar Kreuger, Murdered?* by
Börje Heed and Sven Stolpe; and *Kreuger*, by Poul Bjerre
—the last, a study of Kreuger's personality by Sweden's
foremost psychoanalyst, was especially helpful, as was Dr.
Bjerre himself. Mention should also be made of the memoirs
of Mrs. Ingeborg Hässler Eberth. Books in German that

were useful were those of Adolph Nau, Drs. Alfred Marcus and Paul Grassman, and Anton Mayer. I am indebted to Marquis James's *Biography of a Bank: The Story of the Bank of America,* to J. M. Keynes's *The Economic Consequences of the Peace,* and to J. K. Galbraith's *The Great Crash—1929* for helping me understand the economic and financial climate of the period. Two novels in which Kreuger appears as a prototype are Ilya Ehrenburg's *The Most Sacred Belongings* and Graham Greene's *England Made Me,* and they were both read and appreciated.

ROBERT SHAPLEN

New York, March 1960

Contents

KREUGER

Genius and Swindler

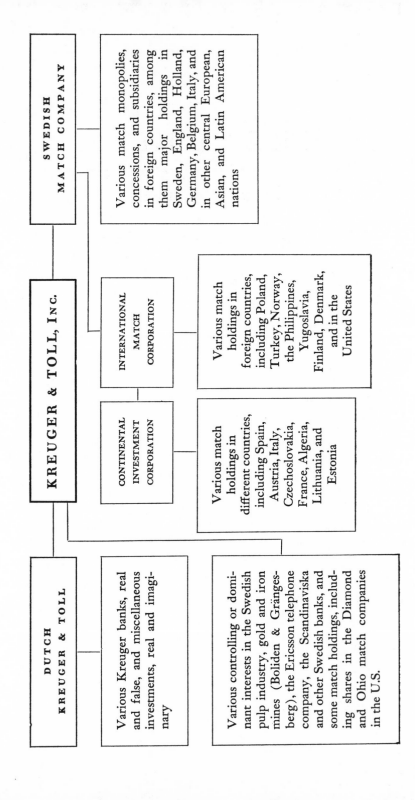

CHAPTER 1

Young Man
with a Mission

IN EARLY AUGUST 1900 a slight, sallow, poker-faced youth who was twenty years old but looked like sixteen arrived in New York aboard a small ship in which he had traveled steerage from his native Sweden for approximately thirty dollars. He had less than a hundred dollars in his pocket when he landed, and for several days, living in a cheap West Side rooming house and watching his money, he walked around the hot summer city and made inquiries about jobs at a number of construction firms. At each office he proudly displayed two degrees showing that his name was Ivar Kreuger and that he had been graduated as a mechanical engineer from the Royal Technical University, in Stockholm, and had then done another year's work in hydraulic-power construction. Although his English was only fair, spoken with a rather heavy accent, he had a pleasant, easy manner and presented himself with a quiet air of self-confidence, but he had no luck; back in his room, he wrote his parents, in Kalmar, Sweden, bemoaning the fact that his appearance belied his qualifications and adding that he would gladly exchange his professional talent for a natural growth of beard.

A week or so later, apparently having decided that a beardless boy might do better out West, he wrote from Chicago that he had rented a room there, for two dollars a week, from a "clean Dutch family" and that he hoped to find some sort of work at once. Chicago had a rural look and tone that reminded him of Kalmar, he noted, but it was obvious that New York had made the greater impression and was still on his mind.

> It is an unusual, beautiful city [he wrote], much more metropolitan than Chicago. . . . All the theaters are stocked with ice, and in all the restaurants, at all the tables, there are four fans driven by electricity, which makes it pretty cool. When in New York, I visited the stock market. There was real liveliness. I have seldom seen people look so absorbed in what they were doing as there. . . . In big buildings there are express and local lifts. The most exciting things I've seen in America up to now, though, are department stores. I don't know what one could ask for they don't have. Clothes, furniture, live animals of all kinds, paintings, statues, all kinds of food, and in the shops there are also all kinds of experts, even dentists. . . . In New York I also visited the summer resort of New Yorkers—Coney Island —a place which I find very beautiful and exciting. The whole city of New York is so fine and clear of smoke. Especially Fifth Avenue is beautiful. . . .

His catalogue of exuberance, including his prophetic fascination with the stock market, was the beginning of a long love affair between New York and Ivar Kreuger, an affair whose denouement was literally to shake the world. Some three decades later, at the age of fifty-two, after he had ostensibly become a multimillionnaire by establishing a series of international monopolies for the manufacture and sale of matches and by gaining control of a number of other valuable industrial enterprises, and after he had kept his thousands of investors satisfied with consistently high dividends while he continued to sell them more stock—the American public alone bought a quarter of a billion dollars' worth over the last ten years—Kreuger was to bring to a sudden, crashing end one of the most amazing careers in the annals of high finance by carefully and coolly shooting himself.

The immediate and natural effect of Kreuger's suicide, on March 12, 1932, in his bachelor apartment in Paris, was to send his stocks, which had been holding up better than most since the 1929 crash, plummeting to record lows on the world's exchanges. But as far as his public image was concerned, there were only paeans of praise for his genius and expressions of sorrow that the strains of the prolonged world depression had led so great a figure to such a drastic act. While his body still lay in the apartment, watched over by a pair of volunteer nuns who insisted on maintaining their round-the-clock vigil even though Kreuger had never shown the slightest interest in any religion, the *New Statesman* described him editorially as "a very Puritan of finance." *The Times* of London declared that he was "no common adventurer . . . cornered at last by the self-defeating ingenuity of his devices" and that "least of all does personal suspicion light upon him," and the *Economist*, after likening him to the hero of an Aeschylean tragedy, characterized him as "a man of great constructive intelligence and wide vision who planned boldly, yet on a basis which seemed to be protected by carefully devised safeguards."

While most of the public agreed, or certainly wished desperately to agree, with these quick and easy encomiums, a number of knowing bankers and brokers in Stockholm and New York and a handful of Kreuger's closest associates were aware that he had lately been having extraordinary difficulties meeting his obligations and that he had begun to cut some pretty dangerous corners. None of them, however, was prepared for the cataclysmic announcement that came three and a half weeks after Kreuger's fatal gunshot from the accountants of Price, Waterhouse, Ltd., the London branch of the well-known firm, who had been hired by Swedish authorities to conduct a preliminary examination of Kreuger's multiple and tangled affairs. The public statement, issued in Stockholm, disclosed that the master financier, the head of a unique and far-flung industrial empire, had deliberately listed assets that were "greatly in excess of the items they purported to represent, entirely fictitious, or duplicative of assets belonging and appearing on the books of associated companies." The facts were already sufficiently documented for the higher-ups in the century-and-a-quarter-old Wall Street brokerage house of Lee, Higginson & Co., which since 1923 had acted as Kreuger's financial agents in this country, to admit that they had been the victims of "flagrant misrepresentations" and to agree that, apparently, "gross frauds have been perpetrated by Mr. Kreuger." On April 13, just a month after Kreuger's canonization in the press, the "Puritan of finance" was further revealed to have ordered and supervised the counterfeiting of one hundred and forty-two million dollars' worth of Italian government securities, and personally to have forged the signatures of the appropriate Italian officials on them.

But this was still only the beginning. Price, Waterhouse eventually wrote fifty-seven reports on the delicate varieties of Kreuger's global manipulations over a decade and a half. After five years of investigation of the financier's four hundred companies around the world by batteries of accountants and lawyers, who conducted the biggest post-mortem of its kind ever made, the final rendering showed that Kreuger, between 1917 and 1932, had inflated earnings on the books of his various real and unreal companies by more than a quarter of a billion dollars. During that period he had received about six hundred and fifty million dollars, mostly from securities he floated and partly as loans from banks, but at the time of his death his companies' net assets came to but two hundred million dollars, which was half of what the statements he drew for them were claiming. The shrinkage was due in part to the low market values of 1932, but most of it was the result of Kreuger's having paid large dividends out of capital over so many years. Many of the millions Kreuger got his hands on simply disappeared and probably will never be traced. Some of the money he squandered in speculating on his own hook, especially toward the end, when, with the chances of making a killing in Wall Street having sunk to an all-time low, he plunged wildly in the market in a futile attempt to bail himself out. Some of it was unquestionably paid to blackmailers, to whom Kreuger, the seeming personification of respectability, was extremely vulnerable, both as a business impresario engaged in some nefarious practices and as a man with catholic tastes in the matter of women and a weakness for some rather grubby forms of semi-public diversion. Finally, a substantial portion of the missing millions inevitably was doled out as bribes to public officials and political parties in nations where Kreuger was already selling matches or hoped to sell them in the future.

Whatever had happened to the missing Kreuger millions, his death left a general legacy of ruin which included lost personal fortunes the world over. These ranged from the sizable investments of the partners of Lee, Higginson & Co. in New York, who had put their own savings into his enterprises, to the hundred-dollar ventures of modest fellow

Swedes who had gone along with Kreuger not only in anticipation of boomtime gains but also because they had felt a nationalistic pride over his having put Sweden on the international financial map. Beyond what individuals lost, there was a universal sense of shock and disillusion over the discovery that a man who had been credited with a truly charismatic gift for making money and doing good with it had turned out to be, if not pure crook, at least crooked enough to have stooped to forgery, fabrication, and fraud while getting people to believe in him and his genius and probity to the point of idolatry. The Kreugerian legend had so many facets, however, that even now there are debates about him, about his true character, about his aims and purposes, and about the good as well as the bad he accomplished. A small but active group, led by his brother, Torsten, not only maintains that Ivar Kreuger was murdered—an argument almost totally unauthenticated by anything approaching proof, though it has its theoretical fascination—but also insists that the key financial structure he created was, despite his having overextended himself, essentially sound and that it should never have been dismantled in bankruptcy.

Part of Kreuger's complicated edifice, the match trust that gave him the name of "The Match King," is still in existence on a considerably smaller scale. So are a number of individual industrial components of what used to be his largest company, Kreuger & Toll, but the central foundation of the house was torn down and the residue of assets distributed in partial payment of debts and obligations. Notwithstanding Kreuger's own dramatic admission of failure and what happened to his properties and to the men who worked for him—a score of persons, including Torsten Kreuger, went to jail for periods of from several months to several years, and, had he chosen to live, Kreuger would surely have gone to jail too—he is no easy person on whom to render judgment.

He was a many-sided, enigmatic man, full of contradictions. Revealed as a fabulous falsifier, he was also, up to a point at least, a brilliant business organizer who created a tremendous *mystique* as a modern fiduciary alchemist somehow possessed of the secret of making gold and willing to use much of his wealth in almost Robin Hood fashion to shore up the economies of poor nations at a time when the European economic and currency dislocation was at its worst. He often came to the rescue, to be sure, at a good rate of interest and in return for profitable concessions; but there is no denying that until the bubble of his false hypothecations burst he was widely respected as a forward-looking international banker who believed that a healthy world economy depended on the free flow of currency in all directions and who developed a highly original formula to make it flow. One of his early post-suicide eulogizers, John Maynard Keynes, the internationally known British economist, declared that Kreuger, beyond possessing "maybe the greatest financial intelligence of his time," had altruistically "deemed it his task amid post-war chaos to create a canal between the countries with abundance of capital and those in bitter need of it [until he] was crushed between the icebergs of this frozen world."

As the port-mortem investigators soon found out, although Kreuger controlled three fourths of the world's match business, traffic on the canal was never as brisk as he led people to believe; a number of the bonds and other assets he listed turned out to be nothing but fabricated collateral for loans or deals he never made. If the depression had not come along when it did, however, and lasted so long, Kreuger might have got away with the falsifications that ran parallel to his bona-fide business. This would not have meant, of course, that he was innocent of wrongdoing, but simply that he might not have been found out and, with the return of prosperity, might have been able to erase evidence of the past, making good on his shortages by substituting new real profits for false old ones. There are indications that this is what he had in mind; on the other hand, there are those who believe he could never have withstood the temptation to falsify and inflate his position, once having begun to do so and having escaped detection as long as he did.

In any case, it is still hard to judge Kreuger solely by the wrongs he committed, because in the speculative twenties, especially in America, he was as much a catalyst as a cause of disaster, and any conviction of him must inevitably cast an aura of guilt on those who helped create him, who nourished him so ardently with their own ambition and avarice, and who saw reflected in his tremendous success their own images of wealth and glory. These are qualities and conditions that thrive on temptation, and it is indisputable that Kreuger became a remarkably clever tempter. In fact, the more he asked, the more he got; but it also is true that the more he tempted, the more contemptuous he became of those who gave, and it was this human frailty of his, as much as anything, that ultimately defeated and destroyed him.

: 2 :

Kreuger's astonishing gift for making others trust him was something he employed all his life, and with it went the ability to adjust himself to any surroundings and circumstances. Even as the jobless boy of twenty on the first of his countless trips to America, he was already a hardheaded cosmopolite, at ease among strangers, always carefully studying them for their strengths and weaknesses, and impressed far more by the material aspects of wealth about him than by anything else in the New World. Outwardly aloof but always curious, he was brimming with conscious purpose. With his tireless energy went a kind of nerveless insensibility that, among other things, seemed to make him impervious to discomfort. For a Scandinavian, reared in a cold climate and never before out of it, the oppressive Midwestern summer was certainly far from congenial, but young Ivar took it in stride. "We had a terrible week of heat," he wrote from Chicago a few days after his arrival from New York. "At 4 P. M., the worst hour of the day, it was 95 degrees in the shade. But I haven't been so uncomfortable because I took off some clothes. People seldom wear vests here, and if you want you can take off your jacket on the street."

He continued his search for work, but soon realized he wasn't going to get the sort he wanted—it was the off-season for construction. So, scanning the want ads, and probably taking the advice of some local Swedes he had met, he applied for a job with a real-estate firm that specialized in selling lots to European immigrants and saw the advantage of hiring immigrants as salesmen. A Swede in the office quickly called him aside and asked: "What did you do on the other side that you're running away from?" and seemed puzzled when Kreuger replied that he hadn't broken any laws, that he had come to America of his own free choice. (Years later Kreuger enjoyed telling his American friends in Wall Street, whose money he was by then calmly manipulating and who never suspected him of anything until it was too late, about this early suspicious compatriot.) Despite the fact that he would have to work without salary on a commission basis, he took the real-estate job because he was intrigued by the firm's offer of a free course in salesmanship designed to teach neophytes like himself how to approach a customer, "make a pitch," and then "close a deal." It was also a good way to improve his English and learn American customs. He got off to a bad start, however, and for six weeks sold nothing.

During this time he may have been able to borrow a little money for food and lodging from some of his new Swedish acquaintances, but he was virtually down and out. Subsequently he confided to friends that, while tramping around trying to sell lots, he had been reduced to begging and on occasion had even picked scraps of food out of garbage cans, but he may have overdramatized his plight—as he occasionally did in recalling his youthful struggles. Finally he managed to sell a scrubby acre or two and earn a commission of fifty dollars, which, at this point, was all he did make out of the real-estate business, though it would not be long before he would be making a great deal more from it in far more grandiose ways.

Shortly after this sale he picked up another fifty dollars in a manner that may be said to have adumbrated the future. His room with the nice Dutch family had been occupied previously by an architect, and Kreuger had found in a bureau drawer some incomplete plans for a small house. One evening a man dropped by and, asking for the architect, explained that some time ago he had agreed to pay fifty dollars for a set of finished sketches. Kreuger thought quickly and replied that, though the architect had gone away, he himself was one and that the job had been turned over to him to complete, which he would do in another few days. He had worked on blueprints as an engineering student, and it was a simple matter for him to tidy up the unfinished drawings. When the man returned, young Ivar handed them over and gratefully pocketed the money. Such opportunistic improvisation and the ability to make split-second decisions were to become dominant characteristics in Kreuger's career.

While still working on the real-estate job he took a cheap short course in surveying—a profession his maternal grandfather had practiced—and, after a brief period working as a lineman for the Illinois Central Railroad near Chicago, he struck out for Colorado. His idea now was to combine his talents as an engineer and his new smattering of knowledge in getting a job in the mines, but once again, probably because of his youthful look, he got nowhere. Thereupon he wandered down to New Orleans, where an incident took place which became one of the minor mysteries of Kreuger's life. He was steaming around the city on an excursion boat when a seven-year-old girl fell overboard. Kreuger immediately jumped into the water and saved her, and four days later the city of New Orleans, as the story subsequently was told, gave him a medal bearing the inscription: ONLY A HERO WILL GIVE HIS LIFE FOR OTHERS. Oddly enough, however, Kreuger's name was not inscribed. What seems even odder is that, although he was in all respects devoid of exhibitionism and even shy about his personal exploits, he usually kept the medal displayed on his desk and, if asked about it, would tell the story with a pretense of reluctance. Ten years after the rescue he claimed to have visited the young girl and her family out West somewhere and to have discovered that she had grown into a beautiful young woman, an item that always interested Kreuger almost as much as a good debenture. The story, in all likelihood, is true; at least, it convinced his mother, for after his death the medal was the only possession of his she wanted for herself.

Although there is no record of what kind of work Kreuger did in New Orleans, he must have done something, for on New Year's Day, 1901, he wrote to his father: "I have a little money now, but as I'm leaving for Mexico I don't want to spend it." He added that he was getting "a free journey and a good salary" and advised his father not to worry because "the climate isn't dangerous at present, and

it's not so bad at any time." He may have put this in to assure his parents that he was feeling all right despite the fact
that, as he related in the same letter, a doctor in New Orleans had examined him as a potential draft candidate for
military service in Sweden and had found evidence of a
slight heart murmur.

His prediction about Mexico proved frighteningly wrong.
He went to Veracruz with fourteen other engineers on an
arduous bridge-building project, and within a few weeks
thirteen of the party had died of yellow fever. Kreuger also
got the fever and, as one of two survivors, was sent back to
New York to recuperate. There he came down with a se-
vere attack of conjunctivitis, induced by his weakened condition, and his eyes were so infected that he could scarcely
see and became understandably panicky. All in all, he was
in such bad shape that his cat-like ability to take care of
himself momentarily forsook him and he made the decision
almost any other young man in a similar plight would have
made: to go home.

There was another reason, beyond his bad health—romance. There was a girl back home, a Norwegian student
of physical therapy young Ivar had met at the university in
Stockholm. Not very much is known about her, except that
she is supposed to have been extremely pretty and that Ivar
had apparently fallen in love with her. He had confided his
passion to an older sister living in Stockholm—an unusual
revelation, for he had never disclosed any of his private
feelings to anyone before. The girl seems to have returned
his affection tentatively, but there had been obstacles to their
marriage. She had a legal guardian in the town of Drammen,
south of Oslo, who was in the true tradition of the tough
and stern protector. When Kreuger had visited him, the
guardian had declared that marriage was out of the question,
as Kreuger did not have the prospect of a job. Ivar had gone
off to America partly to prove himself both to the girl and

to her guardian, but, in a fit of dejection after his illness and his eye trouble, he foolishly wrote her that he was afraid he was going blind and that, though he still loved her, it was no longer right for him even to hope to marry her. He soon regretted this noble renunciation, and back in Stockholm, with his conjunctivitis cleared up and his strength and ambition restored, he tried to undo his abnegation. By this time, however, the girl had apparently lost faith or interest in him, and the guardian was no more impressed with Kreuger than before. The older sister in whom Ivar had confided went to Norway as a romantic emissary, but the answer of both girl and guardian remained no. Ivar was heartbroken, though he did not altogether give up hope. There is no doubt that this was a major emotional event in his life, and that it shaped a great deal of his personal response to other women later on. While there would be many with whom his name was linked, and many more with whom he had relations, he was not to fall romantically in love again.

If this unrequited affair had the effect, once his bout of grief was over, of making him tougher-fibered and more dedicated and ambitious, it also made him more dissatisfied with his Swedish surroundings. It had been as natural for a fledgling engineer to go to America as it would have been for an artist to head for Paris, and what he had seen on the other side of the ocean was far more important than what he had done. "I always had the feeling that one could expect endless possibilities from him, and when he came back from the States that feeling was stronger," a Stockholm friend remarked.

There was little, to be sure, to keep him in Sweden, for at the turn of the century it was scarcely the humming and prosperous industrial nation it is today. Stockholm was a quiet if courtly capital where business was conducted largely along artisan lines and people led solid, peaceful, and well-ordered lives. Young men did not tend to follow an unprescribed course, and success was marked by comfortable, bourgeois contentment. In the villages and in towns such as Kalmar, on the southwest coast, the atmosphere was even more placid and provincial, and obviously would not appeal to one who had already ventured out into the world, especially the New World. Nevertheless, for a period of two or three months, while he was awaiting formal discharge from the draft—his recent illnesses and his mild heart condition were enough to exempt him—the romantically rejected Kreuger went back to Kalmar and worked, as he had done before in summertime, in his father's small match factory in nearby Mönsterås. He was undoubtedly a lot more bored than he had been as a youngster, when he had established a reputation locally as a mixture of a prodigy and Peck's Bad Boy.

: 3 :

After the suicide of Kreuger, when any and all episodes of his life which could be uncovered were analyzed and interpreted *ad infinitum*, his boyhood and young manhood were subjected to scrutiny for early telltale signs of "criminality." With hindsight, it was easy to read into a number of things the premature development of the sneak, the cheat, the liar, and the scoundrel. Some of the evidence was persuasive enough, though without the knowledge of his far greater subsequent wrongdoing, the behavior of the youthful Kreuger would perhaps seem no worse than that of many other rambunctious schoolboys.

More impressive than any specific prank or peccadillo of Kreuger's is the broad picture of a boy and a youth of obviously superior mental agility who was constantly intent on demonstrating it in ways that would, and did, establish him as cleverer than any of his contemporaries. The young man, for example, who made his first fifty dollars in America by doctoring someone else's architectural drawings had done the same sort of thing years before in school, with the same adroitness—and would do the same thing all his life, making no distinctions between right and wrong so long as something "worked." Indeed, from the very outset Kreuger had a signal lack of fear and no thought of what the consequences of his actions would be. His self-absorption and the immensity of his ambitions led him, almost from infancy, to want to prove himself in all sorts of ways, first to his mother, then to his schoolmates, and ultimately to his business associates and to the prominent statesmen of the world. All in all, he was surely one of the most astonishingly amoral men who ever lived, and herein perhaps is the key to his character. Whether Kreuger was dealing with women, with his employees, or with nations, he categorized all objects, animate or inanimate, large or small, purely as they served or failed to serve his purposes, and he used or discarded them accordingly. Not until the end of his life, when he discovered that he could no longer move at will in any direction he chose, did he begin to appraise himself as an individual, and it is interesting to note that his last private letters reveal an effort, at once painful and touching, to come to grips with his personality and his own ego.

The well-known Swedish psychoanalyst Dr. Poul Bjerre, who had never met Kreuger but had always been fascinated by him, was asked by a Stockholm publisher to make an intensive study of him following his death. (Questioned nearly thirty years later, Dr. Bjerre still felt that the financier was one of the most remarkable men he had ever dealt with, even though he never had his subject on a couch.) In searching for clues to Kreuger's character, Dr. Bjerre looked everywhere for facts that would help him understand the man's motivations, especially his amoral drive, and he was struck, in the first place, by the lack of any powerful or important cultural and spiritual heritage in Kreuger's past.

The background of Ivar Kreuger was almost solidly bourgeois. At the bottom of the family tree was a journeyman baker from Germany, Johan Kröger, who emigrated to Kalmar in 1710. He remained a baker there and passed the business to his oldest son; but a second son, Anders, chose to become a coppersmith and, following the custom of the times, used a French spelling of the name, Kreuger. Anders did well enough as a merchant until 1791, when he went bankrupt, but his son, Anders Lorentz, was the first really well-off Kreuger, making his money in shipping and timber and gaining further status by having himself appointed honorary Russian vice-consul in the town (it became the custom, in the nineteenth century, to use prominent local citizens in such posts). His son, Peter Edvard, founded the highly successful commercial house of P. E. Kreuger & Jennings and wisely married the richest girl in Kalmar, Amelia von Sydow, whose prominent cheekbones and general facial contours—long instead of square—Ivar Kreuger inherited. Peter Edvard, among other things, did a rushing business with the Confederacy during the American Civil War. He established several factories, including ones for weaving and papermaking and, most successfully, matchmaking, setting up a small plant in nearby Frederiksdahl. His third son, Ernst, Ivar's father, eventually took over the match business and expanded it by building another factory, the one in Mönsterås.

Whatever glamour there is in Ivar Kreuger's family background seems to have come from his mother's side. Her name was Jennie Forssman, and the Forssmans had a genuine, if somewhat tropically oriented, Viking streak in them. Her uncle went off to the Transvaal and, after making a fortune there as a general merchant, returned to Sweden to transport Jennie's father and a hundred others of his countrymen to South Africa in his own sailing ship, intending to launch a Swedish African colony. After a rough three-month trip the voyagers landed at Durban and began a three-month overland trek into the interior during the rainy season. By the time they got to the Transvaal the Viking blood of most of them had been severely thinned, but some went into the diamond fields, and Ivar's grandfather became a general surveyor for the Dutch.

On the Forssman side of the family, one case of suicide and one of insanity are recorded. The suicide was incited by paresis, a subject that always fascinated Ivar Kreuger, and about which he both read and talked a great deal. There were rumors after his death that he too had suffered from it and that this had led him to overreach himself in impossible financial schemes—paresis has the effect, among other things, of creating an exaggerated sense of power—but it appears that, at most, Kreuger once contracted a mild case of syphilis, which he soon had cured.

Except for the African venture of his two Forssman forebears, there is little in Kreuger's family history to indicate a talent for striking out into new professional fields or even a desire to see new places. Yet from birth Ivar seems to have been "different," and almost everyone, including his parents, thought him so. This may have been due in part to the fact that he was a third child, proverbially the one who requires less attention than the earlier two and who seems better able to fend for himself.

There were already two girls in the family when Ivar was born, on March 2, 1880, in the large flat, the top part of an old mansion, which the Kreugers occupied on East Sea Street in Kalmar. From the very start he demonstrated two of the qualities for which he was to become famous— silence and patience. "He ate three meals regularly a day and one at midnight and never cried if he was fed late, or, for that matter, about anything," his mother later said. "He took care of himself and was just an angel." This meant that he was left to amuse and slowly to educate himself, on the nursery and reading level, and Dr. Bjerre professes to see in this the first signs of a significant character development. "By not being governed or guided in his first educational maneuvers, he was, despite his curiosity, essentially uneducated and quickly became a law unto himself, operating according to regulations he alone devised," he says. "If one conquers one's first difficulties so easily, one gets a sense of superiority that is every bit as dangerous as a feeling of inferiority."

When he was four years old, his brother, Torsten, was born—there were two more girls after that—and, as Torsten demanded greater attention, Ivar was more than ever left to himself. He developed into a shy and solemn child with cool gray eyes that seemed to belong to a much older person and that seldom sparkled with fresh discovery or enthusiasm but appeared to take in and comprehend everything around him. When he started school, he would get up at six in summer and winter, dress and feed himself, and leave the house without anyone even knowing he was gone —all his life Kreuger would be an early riser, and the quality of unobtrusiveness which he developed as a child also became an integral part of his character. As he grew into boyhood, he became tall but frail and not nearly so Nordic-looking as his fellows; perhaps because of this, he felt obliged to demonstrate that he was as good as or better than anyone else. He became daring to the point of recklessness, and the risks he took undoubtedly encouraged him later on to take financial risks no one else would have attempted. He learned how to swim, for instance, by accepting a challenge at the age of seven to jump into the Kalmar bathhouse pool. When another boy dared him to jump out of a tall tree, he jumped, narrowly avoiding injury. Although not athletically inclined, he liked the outdoors and very early acquired a lifelong passion for flowers, spending long hours wandering around the mainland woods and on the nearby island of Öland in the Baltic. The first thing Kreuger ever stole was an envelope of pressed flowers belonging to a schoolmate.

The strange absence of a sense of right and wrong in Kreuger, his adoption of whatever means were available to reach his ends, his equally odd mixture of consideration and contempt for people and his ability to use them for his own purposes without their being aware of it, were all amoral qualities he demonstrated when he was hardly out of knee pants. He was remarkably adept at cutting corners, at finding ways to do things which, while undeniably efficacious and time-saving, were certainly not correct, but he appears never to have had any sense of guilt about what he did, any more than he did later, when he cut accounting corners on a truly colossal scale. In place of remorse, there was always a kind of quiet pride in his own capacities. As he himself later remarked, not in a bragging or omnipotent manner but as if he were just reporting an asset instead of a liability on a balance sheet, "I guess I wasn't quite like the other boys. I thought things through for myself." One of his schoolmates put it somewhat differently: "It isn't that he cheated more than the rest of us, but that he just did it better."

In his later years Kreuger displayed a spectacularly retentive memory that enabled him to rattle off verbatim the fictions in his numerous balance sheets without being flanked by accountants scribbling memos for his guidance. If a story vouched for by the doting members of his family can be believed, this faculty was already fully developed at the age of five, when he recited, word for word, a sermon he had heard in church and then recited it backward. Possibly easier to accept is his parents' assertion that at seven he could add, subtract, divide, and multiply. The fact that he could read a book rapidly and absorb everything in it, however, seemed to make him lazy instead of eager to get his work done well in a hurry. He preferred to wait until examination time and then engage in expert cribbing. Others were spied out, but Kreuger never was. As another of his schoolmates later said, "His thirst for experimenting was frequently due to his wanting to see how far things he had set in motion would develop [and] if something dangerous was undertaken, Ivar had to have a part in it." This remarkably apt summary of the youthful Kreuger held true all his life. His financial maneuvers were always calculated efforts to determine, first on a small scale and then on a larger, how much he could get away with.

Among his schoolmates, Ivar was usually a ringleader. Once he used a set of false keys to enter the school principal's office and obtain final term marks before they were announced—he sold them for the equivalent of a nickel to his fellow students—and an attempt to get some exam papers in advance failed only because they had been locked in a safe (and one thing Kreuger was *not* was a safecracker). Organized cribbing was common. Kreuger also assigned each of a group of boys to study the subject he was best in and, without doing any studying himself but acting as overseer, he then made sure that all the notes were properly pooled before class sessions. "Even in those days he appeared fully determined to arrange all the small, unimportant things into a system," an old friend who knew him as a boy has recalled. "He had a clear realization of the main and fundamental facts. He did not waste time over side issues, but was intelligent enough not to ignore the importance even of trivialities. His principle was the law of least resistance and the realization of the maximum results with the minimum of effort." Kreuger, of course, never lost his early penchant for systematization, and his whole subsequent financial scheme, which he kept chiefly in his head and alone seemed fully to understand, was a natural outgrowth of this early habit of organizing his fellows' school lives.

He quickly demonstrated a knack of appraising his teachers' weaknesses and thereby knowing what he could do, both practically and prankishly. He seems to have been purely devilish at times, a kind of Swedish Dennis the Menace. "It was priceless to contemplate the expression of concentrated innocence on Ivar's face when he had just played some trick or other, as, for instance, on the occasion when he poured all the various acids at the laboratory into one receptacle and the poor teacher failed to get a demonstration to work," a fellow student has recounted. He further learned how to take advantage of any situation and turn bad fortune into good. In later years he used to relish telling how he had been on his way to school one day in Kalmar, worried about passing an examination he had failed to bone up for, when he was knocked down by a man on a bicycle. Badly cut and bruised, he refused all entreaties to go to an apothecary or go home. One of the town officials who had seen the accident walked consolingly to school with him and told the teacher what had happened. Kreuger played the mishap for all it was worth and correctly guessed the outcome: the teacher felt so sorry for him that he got a passing grade.

A significant early interest in girls was apparently encouraged by an older boy who used to visit one of Ivar's sisters and took such a liking to him that they became friends. The young man volunteered to introduce Kreuger to some suitable young ladies, and this prompted considerable teasing by his schoolmates. Typically, Kreuger had a clever counterthrust. When he was named by some of the boys in his class to be an honorary member of a girls' club in the school, he responded with a speech to the young ladies which was printed in the high-school paper (it seems to have been mainly a teen-age gossip sheet that would have been relished by the James Dean generation). "With deepest feelings in my heart, I thank you for your invitation to join your lovely organization," he said. "I hadn't expected this honor. I know I'm considered to be one of the most remarkable curiosities in Kalmar, but not because of my splendid male qualities and my good looks. . . . Maybe it's because I and my friend X [the older boy he had met] are seen so often on the Storgatan [where the girls used to walk after school]. I hope to fulfill all your hopes in carrying out the sweet duties you have enjoined for me. And now, I assure you that . . . as long as my legs hold out, I will hang around the Storgatan at least two hours every day, for what will one not do for what one loves!" Kreuger was thirteen years old at the time. Two years later, it is said, he had his first affair, with a handsome divorcée twice his age who was one of his mother's friends. He had other new interests by then too. He had, for instance, become an excellent shot, and instead of spending so much time hunting flowers in the woods, he hunted animals.

His quick mind and fine talent for cribbing enabled Kreuger to pass his student's examination at the age of sixteen, three years ahead of the average. After working that summer of 1896 in his father's Mönsterås factory, he went to the technical university in Stockholm in the fall, having decided to take up engineering. Here, as in Kalmar, he was soon esteemed for his cleverness—as a classmate afterward put it, he took pleasure in using his agile mind "for the deception of everyone with whom he came into contact"—and his subtle techniques again earned him an odd sort of local fame. When he was asked to build a model drawbridge, he arranged to copy different sections of it from various adept fellow students, who not only didn't mind helping him out but were secretly proud of the fact that his glued-together results were the best. It might be hard to believe that Kreuger actually was able to enlist the loyal and even admiring support of his classmates in selfish schemes of this kind were it not for the indisputable evidence that he later charmed astute financiers into giving him their clients' money and that they made hardly any effort to keep track of what he was doing with it.

Another early example of what might be called corner-cutting, or following the path of least resistance, is provided by the story of how Kreuger passed a mineralogy test that required him to identify a number of stones. The ones he could not name, he calmly dropped into a desk drawer; the professor, as he had surmised, never knew the difference. With this sort of guile went another characteristic that Kreuger developed to a striking degree later on: the capacity to bluff. He once wrote a sarcastic commentary on a lecture on railway building and handed it to the professor, who denounced him for it in class the next day. Kreuger insisted that he had merely set down faithfully what he had heard the professor say, and, accepting the man's dare to deliver a better lecture, he promptly and brazenly stood up and gave a talk that everyone agreed was masterful. Anticipating what would happen, Ivar had all but memorized the textbook the night before. He was later to use such memory tricks to great advantage in winning the esteem of businessmen.

Despite such bravura actions, Kreuger was considered essentially quiet and reserved by his college mates. In fact, they called him "The Quiet One." Though younger than the rest, he seemed older. As he had done before, and would do all his life, he kept to himself most of the time, though, besides squiring his Norwegian girl friend, he apparently went out formally on occasion: in one of his letters home he requested "a set of tails" along with a more prosaic piece of equipment, "a spare napkin ring." He was attracted by the city, an extremely beautiful one, but his response to it was more calculating than aesthetic and displayed little imagination. Such things as the opera, which he dutifully attended with one of his sisters, interested him less than strolling around and pondering his future. Once he and another student, walking beside the inland sea around which Stockholm is built, stopped to watch some fishermen raise and lower their nets. When one of the nets came up with nothing in it but some scraps of orange peel and debris, Kreuger remarked: "That would never suit me. I'd want a netful of fish every time or I'd try something else." When his companion chided him for expecting too much, Kreuger pointed to the Royal Palace across the way and announced that he would own one like it someday—he would, too, his famous Match Palace. He often spoke of making staggering amounts of money in matter-of-fact terms. He had, actually, already learned to deal with money in his own convenient way. In his first accounting home, every item was neatly broken down and listed in a nice round sum. Two of the entries showed signs of having been erased and altered so that the totals of what he had received and ostensibly spent balanced perfectly.

Upon his graduation and the completion of his extra year's course in engineering, he discussed his prospects with his father, who soon realized that his older son wasn't prepared to settle down in a quiet rural match business and had to appease his wanderlust. Ivar accordingly went off to America. When he returned, Ernst Kreuger secretly wished that the one trip, unsuccessful as it had been on several counts, might be enough. But after Ivar worked for four months in the Mönsterås match factory and reached the age of twenty-one, he decided to try his luck in the New World again, and, with a little more money in his pockets than before, he sailed back to New York in the fall of 1901. This time, in addition to feeling older, he made sure he looked older by growing a mustache.

CHAPTER 2

An Empire
is Created

Within a short time of Kreuger's arrival in New York on his second trip to America, he got a job—it may have been the mustache that did it—with the firm of Purdy & Henderson, steel-construction consultants, on West Fourteenth Street. His chief task was to go over structural plans and make sure there were no errors in calculation, something his mathematical mind eminently suited him for, and for which he was paid fifty cents an hour. There were about twenty men in the office, one of whom, a young Norwegian named Anders Jordahl, soon became Kreuger's best friend and was to be one of his close associates in America, a kind of all-round Man Friday, in the big years ahead.

Kreuger lived in a rooming house on West Twenty-third Street and Jordahl lived nearby, so the two often had supper together and spent economical evenings walking around town. It was the dawn of the skyscraper era, and Kreuger was impressed by the new buildings shooting up, but, as had been the case in Stockholm, his response was primarily one of pragmatic, measured assessment rather than excitement or wonder: having seen New York before, he now wrote home descriptive, unemotional letters—almost drab, except for one in which he spoke fervidly of the opportunities he foresaw in the United States. Even in this one there was something calculating in his tone. "There is plenty of room in this country," he wrote. "The people are hard but they give one a chance. At home everyone talks about his love affairs, but here people discuss their prospects. That suits me. I can breathe here." He did well at his job and soon won a promotion by discerning a vital error in a set of plans. Purdy & Henderson had a close association with the Fuller Construction Company, one of the country's building pioneers, and Kreuger worked for Fuller on such early skyscraper landmarks as the Flatiron Building, the Metropolitan Life tower, R. H. Macy & Co., and the Plaza and St. Regis hotels.

The aspect of wealth, in the American image, fascinated him more and more. He again visited the Stock Exchange, and this time noted its operations more carefully. The organization and methods of big business especially intrigued him, and he studied the history of the Rockefeller oil trust and read biographies of such men as Daniel Drew, Jay Gould, and Commodore Cornelius Vanderbilt. At least one prominent person, Per Jacobsson, who is now managing director of the International Monetary Fund and who once worked for Kreuger in Stockholm, believes he got his first real lesson in business shenanigans from watching New York contractors operate under conditions in which political payoffs and kickbacks were rife. It seems just as likely, however, that Kreuger soaked in some of the nineteenth-century American buccaneer past and was much impressed by what the more adventurous and free-wheeling tycoons of that era had got away with. A young Swedish friend who had been with him at the university in Stockholm used to come over from his job in New Jersey to visit Kreuger on week ends, and later recalled how often Kreuger had spoken of the importance of "winning confidence" in business relationships. America was the place, Kreuger kept saying, where one had "to know somebody" to get ahead, and with his usual ingenuity he took advantage of every chance he saw.

When he read one morning that a wealthy industrialist had died, he called at the man's residence and, feigning ignorance, asked to see him. Upon being told what had happened, he begged to be allowed to express his condolences to the son, to whom he handed a letter addressed to the dead man, ostensibly written by Ivar's father in Sweden—"your old friend"—and introducing "my son Ivar" as "a capable young man who may be of use to you." Ivar had, of course, written the letter himself, and though nothing apparently came of this ruse, it was typical of Kreuger's growing gall, which he demonstrated in other ways too, in behalf of friends as well as himself. When another fellow Swede in New York was out of a job, Kreuger stepped blithely into a prominent engineers' club and wrote a letter of introduction under a false name on the club's embossed stationery to one of the firms that, a year before, had turned Kreuger down; the friend was promptly hired.

In time Kreuger came to have an almost mesmeric influence over people and applied it ruthlessly to gain his ends, but he also always seemed to derive pleasure—perhaps as a satisfaction of his own ego or, as has been suggested, as a form of masochism—from going out of his way to help others. The response was exactly the sort of blind fealty he sought and required. He made sure of his friend Jordahl early, as Jordahl himself unwittingly confessed. "It was one of Ivar's characteristics to take not only a purely sentimental interest in his friends, but he utilized every opportunity that came along to help them and further their material well-being," the Norwegian wrote Kreuger's parents after Kreuger's death. "Thus, when a position was offered to him in England a few months after we had met, he took pains to get the post for me. . . . This position happened to be with Waring and Gillow of London, and my duties were to participate in the designing of the engineering work for the Carlton Hotel in Johannesburg, South Africa." Kreuger continued to work as a steel-construction engineer in New York until the summer of 1903, when Jordahl returned the favor by getting him a job supervising the preparation of steel for the Johannesburg hotel at the Bürbacker Hütte steel plant in Saarbrücken, Germany. After spending several months there, Kreuger headed for South Africa himself. He had wangled a temporary subcontracting assignment to oversee the installation of the steel, but he seems to have been attracted chiefly by the romance of the place and by Jordahl's repeated reports of good speculative opportunities.

When he arrived in Johannesburg, he had about three hundred pounds with him, part of which he had borrowed from his father. With this he and Jordahl, who contributed about a fifth as much, decided to open a restaurant near the center of town, where they charged one-and-sixpence for table-d'hôte meals but served no liquor. After he had finished his hotel job, Kreuger gave his full time to managing the place and it made a small profit, though, as Jordahl subsequently noted, "we considered this class of business somewhat below our dignity as aspiring young engineers," and they both resolved to say nothing about the venture in their letters home. Despite the activity in the South African mines, Kreuger, in a letter to his father, spoke of "bad times" and, while an upturn was expected, he added deprecatingly: "I don't consider salaries here high enough compared with those in England and America to make up for the high cost of living and other drawbacks."

He intimated for the first time that he was thinking of returning to Stockholm and applying his knowledge of steel construction to building there, and he asked his father to sound out the possibilities of his getting an interim job back home as a fire inspector. In one of his rare personal asides, he also said that "if one wants to think of marriage some time, it's better to live in Sweden." Presumably he was still thinking of his Norwegian girl—he had falsely told Jordahl he was engaged to her—for shortly after this Jordahl came home one afternoon to the boardinghouse in the hills where he and Kreuger shared a room to find Ivar sobbing on the bed with an open letter alongside him. *"Min flicka är död,"* Kreuger said—"my girl is dead." In his letter long afterward to Kreuger's parents Jordahl recalled: "He was very downcast and mournful for a long time following that and it has always been my impression and still is that his deep love for this girl sweetheart who died was the reason he never married."

It may have been the girl's death that made Kreuger decide to stay awhile longer in South Africa. At any rate, when his period of emotional depression was over, he seems to have had an increasingly good time there, and a profitable one. He made a quick fifteen hundred pounds in a gold speculation, which was an extremely large sum in those days—he didn't report this first monetary success home either—and more and more he enjoyed the get-rich-quick flavor of the place, the colonial morality, or amorality, and the fact that he was now a young man with some money in his pockets and several irons in the fire. He joined the Transvaal Militia and rode around on a horse, with a gun slung over his back, and he resumed his hobby of hunting. He did considerable traveling, and visited his grandfather's grave in Pretoria. He also kept up his reading and became much impressed with Cecil Rhodes, who joined Napoleon and Charles XII of Sweden as the three historical figures

Kreuger most admired. Not even a serious outbreak of cholera, during which he and Jordahl watched bodies by the hundreds being carted out of the East Indian settlement, kept him from seriously reconsidering his earlier inclination to move on; he contemplated settling down instead in South Africa to make a fortune. But there remained one major disadvantage: it was too far off the beaten track, too far away from the world centers of money, and he had not forgotten the excitement of New York and the allure of the Stock Exchange.

In the winter of 1904-5 Kreuger suddenly left Johannesburg and roamed along the coast of East Africa. He shipped over to India, where he did more sightseeing for several weeks and had his picture taken standing with a gun over a large, dead lion, though he later admitted that this had been just a stunt and that the lion wasn't his. From India he went to Paris, where he studied French for a few months. Apparently his savings were giving out, for by the summer of 1905 he was back in London. Unable to find work immediately as an engineer, he became a jobber of a line of cutlery and safety razors. This may have seemed a comedown at the moment, but Kreuger adjusted to it, as he did to everything. In all important respects, he had become a full-fledged citizen of the world.

Now, in 1906, America drew him for the third time. On this trip he went by way of Canada and spent a number of months working for a Toronto contracting firm that was doing some building in Buffalo and Toledo, both of which he visited. For some reason he had become intrigued by restaurants, and he started another one, in Philadelphia; unlike the moderately successful Johannesburg venture, this one soon failed. Finally back in New York, he was hired by the Consolidated Engineering Company, of which he was shortly made manager and vice-president. Among other contracts, the company had one for building Archbold Stadium and some additional buildings at Syracuse University, and Kreuger supervised these constructions. (In 1930 the university gave him an honorary degree as Doctor of Business Administration, which may, in retrospect, have been the most regretted diploma of its kind in academic annals.) The Syracuse structures were of reinforced concrete, a new type of building foundation requiring a special kind of iron which had been invented and patented by Julius Kahn, head of the Trussed Concrete Steel Company. Kreuger went to Detroit to visit Kahn, who took a liking to him and suggested that Kreuger explore the possibilities of applying the new building methods in Europe. The idea suited Kreuger perfectly. As he wrote home in a worldly vein, he was getting tired of "making money for second-rate people," and, in one of his few downright anti-American declarations, he added that "I hate the American outlook." He re-emphasized his admiration for American "methods," however, and, having served his "apprenticeship" and learned "more than the most up-to-date director of any firm in Sweden," he announced that he was finally coming home "bursting with ideas. . . . I am only wondering which to carry out first."

: 2 :

Whatever vision of himself as an important business or financial figure the twenty-seven-year-old Kreuger may have had, he started out modestly enough. On May 18, 1908, he formed a partnership with an engineer named Paul Toll, aged twenty-five, who was also interested in introducing the Kahn method in Sweden. Kreuger put up ten thousand kroner—about twenty-five hundred dollars —most of which he borrowed, as he had done before, from his father. Toll put up nothing, though he was an equal partner. Already Kreuger showed a fondness for commercial nomenclature which eventually inspired him to create his international maze of four hundred companies. The Kreuger & Toll letterhead had THE TRUSSED CONCRETE STEEL CO. written on top, and beneath it was printed IVAR KREUGER & CO., which never did anything and was just his way of getting his name listed; on one side, in smaller type, appeared the name of Julius Kahn.

The partners' first contract was a three-thousand-dollar one for building beams in an electrical plant in the small town of Gullspång, and with their profits they bought a concrete mixer from England for their next job, a twelve-thousand-dollar viaduct. The new building technique caught on quickly, and by the end of the year the firm was hard at work on the city's first "skyscraper"—a six-story department store in the center of town which is still standing. It was on this building that Kreuger pulled off his first big coup. He committed Kreuger & Toll to pay a fine of twelve hundred dollars for each extra day if the work wasn't completed in four months, but he stipulated that if the building were finished ahead of schedule, he and Toll should get the same amount for each day saved. The time was midwinter and no one thought the two young contractors could possibly finish on time, let alone early, but Kreuger set up heavy tarpaulins, installed big searchlights and special heating facilities, and kept a work force going twenty-four hours a day. The nocturnal crunch of the concrete mixer led a group of neighboring residents to complain about the noise, but Kreuger had taken the precaution of getting a certificate from a tension expert stating that it would be unwise to interrupt the laying of concrete in winter, and the police supported this position. One Stockholm paper commented testily: "If this American method of building catches on, the Stockholmer will never have a quiet night again," but when the steel-and-concrete skeleton was completed in a record two months' time and Kreuger & Toll collected a handsome bonus of more than seventy thousand dollars, all of Stockholm marveled. People soon got used to the sound of the mixer and began to take pride in the many fine new buildings the firm was erecting. Within three or four years Kreuger & Toll had gained a reputation as the best building company in Sweden.

Kreuger, who generally drew up the contracts and made all the business arrangements while Toll took charge of the construction, worked day and night himself, often seven days a week. He regularly managed to get along on a few hours' sleep and a cat nap or two, a habit that he kept up for the rest of his life and that never ceased to amaze his subordinates. Unlike most Swedes, he ate sparingly, mainly salads. He lived at first in a small pension called Dehn's, then in a downtown hotel, and after that he took a four-room flat on Strandvägen, by the water, but he was constantly moving about from place to place and often caught a few winks and a quick bite in a construction shack. His punctuality and "American" manner of doing business, which combined efficiency with affability, went over well, and when Paul Toll, who was much more of a plodding, subdued Swede, once remarked that his partner was perhaps unnecessarily ardent and ingratiating, Kreuger replied: "You can flatter so much that you're ashamed of yourself, but you can never make the person you're flattering feel ashamed."

In 1911 Kreuger & Toll was incorporated with a capital in stock of a million kroner, or about a quarter of a million dollars. Its statutes declared that it was "to conduct contracting and building operations and similar business as well as to manufacture and sell building material," and that "the company may in connection with its affairs acquire shares in other concerns as investments, but it may not carry on a regular trading business in securities." Here was the first inkling of the far-flung finance company of the future. Referring to the final clause, one of Kreuger's principal apologists commented after Kreuger's death: "One almost has the feeling that [he] was unconsciously seeking to guard against the temptation to be drawn . . . towards a lurking catastrophe." Despite the forswearing of securities trading, no change in the statutes of Kreuger & Toll Aktiebolaget (Inc.) was ever made when the company itself, as well as the public, later traded its stocks in values of hundreds of millions of dollars on the world's exchanges. (The public trading began modestly enough only two years later in January 1914, when the stock was listed on the Stockholm Exchange.)

Beyond the considerable building in Sweden, Kreuger was once more spreading his wings. He had started a real-estate subsidiary called Capitol City, Inc., which at the outset owned five buildings, and he had begun to cast his eye abroad again. Even before incorporating Kreuger & Toll, he had established branch offices of the construction company in Germany, where he installed his old New York and South African sidekick, Anders Jordahl, and in Finland. The Finnish office, in Helsingfors, soon set up a subsidiary in St. Petersburg (now Leningrad), thereby marking Kreuger's first contact with the Russians, who during the twenties, after the Communists had come to power, were to become a constant competitive goad and a source of anxiety to Kreuger, the world financier, and who would ultimately have a lot to do with forcing him to overextend himself. Even at this early date there was trouble for Kreuger, though of a different sort, from the Russian front. While he held most of the stock in these foreign subsidiaries, he allowed them to be run, or at least seem to be run, quite independently. The St. Petersburg office, in the charge of the man in Helsingfors, began doing so much business that, instead of being pleased and proud, Kreuger developed an odd and overpowering resentment. Summoning the agent back to Stockholm, he planted with the police an astonishing report that the fellow was inflating his records with claims of false profits, and he even went so far as to start personal litigation.

The courts, finding no evidence of wrongdoing, quickly disposed of Kreuger's waspish action and ordered him to reinstate the Finnish representative in his job. Kreuger, angered if unashamed, soon lost interest in the Finnish and Russian ends of Kreuger & Toll's construction business. By this time, anyway, he had far larger game in a much smaller physical product—matches.

꞉ 3 ꞉

It has never been altogether clear whether Kreuger came into the match business by design or by chance. His family, of course, had long been interested in matches. His Uncle Fredrik, even though he lived in London, was co-owner with Ivar's father of the two factories in Kalmar and Mönsterås, and by now Torsten, Ivar's younger brother, not only was managing the Kalmar branch but also had bought one of the two Swedish plants for the manufacture of matchmaking machinery. But the match business as a whole in Sweden was not doing well, mainly because it suffered from too much internal competition.

The industry dated back to 1844, when Gustav Eric Pasch, a professor at the Swedish Royal Academy of Science, invented the modern safety match by substituting red phosphorus for poisonous yellow phosphorus and transferring it from its former place on the match tip to a striking surface. Two brothers named Lundström thereupon started a match factory in Jönköping and began to sell their product in Germany and England as well as in Sweden. The invention of a matchmaking machine in 1872 by another Swede, Alexander Lägerman—a simple mechanism that, incidentally, has hardly been changed since—set off a boom that saw the steady building of factories, most of which did not last very long but nevertheless raised competitive havoc. In 1903 this was partly ameliorated by the amalgamation of six large companies into the Jönköping and Vulcan Match Factories, Inc., but there were still about a dozen smaller fry left, including the two Kreuger enterprises, and they were being increasingly squeezed by the major combine.

It became apparent that, if they were to survive, something had to be done. Early in 1912 Kreuger had mentioned the matter to a young banker named Oscar Rydbeck, whom he had met upon his return from America four years before and who was to become one of the foremost bankers in Sweden as well as Kreuger's chief financial prop and adviser until Kreuger's death brought about his ruin too. The new national banking law of 1911 gave banks, for the first time, the right to invest in industrial enterprises, and Rydbeck had told Kreuger that if he increased the authorized shares of his family concerns, these shares could be used as collateral for loans to facilitate more amalgamations. As Kreuger was then still devoting all his efforts to the building business, he let the matter drop for the time. Various other bankers, looking for new investment opportunities, kept after the match proposition. A group of them approached Torsten Kreuger, but he thought the outlook bleak, and when the bankers formally asked Ivar to study the situation, Torsten advised him not to get mixed up in any scheme to bolster the Swedish match industry. This would not be the last time Torsten tried to hold Ivar in check.

Kreuger announced he would think over the bankers' offer, which amounted to an invitation to join them in a new match enterprise. He was obviously tempted, though Torsten, who had gone into the foreign match business and had just bought a big factory in Finland, was not alone in his warnings. Moritz Kahn, the brother of the Detroit steel man, told him he was crazy to start making penny matches when he was, in effect, selling steel at a hundred dollars a ton. But Kreuger must already have had a private image of what he could do with the little penny product. On March 18, 1913, after his period of pondering, he made his decision. He kept his contracting and real-estate holdings, but he also became head of the United Match Factories, Inc., or the Kalmar trust, as it came to be known, which consisted of nine other small Swedish concerns in addition to the two owned by his father and uncle.

Kreuger undoubtedly envisioned from the outset the possibilities of gaining control of much more than just the Swedish match industry. With typical cold logic, he realized that, in matches, he was dealing with something that everyone used everywhere, and that, because Swedish know-how was superior, he might become the match tycoon of Europe. Dr. Bjerre, in his analysis of Kreuger's motivations, believes that "the day he united the match factories should be called the most tragic in Kreuger's life because the wall that the careful contractor had built up against the consequence of his amoral nature had been broken through. This day the devil tempted him. . . ." Certainly, from this day on, he turned his back for good on engineering. A Stockholm acquaintance who was with Kreuger at the time of decision says that he thought up the whole future match-monopoly scheme in twenty-four hours and blueprinted it in his mind, while Anders Jordahl, who met Kreuger in Copenhagen a few weeks later, recalls that "with a great deal of enthusiasm" his friend revealed his ultimate plan "to consolidate the match business of the world under one control." Jordahl adds: "He had absolute confidence in his own ability to accomplish this goal, and he felt equally assured that once it should be reached whatever sums of money had been borrowed to build up the structure would be repaid with very handsome profits to every investor." Over a fine Danish meal Jordahl listened raptly and, while he thought Kreuger might be "over-optimistic," he was tremendously impressed, as were others, among them banker Rydbeck, to whom the dream was confided.

Kreuger made as much of an immediate stir in the match business as he had in building. With the support of three banks, one of which was Rydbeck's Scandinaviska Kredit A.B. (The Swedish Credit Bank), the Kalmar trust was capitalized at four million kroner, or about a million dollars—less than a third of what the opposition Jönköping-Vulcan trust was worth. Kreuger went to work at once to build the trust into a more smoothly functioning organization. First he bought the second of the two companies that made match machines in Sweden—Torsten still owned the other one—and then he set about lowering costs and raising the quality of the matches produced in his various factories. The outbreak of war cut down the imports of raw materials, especially aspen wood from Russia, and Kreuger made a deal with the Jönköping trust to conserve and promote the development of aspen trees in the northern part of Sweden. But that was the end of his co-operation, for the moment. He beat the more conservative Jönköping group to the draw by selling matches to Germany and her allies, in return for which he got some raw materials shipped north secretly. He also started producing his own potash and phosphorus, and, above all, he began to build up a competitive foreign sales organization.

Here events played into his hands. The Jönköping company had marketed a large part of its product in the Far East, which was now cut off not only by the war but also by Japanese commercial expansion, especially in India. The Japanese were manufacturing matches in large quantities labeled, for prestige, MADE IN TIDAHOLM, SWEDEN. Though the claim was patently false, there was an ironic twist of truth to it, for a year or so before the war a visiting Japanese engineer had surreptitiously let his hat drop into a vat of chemicals in a Jönköping plant and, after fishing it out, had analyzed the secret formula the Swedes used.

The main office of the Kalmar trust consisted of one room in downtown Stockholm, where Kreuger and another man who was destined to be at his side all his life, Krister Littorin, worked with a typist and a messenger boy. Littorin had been a year behind Kreuger at the university. The importance of high-school and university associations in creating lifelong loyalties is probably greater in Sweden than anywhere else, and Kreuger henceforth made good use of this as an excuse to surround himself with weaklings and sycophants who would do what he ordered without question. Littorin, an electrical engineer by training, was no weakling, but he was pliable and, most importantly, he always worshipped Kreuger. A warm, handsome man who was a good mixer and, like his employer, a good linguist, he was a perfect foil for the more somber, seemingly abstracted Kreuger. After college the two men had met briefly in New York, and they had seen each other now and then after both returned to Sweden in 1907. Now, seven years later, they traveled to London to persuade two British sales agencies to join forces with them.

One of the agencies belonged to Kreuger's Uncle Fredrik, who wanted to keep it for himself, and he was obstinate about it. But Ivar, as he did with everybody, played upon his uncle's weakness, which was alcohol, and got him to sign an agreement while drunk. With the help of a lawyer, Fredrik later tried to have the contract set aside, but there had been no witnesses—Ivar had carefully kept Littorin away while he was softening up the old boy—and the deal was upheld. Here was one of the first significant examples of

Kreuger's ruthless business philosophy. The fact that a close relative was concerned made no difference to him. (Much later he was to be criticized for allowing his aged father to remain on the board of Kreuger & Toll until it went bankrupt, even though he knew that a collapse was imminent.) Throughout his career, though he was a kind and generous employer for the most part, Kreuger would betray any of his friends if he saw his work threatened or if he needed something badly.

Even though he knew little of the larger mechanics of the match industry—his experience in the Mönsterås factory had been quite limited—he displayed a genius for dealing with its major problems. From this time on, like an artist, Kreuger poured himself and all his resources, physical and creative, into what he was doing. Dr. Bjerre, looking back on these beginnings, later commented: "There was something special about his work. The strangeness was not only in the power with which he dominated everything [but] we might be uniquely confronted with the fact that for the first time a human being has lived out his capacity for good and evil as completely in a financial creation as hitherto artists and poets have done in their individual ways." It is a fact that what Kreuger fashioned became a kind of fantasy, such a mixture of real and unreal, with the line between increasingly difficult to distinguish, that ultimately he would no longer know where truth left off and fiction began. Once he was enmeshed in his fantastic scheme, it became self-perpetuating, carrying him forward at such a dizzying rate that even he must have been surprised, despite his bold predictions to Jordahl and others.

In the first year of its operation, when a lot of new equipment was bought, the Kalmar trust lost seven thousand dollars, but after that it prospered, making a profit of about sixty thousand dollars the following year. In 1916 it cleared more than half a million dollars and declared a twelve-per-cent dividend. By then it was doing almost as much business as the larger Jönköping-Vulcan combine, and at the close of 1917 Kreuger brought off his biggest coup to date by almost single-handedly negotiating a merger of the two into the twenty-seven-million-dollar Svenska Tändsticksaktiebolaget, or Swedish Match Company, of which he became president. This represented a very large undertaking in Sweden at the time. Included in the transaction were shares in chlorate-of-potash factories, paper and printing mills for making labels, machine-making facilities, and rights to a hundred thousand acres of forest and logging country. Kreuger had been so persuasive in arguing for the merger that he managed to overvalue the shares of the Kalmar trust, so that the smaller organization more or less "swallowed" the larger—it was his first big venture in inflating values, which was to become his prime tactic henceforth. By controlling the votes of a large number of stockholders, Kreuger completely dominated the new concern.

What, in the meantime, was he doing with Kreuger & Toll? It had grown, since its incorporation in 1911, to a company with six building, real-estate, and investment subsidiaries in Sweden, Finland, Russia, and Germany, with total annual profits of some two hundred thousand dollars and paying a neat dividend of fifteen per cent. In January 1917 Kreuger had split the company into two distinct parts. One, called the Kreuger & Toll Building Co. and run by Paul Toll, remained purely a contracting enterprise; Kreuger had practically nothing to do with it thereafter, though he kept some stock. The other and much more important half, simply called Kreuger & Toll, Inc., became an amorphous financial holding company that could be used any way Kreuger wished—in fact, henceforth it was nothing more nor less than his own free-wheeling fiduciary instrument. By 1918, following new stock issues, the authorized shares of this new Kreuger & Toll holding concern amounted to sixteen million kroner, or about five million dollars at the dollar rate then current, and its reserves were seven million dollars. The total was still less than that of Swedish Match, but not for long, for Kreuger would soon start using it for investment and expansion on a massive scale and, above all, for manipulation. The match company, while its affairs grew inextricably entangled with Kreuger & Toll's and even more interwoven with Kreuger's personal accounts, would nevertheless remain the relatively straight spar of his vast and designedly ramified financial structure. The interrelationship between Kreuger & Toll and Swedish Match, which was later to drive a battery of accountants crazy, began at once when Kreuger transferred one hundred and twenty thousand shares of the latter (slightly more than a quarter of the total) to the former, crediting Swedish Match with two million dollars for them.

: 4 :

Just as the war years had given Kreuger a chance to beat down his Swedish match opposition, so the post-war period opened up new opportunities abroad. It was a time when the world's markets were in a state of total disruption, a condition that Kreuger, with his now well-geared machine, could take quick advantage of. He did so with gumption, guile, and relish in a series of swift, open maneuvers and carefully planned secret deals for the purchase of match factories all over Europe. Openly, for example, he managed to recapture most of the markets in Asia from the Japanese, and as soon as import restrictions were lifted in England he was able to sell matches there again. Simultaneously he dumped large stocks of inferior wartime matches in Germany and Russia. Because the German mark was worth very little and it was impossible to get any money out of the country,

Kreuger—through his right-hand man, Littorin—bought up huge chunks of real estate in Hamburg, Danzig, and Berlin. His purchases in the German capital included valuable properties on Unter den Linden, Friedrichstrasse, and Leipzigerstrasse, and when he later sold them he earned a seventy-million-mark profit.

Kreuger transacted at last two good-sized Russian deals, one through a White Russian in Paris, a former officer in General Denikin's anti-Communist army named Nemirovsky, who was apparently acting as a middleman for the Communists. Nemirovsky at first seemed immune to Kreuger's blandishments and even tried to organize an opposition bloc to Swedish Match, but Kreuger kept after him. Nemirovsky had a weakness for fast new cars, and Kreuger bought him one in Paris. Finally the Russian agreed to sell a Polish match factory Kreuger had sought, and then the two men arranged a sale to Russia of a million and a half dollars' worth of low-grade matches. Russian rubles were not considered a very good risk, but with the help of a private Paris bank that agreed to guarantee the payment, Kreuger managed to transfer his return on the sale into hard Swiss francs, about two and a half million dollars' worth, which meant a good profit. Typically—for it was one of his odd quirks that he frequently forgot what he had done with important pieces of paper or even with large amounts of cash —he stuffed the credit slip into a pocket of a pair of trousers and didn't think anything more about it until a week or more later Littorin asked him in Stockholm how he had made out in Paris. A second load of matches went directly to the Black Sea as an out-and-out gamble. A friend of Kreuger's, a former Swedish Olympic oarsman who had become a merchant captain, in effect bartered this batch at local ports for tobacco and other products, which he then sold to several Balkan nations where organized markets and relatively stable currencies existed.

For the other, more important part of his program—the buying of European match factories, especially in countries where depreciated currencies and cheap labor threatened him with serious fresh competition in the export field—Kreuger needed a lot of money. The profits of the Swedish Match Company soared from nearly two million dollars in 1918 to nearly three million the next year (the dividend was jumped to fourteen per cent), but that wasn't nearly enough for Kreuger's purposes, which he regarded as protective at first but which soon became part of his greater ambition to corner the whole match market, or as much of it as he could, and set up a monopoly with himself in Stockholm at the center. He temporarily solved the problem by getting a credit of about twenty million dollars from several Swedish banks that agreed to be part of an underground "international match syndicate," operating covertly because, for the most part, Kreuger necessarily had to function behind the scenes: if he gave any indication of what he was up to, he obviously wouldn't get what he was after. It was just the kind of operation he loved best, and he carried it out with Machiavellian zest. One of his favorite tricks in buying up scattered Continental match factories was to begin by competing directly with better-quality matches in the country in question. Then he would send out secret agents posing as independent buyers, and they would make ridiculously low offers for the match plants. When these were rejected, Kreuger would descend with a much better offer, which would invariably be accepted.

The competition potentially most dangerous to Kreuger in the immediate post-war period came from Belgium, where the match industry, like everything else, had been disrupted or destroyed, but where some excellent factories were salvageable. Early in 1919 he sent a young Swede named Gunnar Cederschiöld on a scouting expedition. Cederschiöld was a personable journalist whom Kreuger had hired on the spur of the moment one day in Stockholm as an "observer," suggesting that while he was working as a newspaper correspondent in Paris he could do odd jobs for the match company on the side. This was the sort of arrangement Kreuger now established with a number of individuals, creating his own "foreign service," and it best suited his strategy to have as his agents men who had other regular jobs so that no one would suspect they were also employed by him. When Cederschiöld had protested that he knew nothing about matches beyond how to light them, Kreuger had smiled and said: "I know, but you speak several languages and you know history and understand Europe, all of which is worth a lot more to me. You can pick up all you have to know about the match business in a couple of hours."

Cederschiöld, who was later to become Kreuger's chief Paris representative, had got his quick briefing, visited London with his new employer, and then returned to France, where he covered the Peace Conference. In Ghent and Grammont, in Belgium, he found a pair of match factories that had been damaged but could be repaired, and he suggested in a cable that some sort of lease or rental deal with the Belgian owners might be worked out. Kreuger replied that he wanted as free a hand as possible, and some equity of his own. A new economic crisis had begun in the Far East, where the price of silver had dropped heavily, and the impact of the slump had spread slowly west, affecting financial conditions in London and, to some extent, on the Continent. Cheap as matches were, in many poor homes they were being split in two and sometimes in four. "Kreuger told me that the situation in the world market was now such that if we didn't soon make an attack we'd be conquered," Cederschiöld later wrote. "A defensive posture was impossible." Quietly, through some small banks, Kreuger arranged to buy the two Belgian factories outright. Over the next several years he bought four others, merged them, just as he had done in Sweden, and then, as he had also done there, worked co-operatively for a time with the leading Belgian trust and ended by capturing complete control of the nation's match business.

What he did in Belgium he did in varying degree elsewhere. In Austria, for example, working with his brother, Torsten, who henceforth would take over most of the match business in eastern Europe, he secretly bought a majority of shares of the most important match company, Solo A. G., which also owned factories in Hungary, Czechoslovakia, and Yugoslavia. Mostly through outright purchases, he soon gained control of the industry in Norway, Finland, Denmark, Holland, and Switzerland, while in England he made an import-and-sales agreement with the largest firm, Bryant & May, and obtained majority control of the second-largest, Masters & Co. His aim was not only to dominate the production of matches wherever possible, but also to guide their distribution, and that meant getting rid of local middlemen and substituting his own people—for the most part Swedes—and his own system. There were temporary setbacks, as in France in 1921, when a large number of leftover, poor-quality military matches were suddenly thrown on the market and imports from Sweden were cut way down, but Kreuger got a stranglehold on, or at least a foothold in, an increasing number of places. He sometimes paid heavily for what he wanted and began the process of overextending himself which he would later carry to extremes, but, for the moment at least, the credit was available in Sweden. Though the profits of the Swedish Match Company remained about the same during these years, it was significant that the name of Ivar Kreuger was everywhere beginning to be heard. Almost overnight an unknown Swede of forty had become one of the new breed of European master industrialists, such as Hugo Stinnes in Germany, men of mys-

tery who flitted across the diffuse economic landscape of
the unsettled Continent like swift chameleons.

⁖ 5 ⁖

Kreuger had now begun to live two lives. One, of which
the public saw something, was that of the emerging business
giant, the quiet, worldly, always polite and considerate man
who listened respectfully to those older and seemingly wiser
than himself, deferring when he went to London, for instance, to his banker friend and champion Oscar Rydbeck.
Rydbeck, who was highly esteemed in English banking and
business circles, gave Kreuger the best of introductions in
the City and spoke of him everywhere as "the coming man
in Sweden." With his uncanny eye for judging people,
Kreuger quickly saw Rydbeck as made to order for him.
The banker liked nothing better than to discuss big issues
in the company of big men, as at the Versailles peace negotiations, where he had been a Swedish observer. With a
vanity that was tempered by a fund of charm, he already
envisioned himself as a kind of roving foreign or finance
minister for Kreuger, who encouraged the image.

Kreuger's other life was compounded partly of his secret
financial schemes and partly of private forms of release far
removed from the relatively prosaic if profitable world of
matchsticks. What this life chiefly represented was his personal image of power; involved were elements of chance
and danger upon which, like the boy in Kalmar who had
cheated in school and the youth in America and South
Africa who had boldly felt his way in a variety of new
fields, the maturing Kreuger thrived, approaching his opportunities like a hunter with an innate seventh sense and
a heightened awareness, a daring to try anything without
fear or qualms.

Thus, for example, in 1918 Kreuger took a tremendous plunge in a dollar speculation which in two years brought him a profit estimated to have been between two and three million dollars. The dollar, when he made this venture, was worth only about 2.80 kroner, but Kreuger firmly believed its value would soon increase. He thought nothing, as would almost anyone else, of the risks involved in gambling with such large sums and made a deal with a Stockholm bank whereby he was able to obtain a huge amount of kroner on loan. As soon as he had bought the dollars, he pledged them for the amount of the loan and got an American bank to guarantee them. By late 1919 the dollar was worth 4.83 kroner and thereafter it kept rising, so Kreuger cashed in splendidly. This was a personal profit—his private fortune that year was estimated by Rydbeck at twenty-five million kroner, or about five million dollars, which made him one of the richest men in Scandinavia. At about the same time he made another speculation that was part of his expanding match business but was also something of a personal coup, the profits of which he was able to use as he saw fit. He bought a majority of shares in a chemical company in Griesheim, Germany—jokingly, he confided to a friend that the stock certificates were all in small denominations equivalent to one hundred marks and that he consequently had so many of them that he had to rent a warehouse room in Berlin in which to store them. Two years later the chemical concern was merged with many others to form the vast I. G. Farben trust. In exchange for his shares, Kreuger got securities in the big new combine, and their value soared so that he eventually made about fifteen times his original investment.

The fact that Kreuger had always got away with what he did, from cribbing in school on, undoubtedly encouraged him in certain odd accounting practices which he engaged in with increasing recklessness. Even his earliest methods of

keeping books were—to put it as charitably as possible—
unconventional. His essential philosophy of accounting, if
it can be called a philosophy, was that a balance sheet existed mainly to paint pretty pictures for the public. He had
an almost poetic approach to annual reports—he usually
wrote them himself—and he believed the function of figures
was not to reproduce a situation as it existed but to create
an impression of it as he wished to portray it. If he had any
basic theory at all, it was one of organic and continuing
growth: neither events nor cycles should retard progress,
and mounting profits, whether they existed or not, accompanied by ever soaring dividends (even if they came out of
capital) were necessary to keep the customers happy and
the credit coming. The other aspect of the principle was
secrecy, and, as the need for it was implicit in the nature
of his operation, he extended the principle to his books.

When they were examined after his death by competent
certified public accountants, and when the liquidators
sought to prepare a chronology of events, a great deal of
pertinent information was missing, but enough was discovered to set the date of his first manipulations as far back as
1917, though his acts then implied purposeful mystification
rather than misdeeds. Certain large debits and credits were
entered that year in Kreuger's personal account with the
match company, for example, without any explanation of
where the profits had come from or how the money advanced to him as managing director of the secret syndicate
for buying factories had been used. There can be little
doubt that money was indeed made and spent, but, contrary to normal procedure, this was done chiefly by one
man, Kreuger himself, and it is pretty hard, when the circumstances are unexplained, to distinguish ingenuity from
questionable practices. There is also some evidence that
Kreuger quietly bought shares in one of his Swedish match
concerns and then sold them at a profit to another company

in his trust, in effect inflating their value and enabling him to announce a higher dividend. He adopted this technique assiduously thereafter.

Throughout his bizarre career Kreuger alone supplied the figures for the books of his various companies, and he mostly kept them in his head and juggled them as he saw fit. Annual reports, as a result, were artistic figments rather than factual statements, and as so much of the money passed through his private accounts Kreuger was able to switch amounts from one company to another and attach any label to them he saw fit, or, indeed, no specific label at all beyond "sundry expenses" or "undistributed profits." Because of the unusual nature of such operations, he was especially careful in picking his accountants. With one exception, the men he chose were almost totally ignorant of professional accounting practices—in fact, they were selected precisely for how little rather than how much they knew. The exception was a former schoolmate of Kreuger's in Kalmar named Sigurd Hennig, and, typically, there was something a little shady in Hennig's past. He had been forced to resign from a bank where he had been a junior clerk because he failed to report immediately a shortage of two thousand kroner. In 1913, when Kreuger made his first amalgamation of match concerns, Hennig went to work for him as a bookkeeper, and by 1919 he was chief accountant and controller of the Swedish Match Company at what was then a high salary of six thousand dollars a year. Though his duties were officially limited to the match business, Hennig's intelligence and his growing comprehension through the years of all of Kreuger's tangled affairs, plus the fact that he handled the income-tax reports of many officers, would finally bring him, at the very end, to the point of openly challenging Kreuger about bookkeeping entries and methods, and about certain phony valuations; but by then it would be too late to make much difference.

Though Kreuger's secret dealings were accepted as necessary by the board of directors of the Swedish Match Company, which included some prominent businessmen and even a famous Swedish jurist, the directors kept after him for information about the company's affairs, as did the bankers who had lent him so much money. But Kreuger had a great gift for satisfying their collective curiosity while still making sure he ran the show. With money flowing mysteriously in and out of new investments, profits and property values were often arbitrarily determined and based on future projections, which Kreuger alone made. In 1919, for instance, the amount of match-company earnings to be listed in the books depended substantially on what worth should be ascribed to certain assets in Germany, where the mark was so highly inflated. Kreuger told one of his subordinates that, on the one hand, he wanted to hold profits down to reduce his tax bill, while on the other hand he wanted to make profits seem higher in accordance with his prime strategy of impressing investors. The second argument won out, and he hit upon a profit figure for the year of 8,753,068 kroner, which in no way represented a true value but consisted largely of Kreuger's projection—including his estimate, in kroner, of what he deemed the profit in marks, say, would have been *if* they could have been turned into kroner under "normal conditions." Kreuger thus disregarded the devaluation of the mark on neutral markets and calmly projected what he thought his German assets would be worth once Germany got on her feet. If anyone questioned him about such easy extrapolations, as happened occasionally, he would simply smile benignly—he was perhaps the greatest benign smiler of all time—and explain his reasoning so persuasively that the reality of it all would seem overpowering and the questioner would feel like a fool.

Kreuger's sovereign nonchalance, which enabled him to carry off such situations with complete aplomb, was not a pose. It was something he had always possessed, since childhood, that charismatic quality that made others turn to him spontaneously for counsel and leadership, and his word was no more doubted when he began dealing with the top bankers and businessmen of Europe and America, or with statesmen and diplomats who consulted him, than it had been when he was a youthful ringleader in Kalmar. "Where's Ivar? He'll fix it," was the lifelong refrain. He ruled his concerns like a benevolent dictator, using democratic forms that gave them a semblance of being old-fashioned family enterprises, comfortable and unhurried. From the very beginning he chose all his disciples, especially in the match company, with prescient care. At the top were attractive, sophisticated men, either engineers or persons with a good business background. On the secondary level, he sent out into the field, as regional or national supervisors of his growing match empire, men whom he had known well for a number of years and whose personal loyalty he could thoroughly depend upon. When a particularly important job had to be done and he couldn't find time to do it himself, he would send one of his chief lieutenants from Stockholm —Krister Littorin, for instance, spent six months in 1920 in the Far East.

On the lowest level, Kreuger had the equivalent of "the boys in the back room" who would simply do as he told them and ask no questions, and whenever possible he sought men for these jobs who were beholden to him personally for some reason known only to Ivar Kreuger and the individual in question. One and all were inculcated with his own passion for secrecy. In fact, when a young engineer was hired by the match company, he had to sign an "Oath of Secrecy" by which he pledged to keep to himself any aspect of the business he might learn about, and the penalty for making any disclosure, not only during the period of his employment but for a ten-year period after departure from the company, was a twenty-five-thousand-dollar fine—a punishment that was doubtless difficult to enforce but that had the desired effect of provoking silence through fear. Kreuger meant that secrecy should be practiced within the company too; carefully compartmentalizing everything made it easier for him, as the sole free wheel, to do what he wished without the knowledge of more than one assistant at a time.

In the case of Kreuger & Toll, which was his own creature and where he had no inquisitive directors in the wings, Kreuger could have hired blind men as his aides for all the difference it would have made. He practically had one in a young fellow named Karlsson, who was the company's original accountant. Karlsson had begun as a storekeeper in Kreuger's building company, and, except for a short course in bookkeeping in Stockholm, he had absolutely no training in accounting and no comprehension of the company's real activities. For that matter, except for Kreuger, no one did. The company's board was a joke. Its original members were Kreuger; his doting father; Paul Toll, who was busy with the building business; and two other old Kreuger buddies, Nils Ahlström and Erik Sjöström. Ahlström did virtually nothing, and Sjöström, another of Kreuger's Kalmar schoolmates, ran the real-estate end of the business at Kreuger's bidding. No board member was ever really consulted about anything. In 1919, for example, Kreuger & Toll's profits leaped from approximately one million dollars to nearly a million and three quarters, and Kreuger declared a fine dividend of twenty-five per cent. Two thirds of the year's profits were set down simply as earnings on "various transactions." Each year when the board met before the annual report was to be issued, Sjöström later testified, "Kreuger would come in briskly, make a short speech about the situation, announce the net gains and how they were to be divided among the subsidiaries, tell us what was to be kept in the reserve fund and describe how fresh capital was to be obtained by new share issues. That was all. The whole performance only took a few minutes and there were never any objections." Ultimately Sjöström, who went out of his mind, couldn't even remember whether he had been on the boards of various subsidiaries—indeed, Kreuger had an interesting habit of putting people on his boards without telling them.

By 1920 Kreuger & Toll had financial interests in a small film company, in a mortgage bank, and in a railway company as well as in large amounts of real estate and in other enterprises—its portfolio was atypically Swedish in its diversity, totaling about a dozen different investments. If the board members had a vague idea of what Kreuger was doing at home or elsewhere in Scandinavia, none of them knew immediately of an important new venture he had begun in America. Late in 1919, with his old friend Anders Jordahl, Kreuger went to New York—his first trip there since 1907—and formed a holding company called American Kreuger & Toll. The initial capital of some six million dollars was represented by shares to that value in the Swedish Match Company, which ostensibly came from Kreuger's personal match holdings or from shares in Swedish Match owned by Kreuger & Toll. In any case, the transfers went totally unrecorded in any books. This was one of the earliest examples of how Kreuger kept the interrelated affairs of his various companies in his head, either, as one of the investigating accountants afterward wrote, because he "forgot," or because he "did not desire to inform the bookkeeper[s] about them." Americans were just beginning to be interested in the post-war European real-estate boom, and one of the chief purposes of American Kreuger & Toll was to buy real estate there and sell it at a profit. As a result of some of the deals American Kreuger & Toll arranged, Kreuger was able to get part of his tied-up money out of Germany at the going rather than the real rate of exchange. American Kreuger & Toll was also designed, according to Jordahl, "to give Kreuger the fresh foothold he wanted in the States," and "we soon had stock in various new companies that were supposed to work up any likely business that came along." There were, among other things, a chemical-and-pharmaceutical import firm, a cigarette-packaging concern, a company that traded in cutlery and surgical instruments, a real-estate brokerage, a general investment business, and something called the Midwest Steel and Supply Company, of Bradford, Pennsylvania, which was principally engaged in importing air filters from Germany. Jordahl, who got a salary of twelve thousand dollars a year plus seven thousand for expenses, scurried around carrying out Kreuger's orders, and every now and then he would get a notification from a bank that such and such a sum, often a large amount, had been deposited in the name of American Kreuger & Toll or one of its subsidiaries by some company abroad Jordahl had never heard of. Kreuger was beginning to proliferate on a large scale, and one of the truly secret things he did during this 1919-20 trip to America—so secret that not even Jordahl knew of it until much later—was to purchase through a private intermediary, his first block of shares in the important Diamond Match Company. It never became clear just where he got the cash for this purchase, but it undoubtedly came from one of his successful personal speculations, perhaps from his gamble in dollars, which may already have begun to pay off.

Back in Stockholm, no one could have guessed the extent

to which Kreuger was already wheeling and dealing abroad. He made a particular point of conducting himself in Sweden as a careful, conservative businessman, reserving his consciously acquired dash and flare for his foreign ventures. The working nucleus of the Swedish Match Company was made up, in addition to Kreuger and Littorin, of only two other men—Carl Bergman, an engineer who had known Kreuger at the university and met him again in America in 1907, and a young man named Berndt Hay, whose father was head of the Jönköping-Vulcan group of match factories. The four ate lunch together every day, and as Bergman, like Kreuger, was a bachelor, the two sometimes spent evenings together. "We never left the office before seven," Bergman, still hale and hearty in his eighties in Stockholm, recalled forty years later. "Ivar's whole life, as far as I could tell, was his work, and he often told me so, adding that the match company was his only child. I remember him saying, 'Most people throw off their work at five o'clock, but I'm at my best after that. That's when I most like to sit down and plan.' Sometimes he'd ask me to his place for a frugal dinner—too frugal as far as I was concerned, and I was always hungry when we got up, but the wine was excellent. Occasionally we'd go on to the theater, and when he decided not to talk about business he could be the most fascinating man and speak amiably about many things. His amiability was never boisterous, and very often it wasn't even the sort that invites response. There was always an inner reserve about him. Even when he wasn't conversing, he seemed to be deep in his thoughts. There was an odd air of greatness about Ivar. I think he could get people to do anything. They fell for him, they couldn't resist his peculiar charm and magnetism. That was his secret, his psychological quality of leadership, his extraordinary intuition. He could grasp things immediately. Above all, there was a look about him that made a difference. I saw J. P. Morgan's eyes many times in New York. They were like fire coals. But Ivar's eyes were not like that. They had another quality. Though small and narrow, they seemed capable, if he desired, of looking right through you."

CHAPTER 3

America the Bountiful

KREUGER'S TRIP to America in 1919, when he set up his subsidiary to Kreuger & Toll, was more than just another foreign venture. It was the start of his new and permanent relationship with this country which would ultimately prove so disastrous to himself and to everyone concerned. At the moment, however, the romance between Kreuger and New York, the financial heart of the nation, was about to flourish. He had already come to feel more at home there than anywhere else outside of Sweden. The city's appeal lay in its very size and in the fact that it offered him anonymity. It seemed ready to accept him, almost as soon as he started making a name for himself, on his own terms, and he was able to find in it a psychological incognito that matched the physical incognito he had begun to use when he traveled. Beyond its sophistication, New York provided a symbolism that suited him admirably. The symbolic aspect had to do with wealth and power, jointly acquired. Already operating above the battle, Kreuger had begun to plot and think and act on a detached, presentimental plane. In Stockholm he was expected to respond to people and events in ordinary human terms, demonstrating fancies and foibles like anyone else. In New York, on the other hand, there was a less personal and far more pragmatic reaction to the unique, many-faceted, and diversified young Swede who walked softly but so obviously carried a big wallet. On more than one occasion Kreuger was to remark that the Americans understood him better than his fellow Swedes. Certainly no one had a keener, more instinctive comprehension of what the Americans wanted and of how far they would go to get it. The attraction for everybody was easy money, and in the fall of 1922, when once again he arrived here, the big post-war boom in Wall Street was just getting under way.

For Kreuger, the situation was particularly attractive, America was eager to lend dollars abroad at high interest rates. Europeans wanted them, and Kreuger would see that they got them—to his own corollary advantage. The situation on the Continent, in the wake of the Versailles Treaty, was growing increasingly serious. Before the war Germany had been a central support for the European economic system. The nation's neighbors had traded heavily with her and, in numerous cases, had looked to her for the capital for their own commercial and industrial development; it was no exaggeration to say that the high standard of living in most of Europe had been the result of German economic strength and efficiency. The organization of the Continental economy, however, had been complicated and delicately balanced, supported as it was by German coal, iron, and transport, and by the importation of food and raw materials from abroad. Thus, Germany's loss of her colonies and her merchant fleet at Versailles was a blow that became immediately serious to the whole of Europe. Her heavy reparations obligations made her recovery all the more difficult, if not impossible.

Further, the Balkanization of Europe by the peace treaty, creating thirty-four separate political units out of twenty-five, set up a whole new series of unworkable units, aggravated by ethnic differences. Vast population groups, already sorely stricken by the destruction and deprivation of war, were now left floating in a vacuum, with their internal productivity almost nonexistent, their transport systems broken apart, and no supplies coming, as before, from overseas. The efficiency of labor was at a low ebb and millions were out of work; the soil was exhausted because of wartime neglect, and a revolutionary ground swell in a number of nations, new and old, was brewing fresh trouble. Finally, widespread inflation was destroying the commercial assets that remained intact, and even where goods could be produced, the breakdown of the European currency system inhibited their sale. As Keynes wrote in his classic *The Economic Consequences of the Peace*, "The inflationism of the currency systems of Europe has proceeded to extraordinary lengths. The various belligerent governments, unable, or too timid or too short-sighted to secure from loans or taxes the resources they required, have printed notes for the balance. In Russia and Austria-Hungary this process has reached a point where for the purposes of foreign trade the currency is practically valueless. The Polish mark can be bought for about three cents and the Austrian crown for less than two cents, but they cannot be sold at all. The German mark is worth less than four cents on the exchanges. . . . The currency of Italy has fallen to a little more than half of its nominal value in spite of its being still subject to some degree of regulation; French currency maintains an uncertain market; and even sterling is seriously diminished in present value and impaired in its future prospects." Keynes also noted: "We are thus faced in Europe with the spectacle of an extraordinary weakness on the part of the great capitalist class, which has emerged from the industrial triumphs of the nineteenth century, and seemed a very few years ago our all-powerful master."

In this atmosphere, as the fluctuating value of Continental currencies brought a new class of ruthless speculator to the fore, the Swedish capital exporter and his Swiss counterpart appeared as *dei ex machina.* Before the war Sweden had been a rather unimportant country economically, despite its considerable national wealth. Now, overnight, it loomed as one of the few exporters of capital. Swedish businessmen, moreover, had always been known for their high standard of ethics. At the top of the list was Ivar Kreuger. On a scale that would seem to give him his greatest stature, he would single-handedly try to create some degree of economic and financial order in the years ahead. If his methods were not always aboveboard, his larger vision remained Napoleonic in scope, and he often said he thought Napoleon was history's foremost figure. As the Emperor used men in battle, moving them grandly if overweeningly, across Europe, so the financier used the dollars he raised like mercenaries in America, and by distributing nearly four hundred million of them loftily, if overgenerously, among fifteen different countries, he did his considerable bit to promote economic and monetary reform and unity in the critical period of post-war readjustment. In this sense, he could be said to have anticipated the much later Marshall Plan. It is ironic that much of the money he lent in return for his match monopolies would be applied to good purposes— that Greece, for example, spent the five million dollars it borrowed from Kreuger to repatriate a million and a half refugees from Turkey, Macedonia, Bulgaria, and Hungary —and that, using American funds as a private person, he

did what the American government and bankers refused
to do themselves as the twenties moved on: lend any more
abroad directly. There is added irony in the fact that revolutionary programs of land reform in Hungary, Latvia, and
Estonia were largely paid for by Kreuger dollars obtained
in capitalistic Wall Street.

In siphoning off so many millions from the eager and
gullible American public, Kreuger's success, on both an al-
truistic and a nefarious plane, was made possible by the
penchant of Americans for evading taxes by transferring or
leaving capital gains abroad and by lax methods of accounting which allowed him, as a free-wheeling operator, to shift
huge funds to Europe and move them at will from one place
to another. It was part of the money-mad mood that Wall
Street's carelessness in guarding the dispersal of its corporate
funds was an open invitation for someone to come along
and fool it, just as it was fooling thousands of Americans
with exaggerated claims of how easily profits could be made
through speculation. As a foreigner whose companies were
not subject to American rules and regulations, loose as they
were, the polite and soft-spoken Kreuger, supposed exem-
plar of a nation known for its honest ways, was a perfect
man for hoodwinking Wall Street. In the overblown era
of financial fantasy, he soon became the tallest representative of the illusory belief that the more money was spent,
the more there was to be made; that vast stock issues, pyr-
amided one upon the other through holding companies, led
to proliferated plenty, to an endless rush of dollars pouring
out of a fabled cornucopia. While he was all but deified as
the greatest of financial wizards, his methods grew more and
more fraudulent; while he kept the Americans happy with
record-breaking dividends that allayed their curiosity about
what was actually happening to the money they were hand-
ing over to him so profligately, most of their capital would

disappear in the fantastic maze of real and make-believe companies and banks he established and ran so autocratically in Europe.

: 2 :

Sooner or later, then, simply because there was so much more money in America than anywhere else, Kreuger was bound to approach the banks and investment houses of New York. But there was a special reason for his return to New York in 1922. Not only had Sweden become too small for him, but he already had overextended himself there, and certain influential persons were aware of it. By this time he had successfully put out stock issues totaling forty-five million kroner in Swedish Match and twenty-eight million in Kreuger & Toll (in dollar terms this was less than it would have been earlier, for the kroner had fallen from a pre-war rate averaging 3.70 to the dollar in 1914 to a 5.70 rate in 1920), but there were indications that he was increasingly engaging in peculiar if not shady practices. In the first place, he was claiming a greater volume of business than he was actually doing, and in a confidential memorandum a government banking inspector had noted that Swedish Match's assertion of having doubled its pre-war rate of export was exaggerated by at least half. Secondly, to bolster such declarations and make it appear that nothing was so good as Swedish Match stock, Kreuger was quietly supporting the market in his own securities. Lastly, and most importantly, in his search for new capital to carry on his foreign-expansion program, he had overborrowed in Sweden to the point where the banks would no longer finance him. Not long ago, while admitting that he spoke from hindsight, Jacob Wallenberg, who as head of the powerful Enskilda Bank in Stockholm is one of the most highly esteemed bankers in the world today, remarked to the author that he had "distrusted the Kreuger set-up from way back." "Kreuger came to see me one day in 1921," Wallenberg recalled, "and his behavior then gave me the impression that something was wrong. A year later, when the Svenskehandelsbanken, with which he was doing business, was in trouble—it was during a post-war banking crisis—we were asked to help out, and we discovered exactly, in the course of our investigations, what he owed that bank and several others in Sweden. His position very definitely was not what a careful banker would call a sound one."

These were very private matters, and the bankers and investment counselors of Wall Street knew nothing about them—among Swedish bankers it might have been considered a violation of the trust they had so far placed in Kreuger if the news of his difficulties at home had been publicized abroad. American bankers and investment men actually knew few details of Kreuger's operations in Europe. He surely knew more about their methods and desires. Not only was his English fairly fluent as a result of his previous experience here, but he also knew how to conduct business in the American style, adjusting himself to an atmosphere that was alternately serious and convivial, wherein confidence, which he was such a born master at creating, was the constant key. Though withdrawn and often purposefully silent, he could banter beautifully when he wanted to, and when the ship-news reporters flocked aboard the *Berengaria* at quarantine to interview the mysterious Swedish match king upon his arrival, he was ready with quips and quotations. When someone asked him jokingly if he had a match, he smiled and—no public-relations expert could have set it up better—replied that he was sorry but, oddly enough, he never seemed to have one with him. He left no doubt, though, that, having established himself all over Europe— and, upon demand, he rattled off the list of countries—he had come to America to talk about matches and to offer his securities on the local market, with a promise of high returns.

Over the next month or so Kreuger spoke with a number of bankers and investment men in Wall Street, almost all of whom responded enthusiastically and with high anticipation. His Continental manner and bearing were polished, and there was a tone of conviction in everything he said. He was always immaculately, if somewhat somberly, dressed, and he usually carried a cane and wore a dark homburg that covered a balding head—for several years he had fought a losing battle, with all sorts of apparatus and treatments, to save his hair. His naturally high brow gave him an intellectual look that his other features, especially his calmly appraising, deep-set, and rather mocking gray-green eyes, accentuated. He had a strange pallid skin that seemed oddly porous and that made his face look fuller than it was. Beneath high cheekbones his mouth was contracted in repose almost to a purse, and when he spoke it formed a small grimace which, while not particularly attractive, implied a special concentration. His fine flow of words and obviously great knowledge of finance—he also knew a lot of history and was generally well read—made an excellent impression, and not the least of his attributes was what seemed to be a genuine modesty.

The result was that Kreuger soon succeeded in doing exactly what he had started out to do—have himself sought out, rather than do the seeking. Among those who approached him were Frederic W. Allen, a partner in the highly respected private banking firm of Lee, Higginson & Co., and Donald Durant, head of its syndicating department. Originating in Boston in 1848, this firm had played a prominent role in the promotion of some of the country's leading railroads and mines, and also of such business giants as General Motors, the American Telephone & Telegraph

Company, and the General Electric Corporation. Allen and Durant had been introduced to Kreuger through a young Swedish stockbroker named Gustav Lagerkrantz, who knew some members of Higginson & Co., a London subsidiary of the American firm, and had come to America to learn more about the brokerage business. Like everyone else, the two Lee, Higginson officers found Kreuger as persuasive as he was charming, especially when he spoke about matches and the limitless possibilities of profit through iron-clad control of their production, price, and distribution.

Kreuger's greatest gift was his phenomenal ability to play upon the mood of his victims, to gauge exactly how and why they would react to something, and he knew how much most Americans loved to project in large figures. To Allen and Durant, his logic seemed irrefutable when he spoke of millions of matches being constantly struck and pointed out what a difference it would make if a few less matchsticks were placed in a box that cost a penny more. Knowing very well how a trust worked and how earnings could mount in such a mammoth undertaking, the two private bankers responded as if they themselves were matches that had just been lit. Having ignited them, however, Kreuger, himself now fired by the tremendous possibilities he saw in the stock market, made his first smart move in his role as a superior American confidence man. He let his two listeners glow with enthusiasm while he sailed back to London, where he made a deal with their English counterparts, Higginson & Co., to handle four million dollars' worth of a new ten-million-dollar issue that doubled the amount of common stock in Swedish Match.

Kreuger was so anxious to make the company an international concern and to get good conservative British money into it for prestige purposes that he gave Higginson & Co. an extremely generous and confidential rebate—it paid twenty dollars a share for the new stock as compared to the thirty dollars that brokers in Sweden had to pay—and the difference was debited to Ivar Kreuger personally. This was to become a typical maneuver. Henceforth, in order to eliminate certain assets or liabilities from the books of his companies because he didn't want anyone to know about them, or to create false assets, or to facilitate the shifting of debits and credits from company to company without any explanation of what they really represented, Kreuger conducted a great amount of business by channeling them through his own account. Ten years later, when the accountants of Price, Waterhouse & Co. tried to unravel the mess, they wrote that the effect of what he had done in his own name "has naturally been to convert what should have been a straightforward record of Ivar Kreuger's indebtedness . . . into a confused mass of figures, the balance of which . . . is entirely meaningless."

Having made his British move, a highly impressive display of public financing which bolstered his reputation all over the world, Kreuger began his private financial maneuvers in an equally bold if less fastidious fashion. From now on, while there would be a bona-fide aspect of his business for the world to see and admire, there would also be a steadily increasing amount of surreptitious activity conducted in a catacomb of subsidiaries, the great majority of which would be nothing more than mute manifestations of Ivar Kreuger himself, through which he would move some large amounts of actual cash but mostly huge fictitious debits and credits back and forth across borders, in and out of some real but mostly phony banks, and, in effect, from one pocket of his corporate suit to another. And while he populated his real structure with impressive persons, such as Donald Durant and his principal Swedish banker and intimate friend, Rydbeck, he would also inject into his largely unreal maze, like settlers from a land of make-believe, all sorts of strange and questionable and frequently bizarre figures who, unknown to the men of position, and often unknown even to one another, would act as glorified messenger boys and pliable yes-men to the Midas-like match king.

One of the first of these darkling fellows was a fair-haired Swede named Bror Bredberg, a former stockbroker and shoe salesman in Stockholm. Bredberg had worked as far back as 1914 for Kreuger's brother, Torsten, who had been in both the shipping and match business on his own for a number of years and was now beginning to co-operate with his older brother on matches. In March 1923 Torsten Kreuger asked Bredberg to go to Zurich, at a good salary of four thousand dollars a year, to start and operate a subsidiary. In Switzerland Bredberg met another secret Kreuger agent, Walter Ahlström, who lived in Paris, where he had been Swedish consul general, and together they founded the first of Ivar Kreuger's fancily named shadow companies, Finanz Gesellschaft für die Industrie. Its capitalization of three and a half million dollars, in Swiss francs, was pledged by Swedish Match and three related concerns, but as only twenty per cent of this amount had to be produced, Bredberg and Ahlström offered up two certified checks for 3,600,000 Swiss francs. Ahlström was listed as chairman of the new firm. A few days later Torsten Kreuger showed up and the Graustarkian trio flitted to nearby Vaduz, the capital of the fanciful and convenient little Duchy of Liechtenstein, where for an annual fee of as little as forty dollars a year a foreign corporation could establish a subsidiary, attribute to it as many parent assets as it wished, and be subject to no further corporate or income taxes, either there or anywhere else. In this happy fiduciary cove, transferring part of the same money that had been applied to the launching of the Zurich company, the three men started Union Industrie A. G., capitalized at a million and a half dollars.

Bredberg became the manager and sole member of Union

Industrie's board, and thereafter he took orders unquestioningly from Ivar Kreuger on running it and several other companies he established in central Europe. He began by listing as an asset an item of one and a half million dollars which he was told represented the value of some real estate bought in Berlin. A few months later Kreuger sent him the note of someone called E. H. Lehmann for three and a half million dollars, which was supposed to be the price agreed on for the sale of this and other real estate in Germany, and was to carry an interest charge of twelve per cent a year. Bredberg never saw the deeds for any of these properties, nor could he ever track down the mysterious Lehmann to send him yearly interest bills—Kreuger kept saying he would handle the matter himself. It later became obvious that, though Lehmann may have existed and Kreuger may have done some business with him, there was no transaction of the size outlined to Bredberg and that, though the properties, or at least some of them, were real, the principal purpose of the "sale" as reported by Kreuger was simply to build up a false profit on Union Industrie's books. By 1931 this "asset" had mounted to six and a half million dollars and by then Kreuger had "sold" what was probably the same real estate and buildings to several other companies and listed the profits on their books as a means of inflating their value and thus attracting still more capital.

From time to time Kreuger would pop into Zurich and give Bredberg instructions as to what should be credited to Union Industrie, which put up a semblance of being a mighty busy company. Occasionally he would actually deposit some securities, but more often he would inform Bredberg by mail that securities or notes to the credit of the concern had been deposited elsewhere. Each year, when the annual report was due, Bredberg would entrain for Stockholm to confer with Kreuger and Anton Wendler, who was the obedient accountant for Kreuger & Toll.

Bredberg would then take the completed company books back to Zurich and show them to an accountant named E. Hess, who had been "elected" by the "shareholders" to certify them. The amenable Dr. Hess would cursorily compare what the books said to what was in Union Industrie's bank vault, and if there happened to be a discrepancy Bredberg would get a personal pledge from Kreuger for the difference.

Kreuger formed these two companies—which, typically, were used in the manner of open-end tubes through which he passed assets and liabilities back and forth whenever he wanted to create a particular situation—as a test of how easy or hard it was to get such concerns going. Having found out that it was simple, he took personal charge of creating a corporation that became one of the two principal sieves through which the millions of dollars raised in America and a good many of Kreuger's other assets slowly disappeared. This was the Continental Investment Corporation, a firm whose mellifluous, broad-sounding title was bound to appeal to the Americans and serves as a fine example of Kreuger's talent as a nomenclator. Helping him with Continental was a young, Swiss-born, naturalized American citizen named Ernst A. Hoffman, who had been working in a bank in New York when Kreuger hired him through a want ad in June 1923. Apparently, though there is no record of the voyage, as Kreuger no longer allowed his name to appear on a ship's passenger list, he made a quick trip that spring to America.

Hoffman's virtues included good looks, a sharp financial mind that, like Kreuger's, was not averse to taking dubious short cuts, and the ability to speak several languages. Kreuger sent him right off to Switzerland to look into the possibilities of starting a Swiss holding company, which he told Hoffman was needed, in view of the generally uncertain condition of the European currency market, to centralize his match operations. Hoffman shortly wired that he thought the prospects looked better in Liechtenstein, whereupon Kreuger came down to Vaduz and, after conferring with the entire Liechtenstein Parliament of thirteen, known as the "Court of Commerce," was given a ten-year agreement under which he promised to form a local concern capitalized at twelve million dollars, or sixty million Swiss francs. To create Continental, Kreuger promptly produced a million francs in cash, nine million in checks, and the remaining fifty million in the form of a personal guarantee as head of Swedish Match—he had the right to do this without consulting any of the other directors. Hoffman originally was the sole member of Continental's board, but a year or so later Kreuger became its president and appointed, as a third board member, his closest friend and associate, the bland and obliging Krister Littorin, from Stockholm. Like all of Kreuger's special companies, Continental, which alone was to mulct the Americans of eighty-eight million dollars, was small and cozy.

: 3 :

Now Kreuger was ready to return to America and deal with the eager gentlemen of Lee, Higginson & Co. They welcomed him cordially, and in November 1923 they joined him in forming the International Match Corporation (IMCO), a Delaware concern whose purpose was to acquire certain assets of the match syndicate. Some of these were to be held directly and some by Continental, which was declared to be a wholly owned IMCO subsidiary that was to act as a go-between with Swedish Match and was to be a repository for joint profits, thereby avoiding taxation both in America and Sweden. IMCO was capitalized initially at nearly thirty million dollars. Swedish Match was credited with being the nominal owner of just over half of its million shares of stock, with a Swedish bank syndicate getting the rest. Though Kreuger told Donald Durant, who henceforth became his principal contact with Lee, Higginson, that he intended to have his world match profits "about equally divided between IMCO and Swedish Match," Durant later admitted that there was never any contract to this effect and that it was understood from the outset that IMCO's main purpose was to bring American capital into the match trust, "thereby giving the concern a broader basis for an extensive program of expansion." Durant and two Lee, Higginson partners—one of them was Percy Rockefeller, a nephew of John D., and a man who was also much taken with Kreuger—were on the IMCO board, along with some other prominent American businessmen whom Kreuger found peculiarly satisfactory because, on the one hand, they lent prestige to the undertaking and, on the other, they knew next to nothing about the match business. The real power was held by an executive committee of three in Sweden, which consisted of Littorin, Carl Bergman, another old Kreuger crony who had been in on the ground floor of the match business, and, of course, Kreuger himself.

Within a short time Kreuger had the IMCO bylaws amended to give him, as president, "special powers to make and enter into all contracts on behalf of the corporation, to execute any and all instruments of transfer of any part of the personal property of the corporation." This gave him complete freedom to do what he wanted with the dollars the Americans now began literally to pour into his lap, starting at the end of 1923 when a fifteen-million-dollar issue of twenty-year, six-and-a-half-per-cent gold debentures was offered to the public at 94½ and was quickly sold out. Of the proceeds, some $12,200,000 was transferred immediately by Kreuger to Continental in Vaduz, where it was credited by him to the account of a company with another odd title, A. B. Russia, a dummy concern that was nothing but a cover for a private Kreuger savings account. A. B. Russia made no mention in its books of owing Continental any such amount—in fact, though it was listed by Continental as a chief debtor, it never acknowledged any obligations to Continental, even though Continental kept pretending to lend it large monthly sums at a high rate of interest, using it, in other words, as a means of manufacturing false interest profits. Once the American proceeds of the IMCO stock issue were in his personal control, through A. B. Russia, Kreuger used part of them to pay off the Swedish members of the banking group that had got him started in the match business by lending him money to buy factories in Europe.

Kreuger once defined gratitude as "the feeling one has that one can get more from the same source," and it didn't. take him long to be persuaded that he would be able to get just about as much money abroad as he wanted. Early in 1924 he came up with the first of several securities gimmicks: Swedish Match B shares. In contrast to A shares, which had full voting rights and by law had to be held in Sweden, B shares represented one one-thousandth voting rights per share but had the same face value and dividend rights as the A shares. Eventually, through this and similar devices, Kreuger controlled his six-hundred-million-dollar match empire with shares of his own which totaled less than one per cent of the total. As he had done before, he tried out his new certificates in England, where they were gobbled up, and then threw them onto other world exchanges. He was no longer worried about being overextended in Sweden, figuring that he could easily pay off what he owed there by floating new foreign issues.

"You Swedes are blockheads," he told a friend. "You haggle about giving me money, but when I get off the boat in New York I find men on the pier begging me to take money off their hands."

It was unfortunately true, and between 1923 and its bankruptcy in 1932, IMCO alone sold $148,500,000 worth of securities to the American public, and all but four and a half million of the total was transferred by Kreuger to Europe and disposed of in one way or another. Kreuger always gave a convincing explanation of where all the money was to go. In 1926, for example, when a block of IMCO shares netted nearly twenty-two million dollars he declared that this money would be used for "transactions in Greece, Portugal, Algiers, Norway and Manila," none of which took place, though the funds were used in part for some other match purchases. Meetings of the IMCO board in New York, according to Samuel Pryor of Lee, Higginson & Co., were always "expressions of implicit faith in Mr. Kreuger," and, as for allocation of profits, "We depended on the equity of Mr. Kreuger's judgments." From time to time American members of the IMCO board visited Kreuger in Stockholm, and he always managed to entertain them so graciously that they were more bewitched by him than ever. When Percy Rockefeller returned from one of these trips to Kreugerland, he told his fellow directors in New York: "I have never been more impressed by anything than by this organization. It seems almost too good to be true. We are fortunate indeed to be associated with Ivar Kreuger."

Though IMCO had its own accountant, a taciturn Swede named Ben Tomlinson, and though its books were inspected annually by the top-flight accounting firm of Ernst & Ernst, they never consisted of anything more than what Tomlinson was ordered by Kreuger to draw up. In the twenties, in contrast to what is now required under the regulations of the Securities and Exchange Commission, foreign companies whose affiliates sold securities here were not required to submit their books to examination by certified accountants. In the case of IMCO, it was later brought out that *none* of the books or balance sheets of any of the foreign companies it dealt with or "controlled" were ever seen in America, and the directors never even knew just what their company's earnings were. As regularly as clockwork, however, Kreuger saw to it that just enough funds were transferred from Europe each quarter to pay IMCO's dividends due on stock issued here, and the transfer would usually be made via its chief subsidiary in Europe, Continental. These payments were always depicted by Kreuger as being partial earnings from IMCO's European match enterprises, and they always averaged about $2,300,000 per quarter—just sufficient to pay the dividends due with a little left over.

During the receivership hearings on the Kreuger debacle, James N. Rosenberg, the counsel for IMCO, questioned Donald Durant about the degree to which IMCO and Lee, Higginson had placed their trust in Kreuger and his system, and the following colloquy took place:

Q: . . . Did it ever strike your mind that there was anything calling for inquiry or study in that regularity in the amount of [IMCO] earnings?
A: The reason, I understand, was not to bring into the parent corporation all the dividends and earnings from the subsidiaries. By not bringing the earnings into the parent corporation each time, but keeping them in the subsidiaries, it was not necessary to pay an income tax on earnings which were not brought into the country.
Q: And it was because of that general scheme that it never aroused any suspicion or wonder?
A: That is right.
Q: Did you ever go back of the Ernst & Ernst quarterly reports?

A: We relied upon them.

Q: You accepted these things without going to the original source?

A: Yes, we relied on Ernst & Ernst.

Q: And you knew, of course, did you not, that Ernst & Ernst in turn relied blindly on what was cabled over from Europe?

A: I don't know what Ernst & Ernst relied on.

When A. D. Berning, the Ernst & Ernst accountant who handled IMCO, was questioned, he made it clear that, while he was called upon each year to make "merely a qualified statement of opinion as to the audits of the subsidiaries" abroad—based on the summaries of Kreuger's own accountants—he tried on several occasions to persuade Durant and other IMCO directors to allow Ernst & Ernst to pursue such matters further. "As far as I could see, Kreuger & Toll had no American accountants or English auditors," Berning noted, "and naturally being desirous of expanding the business of our own firm, we thought this was a proper part of the picture for us to take care of." But, as Durant put it afterwards, "Kreuger & Toll was the leading company in Sweden, and Sweden did not relish having foreign accountants come in and look over its affairs."

The man who really ran the IMCO show in its early days was the Swiss-American jack-of-all-trades Ernst Hoffman. In addition to being director, secretary, and accountant of Continental, Hoffman was also secretary of IMCO and an officer of three other Kreuger corporations in America, two of which were established to help buy up match factories in and around Poland. Successful as Kreuger had been, he had from the start been subject to certain competitive difficulties. In Finland and in Czechoslovakia, for instance, fractious elements had refused to co-operate with him, but his brother, Torsten, had managed to compromise the disputes.

The stubborn Poles were the next to raise a ruckus, and it was a more serious one that demanded a longer-range solution. There was always a certain jealousy between Torsten and Ivar Kreuger, and it partly had to do with credit for conceiving the idea of obtaining match monopolies *de jure* as well as *de facto* in order to remove, once and for all, any competition.

The first such legal monopoly was the Polish one, and it was arranged by Torsten in October 1925. Though he profited personally from it more than Ivar, he had to get money from his brother to implement it. Ivar put up six million dollars, part of which he had raised in America. This was lent to the Poles at seven-per-cent interest in return for a monopoly in the manufacture of matches. Ten Polish factories, including a couple the Kreugers already owned, were amalgamated, and the combine was then, in effect, rented to the Kreugers for twenty years, after which the Poles were to own all the properties. During the monopoly period the income from the business was shared by Swedish Match and IMCO, but the monopoly was regarded as one of those belonging to IMCO.

If Torsten deserves the credit for devising this primary plan, it was Ivar who worked out the details of the unique formula that became the basis of other monopoly agreements which eventually embraced twenty-four countries around the world. It was a formula so seemingly foolproof, as Kreuger outlined it for the special benefit of his American friends, that it could not help luring hordes of investors. In each country, either Swedish Match, IMCO, or a subsidiary of one or the other administered the state-created monopoly and paid a regular royalty to the state treasury. The proceeds of the royalty were used to secure a Kreuger loan to the government, and the amount of the loan was so calculated that the amount of the royalty payable to the government each year covered the annual debt services and gave the government a profit margin of from twenty-five to fifty per cent. As match consumption increased, the royalties also went up, but while the government shared in the match profits, it could not actually take out any earnings until it paid off its interest obligations to Kreuger, plus what it owed on the principal of the loan. As Kreuger himself proudly pointed out once, in emphasizing the soundness and safety of the scheme, "It may even be said that the loan itself is nothing but an advance of future royalty payments."

The arrangement benefited governments and saved many a regime from bankruptcy and political defeat, but did not always prove a blessing to ordinary people, who often had to spend more money for their matches than they had before Kreuger appeared on the scene. In some cases the use of any other than Swedish matches was forbidden as part of the monopoly deal Kreuger made, and a fine was imposed if "foreign" matches were brought into the country, with a reward offered to anyone who reported a violation of the ban. The result was that beggars sometimes went around asking visitors for a match; if the match wasn't a Swedish or a monopoly-sponsored one, the beggar would report this to the police and receive what amounted to an informer's payoff.

There were thus some disadvantages as well as advantages to Kreuger's match loans. The monopoly in Poland, for instance, was one of the most profitable ones for Kreuger, and the government used its profits to good purpose, chiefly for flood relief in Upper Silesia, but the price of matches was raised so high that many people began splitting them in order to save a few pennies a week. Subsequently this happened elsewhere in eastern Europe too.

As with so much else in the Kreugerian saga, it developed that there had been something crooked to go with something straight in Poland. On July 2, 1925, Kreuger supposedly signed a secret agreement with Dr. Marjam Glowacki, deputy director of the Polish Ministry of Finance, whereby a Dutch company impressively called N. V. Financeaelle Maatschappij Garanta was to have a highly profitable monopoly for the sale and distribution of matches in Poland to complement the newly established monopoly for match production. IMCO in New York agreed to finance Garanta by lending it seventeen million dollars on October 1, 1925, and eight million more the following July. The total was to be repaid in thirty-two semi-yearly installments, and interest payments, compounded at the munificent rate of twenty-four per cent in view of what Kreuger said would be exceptionally high profits, were to be made once a year.

The stock in Garanta was to be held by Polish citizens, and the company, in addition to having all rights for retail distribution of matches in Poland, was to have title to certain other assets of the Polish match industry. Apparently Kreuger and Dr. Glowacki did work up some such deal, but it was never approved by the Polish Diet and nothing ever came of it. That didn't stop Kreuger from pretending it did, and he took advantage of the unimplemented agreement to get credits out of IMCO, which he booked in a way that helped him give an overblown picture of his match activities.

Garanta was even "created" physically in the fall of 1925 in Amsterdam, another favorite place for surreptitious wheeling and dealing because, as in Switzerland, there were no currency restrictions in Holland, no annual auditing of firms was required under Dutch law, and no taxes had to be paid on undistributed profits. After Kreuger had invented the Garanta name, he wrote to a prominent Dutch bank director and arranged to get the company a good banking address. Meanwhile, in New York, with the help of Lee, Higginson & Co., IMCO quickly sold a new issue of four hundred and fifty thousand shares in bullish Wall Street, and of the twenty million dollars received, seventeen million was supposedly earmarked for the first payment to Garanta, which had to be located in Holland, Kreuger explained in New York, because of "unsettled Polish political conditions." What followed is a perfect and prolonged example of Kreuger's financial capers. Actually, IMCO never paid out any cash to Garanta. Instead, the IMCO directors in New York were led to believe that Swedish Match was handling the Garanta financing and that the seventeen million representing the first and biggest payment to the Amsterdam company had been duly made by Swedish Match to wipe out a debt it owed IMCO. It was still IMCO's right, however, to list the amount as an asset owed it by Garanta, and as it never got any of this money back from Garanta or from Swedish Match, it ended up being out the seventeen million. IMCO did receive half a dozen interest payments on the debt, of about one million each, which helped pay dividends due American investors. Swedish Match made no cash payments to Garanta either, but pretended that it had. The whole thing, in other words, was an elaborate hocus-pocus that enabled Kreuger to pretend he had a big Polish distribution business in matches and, incidentally, to wipe out a book debt Swedish Match owed IMCO.

The use of "suspense accounts" in private banks was another favorite Kreuger device, and the investigating accountants later concluded that it was the only really new ruse he developed. It enabled him to make an asset out of something that was either totally false or had not yet materialized—in this case, even though it seemed doubtful that the Polish Diet ever would approve the Garanta contract, he could at least pretend to have hopes indefinitely. Meanwhile, he could go on creating the illusion that he was doing a vast Polish sales business to the benefit of the whole match trust but especially to IMCO's advantage, and it all looked bona fide because he saw to it personally that the interest payments were kept up. Controlling so many companies that owed one another money as a result of different sets of transactions, Kreuger was easily able to keep shifting these multiple obligations around on a sort of barter basis, or on the basis of the swindler's classic borrowing from Peter to pay Paul. As he made all the arrangements himself, his manipulations were essentially a one-man show, but in order to keep up the pretense of having physical companies and physical sets of books, he needed simple dupes to sustain his masquerade.

The Garanta dupe, as New York's late Mayor Fiorello H. LaGuardia would have said, was "a beaut." He was Karl Lange, an imposing-looking, elderly man with a white beard, and like a number of other lower-level Kreuger henchmen, he had been in trouble when Kreuger hired him in 1923. He had been fired from a bank in Stockholm (of which Kreuger was a director) after arranging a loan for himself through a cover. Kreuger gave him a confidential job boosting sales of stock in Sweden by offering brokers double commissions, and later sent him to work in Berlin. Lange was then deemed ready for his "big job" as head of Garanta. During the period of its incorporation in Amsterdam, he opened a two-room office there, but this was quickly abandoned and Garanta thereafter consisted of nothing but a set of books that Lange, as the sole officer and employee, carried around with him from capital to capital as Kreuger directed.

He got his first set of figures one evening in the fall of 1925 when he went to Kreuger's apartment in Stockholm. Kreuger handed him a balance sheet and bluntly told him to sign it. In the only show of protest Lange ever displayed, he demurred momentarily and said he'd like to look it over first, as such huge sums were involved. Kreuger stared at him stonily, and when Lange murmured that it would be nice to know where all that money was going, Kreuger replied that it was being spent secretly in Poland and shouldn't be talked about. "If you don't believe me, go to Poland and see for yourself," he said coldly. The bluff, as always, worked. Lange—one of the Kreuger employees who later went to jail—took out his pen and signed and never again questioned his master.

Despite the huge sums that went through Garanta's books, Lange never handled any cash. When he asked Kreuger how to balance the seventeen million Garanta allegedly received from IMCO via Swedish Match, Kreuger snapped: "Just debit it to me," which Lange promptly did. At the end, Garanta's books showed that it had received a total of $25,421,875 from IMCO and Swedish Match, all of which was entered as having been paid out to Kreuger—and that was that. It could not be traced.

Torsten Kreuger and others in the top echelon in Stockholm surmised that Garanta represented Kreuger's private fortune, which they figured he kept in Holland to avoid Swedish taxes. However, when Sigurd Hennig, the top Swedish Match accountant, asked about this one day, Kreuger laughed and said it was nonsense, that Garanta did in fact own a lot of real estate and factories in Poland. This was an outright lie, but Hennig had to accept it and was satisfied. As for Lange, he later told the investigators sorrowfully: "To me, Kreuger was a great man, admired by the whole world, whose business genius and honesty were the pride of nations. He was the noblest man who ever lived, and his like was nowhere to be found." And then, to prove his faith, he recited a list of Kreuger stocks he owned, including some shares he had bought only a few months before Kreuger's crash and death in March 1932.

It was a mark of Kreuger's peculiar genius that he could keep the loyalty of a dozen undercover men such as Lange and at the same time retain that of the dozen highly sophisticated and respected bankers and businessmen with whom he worked, for the most part, above ground. He juggled the two groups beautifully. There was a third group. Because so much of Kreuger's business had to be carried on clandestinely—not all nations willingly gave him concessions or monopolies—he sometimes had to buy his way into a position of prominence or power through fronts and dummies. The erratic political and economic weather in Europe during the twenties didn't make his operations any easier, and in seeking to win confidence Kreuger invariably had to move confidentially. As a consequence, the first question he would ask about any prospective employee was: "Can he keep a secret?" He was fond of quoting his own motto for success—"Silence, more silence, and still more silence"—and, in passing this on to his staff, he meant it to be more than just a nice business maxim; by sealing the lips of all his workers, he was able to keep to a minimum their knowledge of what was really taking place. As time went on, Kreuger became increasingly secretive about everything, his legitimate as well as his illegitimate enterprises. And as his unique economic and financial state became a supranational entity of its own, affording him his most impressive role, he became more and more of a lone wolf. Gunnar Cederschïold, his chief Paris representative, afterward commented: " '*L'état, c'est moi*' applied to Ivar Kreuger as much as to Louis XIV. We assumed, all of us, that it was as natural for him to transfer assets from one company to another as it was for a King to send troops to whatever part of the empire he wished. And we all thought the King could do no wrong."

CHAPTER 4

Palaces
and Plots

LIKE CLUMPS of wild garlic, Kreuger match companies, holding companies, and shadow companies began to sprout and multiply by the mid-twenties, and Sweden's conservative banking and business community watched with admiration and some degree of trepidation. Almost single-handedly, it seemed, Ivar Kreuger was turning Sweden into a front-rank financial power. Nothing, apparently, could stop him, and in 1926 "the match king" ordered work begun on a "palace" suitable to serve as "the seat" of his "far-flung empire," to cite a few of the references in the press to his new corporate home.

Located in the center of Stockholm, at No. 15 Västra Trädgårdsgatan (West Garden Street), the famous Match Palace was, and is, a beautifully designed, long, four-story building of pale marble and granite erected around a large, open courtyard. In the middle, one of the most graceful groups of the late Carl Milles shows a bronze figure of Diana wakening some forest creatures to life while a hind and a boar watch from the sides. A portico of columns forms the approach to the court and is in turn entered from the narrow street outside through a fine pair of wrought-iron gates. From opposite ends of the portico, circular stairs ascend to the hundred and twenty-five offices. The tone of the entire building is one of simplicity of line and furnishing, and the work of Sweden's foremost architects, artists, and designers went into it.

Kreuger's second-floor office, paneled in rosewood and mahogany, contained a specially made, super-sensitive telephone that enabled him, while walking around the room, to carry on a multiple conversation with his various directors. An elaborate system of signs in all parts of the building flashed the name of any top executive Kreuger wanted to reach, and red and green lights outside each director's office told whether the occupant was engaged or not—a signal Kreuger himself obeyed as carefully as he expected it to be observed in his case. One of his pet devices was a world clock that showed the time in various cities of the world; its innumerable hands moved, not circularly, but from east to west, like the sun, across the top of the board.

On the top floor was a sanctum called the "Silence Room," to which he occasionally retired when he didn't want to be bothered by anyone. Here he kept his most secret documents in a large safe. When a caller overstayed his time, Kreuger pressed a button under his desk which rang a bogus telephone, and then he pretended to accept a confidential long-distance call. (He also used this phone to impress such American visitors as Percy Rockefeller with pretended calls from leading European statesmen.) Probably the most beautiful room in the building was the curved board room, with a curved table, both symmetrically following the semicircular line of the interior courtyard below. Here, on a series of panels, Isaac Grünewald, one of Sweden's best-known artists, painted a composition called "Dawn," which, carrying out a theme that appears elsewhere in the building, shows Prometheus emerging from a rainbow on a winged horse and rushing down to earth, bringing fire to man and bidding darkness flee. A popular Stockholm jest maintained that the central figure was really Ivar Kreuger and that the eager crowd represented greedy shareholders clamoring for even higher dividends than they were getting.

The cool, softly lighted corridors of the Match Palace were so quiet that the building suggested an institution of learning or even a hospital rather than the hub of a vast industrial empire. Next door was the headquarters of Kreuger & Toll, but Kreuger carefully kept the two separate, and there was not even a connecting passageway. When he was not at his Stockholm offices, he was most apt to be in Berlin or Paris, and after 1925 he seemed to spend an increasing amount of his time in the French capital, where he regularly held conferences with his many Continental employees.

As his principal confidant there, Cederschïold, the former journalist who was now working full-time for Kreuger, was in a position to observe him and his methods more closely than anyone else, and to gauge the response of other employees to Kreuger as well. The public looked upon "the Kreuger men" as an elite corps whose members, through their fortunate contact with the wizard, gained a special insight into all important matters of the day. Though his salaries were not sensational, there were always two or three hundred names on the waiting list for positions in his organization, including many from the best families of Europe. Kreuger welcomed this wide approbation, and responded by ruling his roost with quiet, benevolent authority. Toward everyone who worked for him he showed consideration and tact, though privately, as so much of what he did involved fooling his own staff as well as outsiders, he must also have felt considerable contempt. He was too wise, however, to show it, and always went out of his way to foster a happy family feeling. "There was never any intrigue," Ceder-schiöld recalled afterward. "Kreuger wouldn't have stood for it, and he hated to hear criticism of anyone who worked for him. A wonderful control and inner coolness ran through everything he did. When something had to be decided, he always proposed and never disposed, and two of his favorite phrases were, 'How would it be if such-and-such were done?' and 'Don't you think it would be better if?' etc. The result was a remarkable loyalty and belief in him, as attested by the fact that we all had our savings in the firm. If we had been asked to offer our lives, no one would have hesitated, and we felt that he would never let any of us down. Yet we all feared him because of his exceptionally sharp mentality, and because he was reality personified. We thought he could see into the future better than anyone else."

Those who worked for Kreuger became accustomed to being sent on the spur of the moment to distant places where they might remain for years—more than one person he thought had found out too much about his operations was sent especially far away. Working for Kreuger in the field was often lonely, with no word from him for months at a time. "I sometimes get an interesting and kind letter from Mr. Kreuger, and to read it is my main work," one far-flung agent remarked. The chosen few who saw him more regularly in Paris or Stockholm grew accustomed to watching him work almost completely by impulse. "He would talk about things that seemed to have no relation to what he was doing," Cederschiöld said, "but he enjoyed associating ideas in his own peculiar fashion. Probably some of his biggest concepts were born that way, as thought experiments. The process might take years. An idea would often burgeon and change, and reappear much later in perfected form." Another observer said: "Beyond logic and quickness, he could combine things into organic wholes that seemed but were not incoherent. People often wondered why he did something and suddenly found themselves watching a fantastic demonstration, wherein everything beforehand had been a necessary part of the procedure."

His propensity for throwing out ideas in an almost off-hand manner was marked by his odd way of addressing people. "He rarely looked at the person he was talking to," Cederschiöld recalled. "Usually he looked at the person nearest to him. If he did look at us directly, it seemed to be without really seeing us, or as if he were looking right through us. Yet he had a great need of approval from a sympathetic source." On some occasions Kreuger could be deliberate and slow to the point of madness. In dictating a telegram, he would often pause for ten minutes over one word, and the simplest message might be written ten times before he was satisfied. He composed telegrams and cablegrams like letters, never leaving out an article. "There's no time to solve puzzles," he would say. "A misunderstanding can cost more than you could save." For those who didn't know him, his long silences could be embarrassing, and when he got on the transatlantic or long-distance phone, they could also be expensive. A hundred dollars' worth of silence was not unusual.

Kreuger's apparently phenomenal memory never ceased to amaze both his intimates and strangers. He could recite the exact rise and fall of stocks over a period of twenty years and could rattle off verbatim the lines of a play he had seen as many years back, and he invariably remembered faces. As one of his non-admirers later put it, "Liars have to have good memories," and undoubtedly Kreuger's special gift helped him immeasurably in juggling his books. He often impressed his Wall Street friends by reciting his phony balance sheets out of his head, down to the last decimal. At the same time, as a born muser, he could be very absent-minded and forgetful. He mislaid keys and papers so often that Cederschïold and others got in the habit of giving him only duplicates and carbons. He mislaid people, too. In Paris he frequently used Cederschïold's car and chauffeur, and he particularly liked the driver because of the man's great patience. He would never remember, however, where the car was parked, and sometimes he even forgot that he had it with him; the chauffeur once passed a whole night on a St. Germain street when Kreuger absently took a cab home from a dinner meeting.

: 2 :

Cederschïold, even though he was one of Kreuger's most trusted aides for thirteen years, knew only a segment of his employer's total business, and, as it turned out, he was only partly informed about some things that concerned himself. Among the important assignments he was given was the conduct of negotiations with Spain. As in Poland, there was a bona-fide Spanish effort by Kreuger to match a fraudulent one. Beginning in 1925, he tried secretly to buy several of Spain's major match factories. As a result of a number of conferences with Spanish agents in Paris and Madrid, some headway was made, but Kreuger failed to get what he wanted, and as late as 1930 he was still negotiating to obtain a match concession in return for a ninety-five-million-dollar loan to Spain.

But Cederschïold, who was sent to Madrid on that mission, apparently knew nothing about another of Kreuger's long-term hoaxes that dated back to January 1925, when he claimed to have signed a twenty-five-year match-monopoly contract with Primo de Rivera, the Spanish dictator. After Kreuger's death an English translation of this supposed agreement was found in Kreuger's safe in Stockholm which had Rivera's broad signature on it, but Kreuger is believed to have forged the Spaniard's name. As Rivera was dead, nothing could be proved. It seems likely that, as had been the case with Dr. Glowacki, the Pole, Kreuger did confer once or twice with Rivera; if so, the results must have been even less conclusive. As with Garanta, however, Kreuger pretended in America that the contract had been signed. Among the "assets" of the Continental Investment Corporation, and thus of IMCO, was an alleged "receipt" from Rivera showing that about three fifths of the payments had been made on schedule; the amount of the loan—one hundred and sixty-five million Swiss francs, or about thirty million dollars—plus accrued interest at sixteen per cent a year, was listed as an "asset" for Continental totaling nearly sixty million dollars. All of this was booked through a so-called Spanish "suspense account," and most of it allegedly reposed in a phony bank Kreuger established in Amsterdam called the Nederlandische Bank voor Scandinavischen Handel, which another convenient dupe named Sven Huldt ran. Late in 1925 this bank was listed as owing Continental a large sum even though it wasn't founded until March 1, 1926—a minor discrepancy in Kreuger's grand scheme which didn't seem to bother him, for he did the same thing on other occasions. It was enough, as far as he was concerned, that he *intended* to have both a bank and a firm agreement.

While he kept knowledge of the Spanish deal from Cederschiöld, Kreuger showed the Rivera contract to others in his organization from time to time in order to give an impression of its genuineness. To the Americans who were supposed to be profiting from the monopoly, he simply pleaded secrecy until the very end. Spain ultimately became "Country X" in the famous "XYZ Memorandum" he reluctantly produced upon request in New York in 1930. This purported to show that IMCO was doing seventy million dollars' worth of business in three separate transactions, two thirds of which turned out to be fictitious. When Donald Durant was asked at a hearing afterward: "Did you consider the memorandum on the whole as satisfactory or unsatisfactory?" he replied: "On the whole, I think, it was regarded as satisfactory." As a further indication of how much they had believed in Kreuger, the men of Lee, Higginson & Co. had promptly gone out—in that post-crash year—and underwritten additional debentures worth fifty million dollars.

There was a final twist to the weird Spanish story. Sometime in 1929, apparently without telling anyone, Kreuger gave a Spanish senator named José Serran a quarter of a million dollars' worth of pesetas for the secret purchase of a big Spanish match property. In the spring of 1930 Serran vanished from Madrid and was arrested several months later in northern Italy, with the pesetas. He was brought back to Madrid for a hearing, where he pretended to be a hero and claimed he had absconded to save his country from Kreuger's depredations. When he hinted that he knew something more about Kreuger bribes to high officials and even to the royal court, the proceedings were halted and Serran was tossed into jail. He lingered there until the Spanish Revolution started, when a new effort to try him petered out, and eventually he was released. The Spanish government recovered part of the money and kept it, while Serran kept the rest, so the result of this bit of hugger-muggery provides one of the few instances of Kreuger himself being robbed. He wouldn't admit it, however: while he debited himself for what Serran had stolen, he kept listing the pesetas seized by the Spanish officials as an "asset" in the books of Kreuger & Toll. He reasoned that this sum was, in effect, "liquid grease" and that such a payment on a deal was a plus instead of a minus factor because he retained every expectation of someday bringing the Spaniards to heel. In other words, bribery was essentially a sound investment even when a bribe went awry.

Wrong as Kreuger was in carrying this principle as far as he did, the argument can be made that businessmen have frequently operated in similar fashion—that, for example, a political contribution to a campaign that fails, or a contribution to a faction in an undeveloped country which either loses out or breaks its promises is not much different, theoretically, from Kreuger's habit of paying out or pretending to pay out huge sums on deals that never materialized. Less defensible, however, was Kreuger's private purpose, what became his imperative need: to create false profits so that investors would think he was a particular kind of genius and go on buying his stocks. He was always smart enough to keep the real separated from the false. In anything that concerned Swedish Match, which remained throughout the most bona-fide of his companies (he called it "my son"), he maintained a show of proper accounting and saw to it that profits kept pace with the increase in authorized share capital and that few false entries passed through the books.

Starting in the mid-twenties, however, when he formulated his plans for world-wide expansion based on getting an increasing number of monopolies in return for large loans to governments, he needed far more capital than he could derive from a mere match company. Even with his clever formula for servicing each debt to him out of royalties, the more loans he made, the more initial outlay he required. On top of that, the expenses of running such a large enterprise were tremendous, and not the least of these were bribery and political payoffs. Furthermore, Kreuger wanted funds to expand in new directions so that he could constantly cite fresh resources in America. In 1925, for example, he acquired his first holdings in the Grängesberg-Oxelösund Mining Company, which was Sweden's greatest iron-ore

producer, and the same year he bought a considerable number of shares in the Scandinaviska Kredit A.B., the big bank
in which his friend Rydbeck was increasingly the dynamic
influence. He also used some of the swollen profits from his
real-estate deals to launch another company in the United
States: the Swedish-American Investment Corporation, created by Kreuger & Toll in collaboration with Lee, Higginson & Co. late in 1925 as a more ambitious successor to
American Kreuger & Toll, then six years old.

The Swedish-American Investment Corporation, whose
board of Wall Street luminaries interlocked with IMCO's
and which used the same accountants just as cursorily—it
was later found that its book entries never had agreed with
those of Kreuger & Toll in Stockholm—was responsible for
some eighteen million dollars' worth of issues to the American public between 1925 and 1928. Such concerns were extremely popular in America during the heyday of the boom.
Less controlled forerunners of today's mutual funds, they
ostensibly gave small investors a chance to invest in a manner that minimized risk because equities were offered in a
number of different fields. A European counterpart of this
new American subsidiary, one which slowly took over its
role and assets, was formed in Amsterdam in the fall of 1926.
This corporate concoction was called Financieele Maatschappij Kreuger & Toll—it became known more simply as
Dutch Kreuger & Toll—and it eventually was used, like
Continental, as a major sieve through which money raised
in America and elsewhere vanished.

Dutch Kreuger & Toll was created, again with obedient
dupes, "to perform and execute all kinds of financial transactions in the widest sense of the word." Its real purpose,
however, as the liquidators subsequently set forth, was "to
raise large book profits for balance sheet purposes" to give
the impression that Kreuger & Toll and its ever-growing
number of daughter concerns were earning much more

than was the case. The only legitimate business the Dutch company did was to act as a sort of broker for its Stockholm parent, taking over new issues of debentures at par and re-selling them at a premium, the difference theoretically being held in Holland because of the favorable tax situation there. Actually, these bona-fide profits of Dutch Kreuger & Toll were shifted and reshifted and used several times over in the books of various companies. The really fictitious investment business done by the company didn't begin on a massive scale, however, until toward the end of Kreuger's career, when, because of the declining world economic situation, he more than ever had to show large paper profits.

: 3 :

Notwithstanding the imaginary match deals and the phony and double entries having to do with real-estate and security holdings, Kreuger, as of 1927, had enough real values to be considered solvent. He was obviously aware that he was in-flating his values, but it seems possible that this amoral and visionary man believed he was not doing anything terribly wrong or, at least, anything unrectifiable. And, considering the peculiar financial morality of the day, perhaps he was not very different from the *genus speculans* all around him. He was a man who relished financial philosophizing—it was the only sort of conversation he enjoyed—and a revealing bit of unorthodox conceptual thinking has been recalled by a Swedish businessman and displomat named Björn Prytz who, luckily for himself, never got involved with Kreuger until after the collapse, when he was a major figure in the investigation and reorganization of the Kreuger properties.

Prytz, who looks upon Kreuger as "very much of a Con-quistadore, the kind of man you had in rougher centuries," remembers clearly a conversation they had one day while

riding across Germany in a train. Kreuger was reflecting
about accountancy. " 'You know, it's a curious thing how
every period in history has its own gods, its own high priests
and holy days,' he remarked. 'It's been true of politics and
religion and war, and now it's true of economics. We've
created something new. Instead of being fighting men, as in
days of old, we're all in business, and we've chosen some new
high priests and called them accountants. They too have a
holy day—the 31st of December—on which we're supposed
to confess. In olden times, the princes and everyone would
go to confession because it was the thing to do, whether
they believed or not. Today the world demands balance
sheets, profit-and-loss statements once a year. But if you're
really working on great ideas, you can't supply these on
schedule and expose yourself to view. Yet you've got to tell
the public something, and so long as it's satisfied and continues to have faith in you, it's really not important what
you confess. The December ceremony isn't really a law of
the gods—it's just something we've invented. All right, let's
conform, but don't let's do it in a way that will spoil our
plans. And some day people will realize that every balance
sheet is wrong because it doesn't contain anything but
figures. The real strengths and weaknesses of an enterprise
lie in the plans.' "

Aside from the fact that Kreuger did think and act cre-
atively in these terms, and that corporate publicity in Europe was customarily kept to a minimum, largely because
the public as a whole did not invest very much in securities,
his cavalier use of figures sprang from an odd miscompre-
hension of the true meaning of money. Even though he dealt
with it all the time, it had a remarkable unreality for him.
While he sometimes threw it around, he was never a conscious user of it in the sense that other wealthy men, or even
most people who spend it systematically, are. In some ways
it embarrassed and encumbered him, and he often looked

upon it disdainfully, as an odd sort of international toy. "Making money is child's game," he once said. "The fortune of nations can be made to turn on apparently trivial things. I have made countries swing upon a match. It could just as well be hairpins or buttons."

He usually carried large amounts of money around with him without being aware of it. Once, en route to Berlin with a friend, he had all kinds of bills to declare, including some worthless Tsarist rubles that had probably been in his wallet for years, and fifty Swedish notes of a thousand kroner each, as well as a lot of dollars. The total came to an astonishing thirty thousand dollars in value. When the friend asked why, among other things, he had so many dollars with him, Kreuger shrugged and said: "It's good money, it doesn't take up much room."

On another occasion, boarding a streetcar in Stockholm, he found that he had nothing smaller than a thousand-kroner note. When he announced this nonchalantly to the conductor, the man laughed and said: "I've never seen one, but if you let me look at it I'll let you ride for nothing." Kreuger's essential lack of feeling for money may have had something to do with the casual manner in which he both gave it away and took it. Just as he distributed it like chunks of candy to second-rate artists or friends in need, his attitude enabled him to keep coming to Wall Street for vast amounts of paper which he didn't feel obligated to account for because, as he said to Prytz, what alone mattered was the soundness of the long-range "plan." The reputation of a person or an institution was all-important, he insisted, and he often cited the Bank of England as an example. "People know that in its vaults are huge reserves of gold, and their confidence springs from that," he would say. "But suppose all the gold were dumped into the sea tomorrow. Don't you think that great institution would remain? Probably no one would even know the gold was gone."

Notwithstanding his philosophical cynicism about money, Kreuger never lost sight of its practical importance to other people. As he operated without surveillance, it was a simple matter for him to make the public think his income was always rising. And if he used capital to pay high dividends, as we have seen he did from the outset, his credit remained unchallenged, for by switching his many current accounts around and balancing them as he saw fit in his private game of financial charades, closing one set of books one day near year's end and another set a few days or a week later, and by generally following the formula he outlined to Prytz, he more or less succeeded, by 1927, in making his position seem sound.

Most importantly, his real profits—or at least "real" in the language and meaning of the times—had soared to great heights with the constant rise in the market value of his securities, and personally he had become an extremely rich man. The question was, could he continue to show profits that would justify the prices to which his shares had been pushed on the world's exchanges? There was only one way to find out, and that was to do what everybody else was doing: keep pushing ahead.

Kreuger never had any controversies with his nonexistent conscience, and he figured that if his stockholders wanted to use him as a vehicle to obtain unreasonable profits on their investment, that was their business. At the same time, as long as the customers lined up to give him their money, he saw himself as bound to go on growing. And indeed the money did keep coming for a couple of years more, and during those years Kreuger's ability to double and triple its value and his munificence in dispersing some of his profits for good and sound purposes were everywhere admired.

He was now, in all respects, approaching the height of his career, when his slightest pronouncement would be listened to attentively by the heads of nations as well as by the heads of business. Yet he was also becoming more and more a man of mystery who moved fleetingly from capital to capital, emerging from the wings like a great actor when he had some public or quasi-public mission to perform, but who, for the most part, remained in the background, and lived there a private life of almost tragic emptiness.

CHAPTER 5

The Man Who Needed Nobody

DESPITE the initial impact of Kreuger's charm, people who came to know him felt that beneath his graciousness there was something inherently remote, even cold, and this impression was strengthened as the years passed and they saw more of him. His smile grew bleak and his handshake clammy, and the warmest thing about him remained his voice, which was always quite beautifully modulated. From birth on, he had been different from others, and as he became older he was increasingly aware of his isolation. "No one ever broke through the wall he built around himself, and each year it became thicker and wider," Cederschiöld said. "No one shared his dreams and worries, and he didn't seem to need anyone." In his own odd way, perhaps he did, but he had an innate shyness that sprang from a realization that, while he was indeed bigger and better than most people, and certainly smarter, he was unable to share their common pleasures and problems. At the same time, by withdrawing he tended naturally to enhance his air of mystery, and he was wise in using this professionally as a cloak to hide behind.

He was also honest enough to dislike publicity and praise because he felt that most panegyrics were false, ritualistic displays. They embarrassed him particularly toward the end of his career, and it was either fear or guilt that prompted him to duck the party his friends gave him on his fiftieth birthday, a traditional date for celebration among Swedes. He left town a week in advance without telling anyone he was going—and later he confiscated copies of the elaborate volume his friends published to commemorate the occasion. This didn't stop an outpouring of encomiums, typified by that of Gustav Cassel, Sweden's leading economist, who said: "Ivar Kreuger needs no peace prize. He has awarded it to himself through his work. He has opened the doors to the world and given his nation joy and self-confidence. What he has done during his first half-century is incredible, and of his work one can justly point everywhere and say *si queris opera circumspice*—if you want to know what he has done, just look around."

One important key to Kreuger's isolation, and to his whole character, lay in his peculiar insensitivity to pain. He never seemed to feel any—dentists, for example, could work for hours on the most tender nerves of his mouth and he would neither complain nor ask for novocain. Dr. Bjerre, in his study of Kreuger, sees in this, and in a lifelong lack of any sense of danger, "a kind of blindness" that blunted all his sensibilities and that was mainly responsible for Kreuger's lack of concern for individuals who got in his way—he out-maneuvered and often destroyed people without any feeling whatsoever. "The blind live in their own world," Dr. Bjerre says. "For one who has a low reaction to pain, there is a lack of contact with life. Kreuger didn't look on suffering souls as men and women with pounding hearts but as inanimate objects, a sexual mate or a shareholder. They were all colorless chessmen." Cederschïold carried the image further. "The whole world was his chessboard," he noted. "He valued the queen more than the pawns because she was worth more, but he didn't love any one more than the other. His watchful eye was always on his opponent's knight and castle, but he didn't hate them or his enemies. He was unable, congenitally, to hate, just as he was unable to love. It was therefore all the more puzzling that he could inspire sympathy and even a kind of adoration."

The fact that Kreuger was everywhere regarded as the personification of soundness and stability was attested by public-opinion polls that repeatedly chose his securities as the best and the safest to invest in, while Kreuger himself was named as "the man I would most like to be." The god of money to some and a father image to others, especially to those who worked for and with him, he also personified the typical Horatio Alger hero, for he had done it all from scratch, and by dint of hard work.

To Kreuger the hard work was routine. He thought nothing of going eighteen hours at a stretch, not stopping to eat, and would not become aware of the ordeal he was putting others through until someone literally begged him for food. When he was asked what he did when he wasn't working, he would look positively surprised, and when someone once inquired if he didn't desire a good rest on occasion, he replied: "Unfortunately, I can't rest, even if I wanted to. Something inside me goes on thinking all the time." His rare non-admirers, chiefly those businessmen and bankers who, for one reason or another, had nothing to do with him—the Warburgs in Germany and America, for example, and men such as Prytz in Sweden—resented and perhaps envied this supreme dedication to work. "He was one of those queer men, one of those dangerous men, who had no family, no real feeling for any woman, and no belief except in himself," Prytz has remarked. "Everything, down

to the way in which he conducted his private life, was reduced to a formula."

To a large extent, Kreuger did live by rote. Though he
appreciated good food, he customarily ate very little—"Eat-
ing makes one lazy," he liked to say—and he went about it
systematically. Breakfast consisted of a cup of tea, fruit, and
toast or a bun; lunch was often the same, while dinner as a
rule comprised one main course and dessert. He liked good
restaurants, but even there, except on special occasions, he
dined simply, though waiters were among the few people
who could intimidate him: he once went into Maxim's in
Paris for a cheese sandwich, but the headwaiter was so im-
posing that he ordered lobster and champagne, and then
some cheese and beer. Because of a family tendency toward
obesity, he watched his weight carefully and checked it
every morning. He was a nervous nibbler, however; if left
to himself, he could absently devour a whole dish of nuts
or chocolates or a basket of hard Swedish bread, and he
asked his friends to guard him against this weakness. He was
very fond of wines and knew a great deal about them, pre-
ferring Bordeaux and champagnes; with part of his first
speculative gains in the early twenties, he bought Paillard's
wine cellar and restaurant in Paris, and frequently, at din-
ners, he served two or three twenty-year-old vintages, but,
while he could drink a lot and not get drunk, he became unusually voluble and therefore watched himself.

Smoking was one of the few things he did irregularly; he
would go for weeks without smoking at all, and would
then go through a pack of Turkish cigarettes in an afternoon. He dressed much as he ate, without variety, ordering
eight or ten dark, expensive suits of the same cut at once,
and he did the same with shirts and other garments, although
he once remarked to Cederschïold: "I can't ever learn how
to be a real gentleman because I can't sleep in pajamas." He
was inclined to form attachments for certain objects; his

shaving equipment, for instance, consisted of an old Gillette razor that dated back to his first trip to America, and a brush that was almost bald.

Kreuger lacked the acquisitiveness that most rich men have. "My desires are usually of the moment," he once said, "and they die almost as quickly as they arise. For me, possession takes the edge off appreciation." While he could spend a lot of money impulsively, he was no real collector, except of unlikely objects such as leather suitcases, walking sticks, and cameras and snapshot albums (though he hated to have his picture taken, he was an ardent photographer). He had to be persuaded that his status demanded that he have an automobile or two, and he finally bought an Isotta-Fraschini to match an earlier Rolls Royce. He seemed to get more enjoyment out of his three motorboats, one of which could do sixty miles an hour, but boating is a national pastime in Sweden and it was not unusual for well-to-do people to have more than one boat.

Kreuger had no real appreciation of any art, except perhaps certain kinds of literature. He was no music lover; though he liked to listen to records or to a good pianist, classical or jazz, his tastes were plebeian and his favorite song was "*La Paloma.*" When an energetic art dealer in Paris once got him to look at some fine Cézannes and Gauguins, he seemed impressed, but begged off purchasing any with the remark: "No, I have just two interests, the match and Kreuger & Toll—a third would split me." The comment was not altogether true, but it reflected his general attitude. Basically, Kreuger didn't want to be bothered. The dozens of paintings he bought, mostly to oblige friends or because a dealer happened to corner him at the right moment, were almost all lesser-known works of famous artists or those of second- and third-raters. They hung on the walls of his apartment, as someone said, "unsung, unlit, and unlooked at," or were stored in empty rooms. He had one real prejudice: when a dealer once placed a madonna on a pedestal above a fireplace, Kreuger waved it away, remarking bleakly: "I don't like madonnas."

Similarly, he bought beautifully bound books by the shelfload which neither he nor anyone else opened, though he did a fair amount of reading. Biographies of famous men particularly appealed to him, and his admiration for Napoleon was demonstrated by his designing a bookplate with Napoleon's head on it. He had a dog-eared copy of a book on Charles XII which he had minutely annotated and often restudied. He liked detective stories and some poetry, especially Baudelaire and—not unexpectedly, in view of his own empire-building—Kipling, and he was fascinated by books on sex and love, ranging from Michael Arlen to Van de Velde, and including volumes about that subject which had always intrigued him, syphilis.

Kreuger's twenty-three-room duplex apartment at Villagatan 13, in Stockholm, lacked any personal touch and was compared by more than one visitor to a hotel suite. "It was hard to believe that the same man had lived there for years without leaving any more real trace of himself than a slipper," Cederschiöld commented. The extravagances were meaningless, and, in contrast to his corporate personification, the splendid Match Palace, his home was a cluttered, unartistic hodgepodge of old, dark, heavy furniture and a few graceful pieces tucked into obscure corners. In the midst of all this indiscriminate luxury Kreuger remained uncaring and oddly Spartan. He had a small Renaissance table which he used to tap lightly and murmur: "This is the loveliest table in the world," but the only other thing that seemed to appeal to him was a small wooden bear on the banister at the foot of the staircase to the second floor. Whenever he walked up from the dining room to the library, he patted the bear's heel for good luck—he was a man with a collection of such small superstitions.

His favorite room was the library, and he was content to sit for hours in a soft chair there; if the telephone rang, he would invariably pick it up himself, not waiting for a servant to answer. The only other room upon which he lavished attention was the bathroom, where he had a sunken marble tub, a divan, a tea table, and a thick Oriental rug. Often he would take his tea and use a sun-lamp there for a couple of hours before bathing in the morning or evening. His bath was always a great ritual, in keeping with the almost psychopathic fear of germs which was exemplified by his putting a handkerchief behind his head when he leaned on anything, washing his hands after petting an animal, and kissing a woman's wrist rather than her hand.

To the observant Dr. Bjerre, the whole Stockholm apartment was "like an exhibition hall. . . . The dining-room looked like it belonged in a clubhouse, and the salon as if Paris mannequins might suddenly appear. I have seen homes richer and poorer, but never one that oppressed me so much as Kreuger's. Never have I had such a feeling of inanimate objects crying for love and understanding as in his home of waste." Kreuger's apartments elsewhere were much the same, though smaller. He rented a six-room one in Berlin in 1927 on the Pariser Platz, and in Warsaw he had a five-room one on top of the Bank Amerikanski, which he owned. In London he rented a permanent suite at the Carlton Hotel, and in Paris he had a five-room furnished flat at No. 5 Avenue Victor Emmanuel III, near the Seine. His most lavish place was his apartment in New York, a penthouse at 791 Park Avenue, at the corner of Seventy-fourth Street, which he also took over in 1927.

Here he kept some of his better pictures, including a Rembrandt and a Rubens—all in all, some two hundred thousand dollars' worth of art. But what intrigued him far more, satisfying his engineer's soul, was an intricate system of switches and rheostats which enabled him to bathe any of the nine rooms in white, red, blue, or amber light, or blendings of these colors. He especially liked red, and by a hidden button at the head of his bed could put out all the lights in the room except four red ones left softly glowing in the corners. The walls were covered with expensive cloth, and the reception hall was paved with flagstones and lined with mirrors. The place was full of labor-saving devices, and for his roof garden Kreuger imported tons of soil from France, which he spread seven feet deep for elaborate beds of flowers, for fruit trees that burgeoned and a willow that spread its branches twenty feet high and extended out over Park Avenue. In the center was a Japanese rock garden where a blue light played on a nude, while a white stone Cupid spouted what looked like blood when a red spot shone on it at night.

One of the few things Kreuger seemed to care about all his life was plants, but there was something unimaginative and formulistic in the way he dealt with them too. He had a roof garden in Stockholm as well as in New York, and raised flowers at his three country retreats in Sweden. Even so, his Stockholm florist had a standing weekly order for a thousand lilies of the valley, his favorites, and if Kreuger was out of the city they went to his mother. He was extremely particular about flower arrangements, and if a guest criticized them he would have an entire display removed and would reprimand his gardeners. Despite his professed love for plants, he treated them as if they were inanimate objects. One April, in Stockholm, when the wife of an American visitor complained that there were no flowers blooming anywhere yet, Kreuger called every hothouse in town, had row upon row of plants put in at one of his summer places, and surprised his complaining guest and the rest of the company by taking them out there; he wasn't at all disturbed when, within two days, all the flowers froze to death. On another occasion he sent his florist to London to buy forty Japanese pear trees, each of which had to be separately wrapped, for a large party he gave, after which he had them carted away.

Dr. Bjerre believes Kreuger's approach to flowers and plants was a clear example of his essential amorality. "There is something deeply moral about horticulture," the analyst has noted. "The weakest of all living things are plants, and therefore the communion of flowers and people is a special source of the life process for those who are aware of the relationship. But to throw away the equivalent of a year's salary for a thousand lilies a week and to let flowers freeze to death without caring is not only a meaningless luxury but a kind of barbarism. Kreuger's relationship to flowers is an expression of the poverty of his spirit."

Just as he spontaneously decided to put on flower shows for his guests, Kreuger liked to offer sudden gifts to people, often to virtual strangers. The act of giving often became ludicrous. When three Oriental visitors once admired a sofa of his, he saw to it that before they returned to their hotel suites in Stockholm there was a similar sofa in each man's room. On another occasion he bought a roadster for a girl he had met in a restaurant who had refused to believe he was Ivar Kreuger. This predilection for bestowing sudden favors was undoubtedly a form of compensation for his incapacity, which he was aware of himself, to establish a permanent or even temporarily close relationship with any person. He had been that way as a child and remained so all his life. If this removal was partly bred of contempt, it also sprang from a deep inner sense of self-sufficiency, or perhaps from a desire for deprivation which was essentially masochistic. Self-protection may have been at the roots of his subconscious. Beyond satisfying his basic needs for physical companionship with women when he required it and for what might be described as monetary companionship with men, he would not let himself be drawn into anything approaching spiritual affinity with anyone.

His constant effort to keep himself apart from others applied even to his family. When he started to make a lot of money, he brought his elderly parents to Stockholm from Kalmar and saw to it that they had everything they wanted. Once a week, ritualistically, he would go to their house for dinner, but he seldom told them anything about himself, and not infrequently would sit in almost total silence for a couple of hours before going back to work or off to some secret pursuit. His sisters never felt that they knew him well, and though their husbands were given important jobs in his organization, he was close only to his youngest sister, Britta, who remained unmarried and sometimes acted as his hostess. Bold and daring in his business operations, where he could present the most convincing bluff or front, he was inordinately shy and was forever fearful of being the center of attention in public. At a railway station he refused porters and carried his own bags, like any country traveler. ("That fellow doesn't travel with any battery of secretaries—he takes the night train by himself," one of his American admirers remarked.) When he went to a theater, he always sought an aisle seat so he could make his escape in a hurry if he felt he was being whispered about. On a number of occasions he got up and left a restaurant before his food arrived because he had seen people turning to stare at him or felt that waiters were dancing too much attendance on him. Yet, despite his determination to reveal as little of himself as possible, he was by no means insensitive to what others, even fools, thought or said about him. When he was already very successful in Sweden, a drunken count came over to his table in a Stockholm night club one evening and borrowed a thousand kroner. The unwelcome visitor then sat down and, sipping Kreuger's champagne, stared at him for several

minutes. Finally, the man exclaimed: "You don't look like
the match king to me. You look like a big cheese." For
months afterward, according to Kreuger's early Stockholm
mistress Inge Hässler, she found him staring at himself in
mirrors, muttering moodily: "So, you're a big cheese."

: 2 :

If Kreuger's capacity for love was blighted after the death
of the Norwegian girl he had met as a student, he remained
all his life an active man whose physical needs were strong,
and the older he got, the more immersed in his schemes and
the more isolated within himself as the financier, the more
he looked upon women as his chief form of escape. After
his death his private life became a source of sensational copy
—the public seemed to want the swindler to have been a
libertine as well. Many of the newspaper stories were exaggerated, but it is true that he had mistresses in practically
every major city of Europe. There were girls he met in passing, including streetwalkers to whom he took a brief fancy
and whom he paid off at what sometimes amounted to black-
mail rates. There were also highly sophisticated and intelligent women who were thoroughly charmed by him and
who, beyond being impressed because of his eminence, were
attracted by his odd combination of rough masculinity and
an almost feminine quality that found expression in his mellifluous voice.

Inge Hässler was a tall and moderately attractive Swedish physical therapist—he seems to have had a weakness for
the type—whom Kreuger met one spring evening in 1912
in the Djürgården, Stockholm's largest park, but he didn't
start taking her out until the following year, when she was
nineteen and he was thirty-three. Their first evening together, she recalled in a book she wrote after his death, was

spent, prosaically enough, over a can of sardines and some
tinned pineapple, washed down with champagne, in Kreuger's harbor-view apartment on the Strandvägen. The
courtship was marked at first by "lots of roses and shyness,"
Inge wrote, and another year went by before she gave in to
his advances. Thereafter they spent many long week ends
together at various places in the archipelago that forms the
southern approach to Stockholm. Inge loved the outdoors,
as all Swedes do, and whenever she could she cultivated a
tan. In her book, as one of several samples of Kreuger's correspondence with her, she includes a letter she received from
him while she was vacationing at a seaside resort and he was
working away in Stockholm. It is a banal bit, scarcely worth
notice except, perhaps, for these few lines in which the almost middle-aged Kreuger managed to sound just as gauche
as the average adolescent in roughly the same situation:

> My dearest Nigger-baby: I suppose that you are now
> lying in the sun on some rock while I, poor boy, have to
> sit here and long for you. I'm sitting in the office all day
> and, like a good boy, go to bed at 9.30 every night, so
> I'm sorry that I have nothing of interest to tell you.
> . . . I hope there are men enough out there so you can
> get all the dancing and flirting you need to be able to
> live. Greetings, Ivar.

Despite the almost empty, dispassionate tone—Kreuger
seldom sent his "love" to anyone—Inge claimed that he became extremely jealous and even went so far as to post a
guard at night in front of her apartment door. Kreuger, for
his part, was scarcely a faithful swain and Inge was fully
aware of it, but whenever he had been out with another woman he was so profuse in his apologies that Inge, obviously
a girl who could be won over and over again by flowers and
gifts, forgave him. "Even if one had proof of his duplicity,"
she wrote, "he seemed able to convince one that he was

telling the truth." Inge didn't seem to mind his roving eye until another woman's threat to create a scandal led him to beg off marriage in 1915. The next year, fed up with Kreuger's procrastinating, Inge married a Dane named Eberth. When she announced that she and her husband planned to live in Hellerup, Denmark, Kreuger's bland response was that perhaps he'd buy a match factory there. He also predicted, cynically, that she'd come back to him, and less than two years later she did. After this hiatus they settled down to a fairly constant relationship that didn't sputter out until the mid-twenties. Kreuger set her up in a five-room, loft-like apartment in Stockholm behind a heavy iron door with no name on it, and part of the time they also shared a summer home he built at Ängsholmen, an island in the archipelago. Though he was no sportsman beyond enjoying the motorboating and an occasional bit of shooting, Kreuger liked to go to the island and just think, and he often left Inge to her own devices for hours at a time.

If Inge was possibly as amoral a person as Kreuger himself, she was, withal, an observant woman with a good sense of humor who came to know and understand Kreuger and his idiosyncrasies better than most people. He seems to have responded by sharing more confidences with her, at the beginning of his business career anyway, than he did with anyone else. He told her, for example, about his private dollar speculation, and when they went to the Continent together he seemed not to mind introducing her to his business friends—many of whom, she commented, were "strange and came from all walks of life." He was inclined to be moody, she noted, and, in a particularly abject frame of mind, he once remarked: "All human beings are reprehensible, especially those who can get everything they want." Another time he told her: "If you marry again, which I hope you never do, marry an American. The Yankees are the only men who respect women."

Kreuger's odd interests were a source of fascination to Inge. He loved unusual jewelry, which he kept wrapped piece by piece in little leather bags and gave away as gifts, often just to dinner hostesses he liked. His supply of stick-pins numbered in the dozens, and he kept replenishing it. "If you didn't know who he was, you'd think he was a stick-pin salesman," Inge later wrote. Mechanical toys greatly amused him, and he kept these for himself; his two favorites were a peacock and a little jumping pig with rolling eyes. Someone once gave him a toy abacus and Kreuger played with it like a child. "With this abacus, I can count many millions," he would say, with his peculiar, gray smile.

It seems doubtful that after the death of the young Norwegian girl Kreuger ever thought seriously of marriage, but there were plenty of rumors from time to time linking him with well-known women of society or the arts—Greta Garbo, with whom he was seen once or twice, was one of them—and also with royalty. Kreuger was honest enough with himself to know that, while he needed women as a form of release, he could never devote himself to one woman with any real sense of moral obligation. Sometimes he would joke about his lack of permanent attachment. A New York banker once prodded him about falling in love with an American girl, and he quipped: "I prefer a Swedish match." To the wife of one of his top directors in Europe, who asked him why he didn't get married, he replied: "I need at least eight days, and I haven't got time." On another occasion he remarked contemptuously: "Marriage is for my employees, not for me."

In a letter he wrote late in his life to a particular friend of his, the following unusually revealing paragraph appears:

You asked me once whether I could tie myself permanently to a woman. I believe I could, externally—because I should only see her occasionally anyhow. But spiritually, I must honestly say, no. I don't care about children. I don't know why, except that they always do things differently from what one would like, which must be so annoying. Nor do I wish to be burdened with love. . . .

Dr. Bjerre agrees thoroughly with this bit of self-analysis. "Even a woman with the patience of an angel and the wisdom of a Sybil would have fallen short, always groping in empty air when she tried to reach what she loved or tried to make him express himself through love," he wrote. "No woman could have stood it. For Kreuger there were no other possibilities beyond transient, loose relations."

There were always women to be had for the asking if one had as much money as Kreuger did, and undoubtedly the classic life of a rich bachelor, with all its wastefulness and ever-shifting monotony, was all he ever expected. As time went on, he conducted his affairs with women with the same combination of secrecy and guile and careful calculation that he applied to his business, but with considerably less imagination. He kept drawers of expensive brooches, cigarette cases, gold handbags, and small gold boxes, watches, silks, and perfume, all of which he gave away generously and kept replenishing, as if he were filling a freezer. The gifts seldom varied, except that they were sometimes accompanied by envelopes containing stocks or debentures. When Inge Hässler one day in his Stockholm apartment opened one of the drawers containing cigarette cases, he remarked nonchalantly: "I know a lot of girls, I'll use them." In two months they were gone. Another time Inge remarked about his gifts of stocks and money, and he replied: "When I give a woman a large sum, it is not because I love her but because I'm tired of her and want to get rid of her." That he systematized even his relations with women was shown by the discovery, among his papers, of a small black book containing the names of a score or more girls. There was one page for each, and the girl was classified according to her personality, her likes and dislikes, how much she cost and whether she was worth it. At the bottom of the page was what amounted to a final grade—A, B, or C.

On a grand level, Kreuger willingly went all out for some women, sometimes out of kindness as much as from desire. He financed at least two young Swedish girls in musical careers, set an Irish girl up in a fashionable shop in Paris, and supported a former Stockholm actress there. He also kept at least a dozen other women on regular allowances all over Europe, a fact that came out only after his death when they started complaining about being cut off and when his apartment safe in Stockholm was found to contain scores of letters from these various ladies in which they addressed him in such realistically endearing phrases as "My Own Match King."

Less grandly, and more sporadically, he maintained a stable of musical-comedy stars, night-club dancers, and such, and it was not unusual for him to give hundred-dollar bills to performers he liked, whether he asked them out or not. Watching such entertainments was apparently a form of relaxation from his endless round of business meetings. At sumptuous parties for his business friends in New York and Stockholm, he surprised them by having a dancer such as La Argentina suddenly pop out from behind a curtain or arranged for an entire chorus line or well-known band to be on hand, but, significantly, he preferred to be alone when he went out on the town. He always took in all the musical shows when in New York, and during a three-week stretch there in the mid-twenties he made the rounds of virtually all the night clubs by himself, sipping champagne and rewarding the performers as he went along.

Finally, on a low level, Kreuger seems to have been inclined on occasion to sheer debauchery, and it is not surprising that his favorite haunt for what amounted to a Jekyll-and-Hyde transformation was post-war and pre-Hitler Berlin, which was steeped in its own forlorn amorality. In addition to carrying on a sordid affair there with the wife of one of his associates, he is said to have enjoyed frequenting low dives, where he partially disguised himself by wearing workingman's clothes. According to stories that remain flimsily documented but were widely printed after his death, he went to Berlin once or twice a year for gambling sprees—he was a truly great poker player, but preferred quiet tables in out-of-the-way places to casinos of the Monte Carlo type—and to visit private clubs of ill repute, where, among other things, he liked to watch others drink copious amounts and to lay bets on which alcoholic customer would last longest. In Berlin once, and another time in Paris, when he was recognized in pursuit of pleasure in the poorer sections of these cities by fellow Swedes, he pretended that it was a case of mistaken identity. "My name is Lee," he muttered, which at least was better than saying it was Higginson. After a day or two of letting off steam in this fashion, he would reappear in public as the suave and self-controlled financier.

Kreuger once remarked to a friend: "I prefer to throw the world a few names, to give it something to talk about. At least people don't nose about my real private affairs then." Despite his apparent unmarriageability, he did have full and mature relationships with a few women. One was a society matron in Cleveland and New York. Another was a woman in London with whom, among other things, he practiced thought control, or telepathy. A third was a German woman of French extraction, known by the pseudonym Itta Sandt, perhaps the person he became closest to toward the end of his life and certainly the one woman with whom he established a serious and regular correspondence over some years. She was a small, attractive, bird-like creature, a fine linguist interested in art and psychology, and though she was also quite an admirer of the Soviets, with whom Kreuger was always fencing, he seemed to respect her judgments about business matters—at least, he hired and fired some people according to her whims. In addition to an obvious physical attraction, he appeared to feel a particular rapport with her, maybe because she was as aloof and removed as he was. When she complained in a letter about sitting at dinner parties with people who were "really all dead," he replied:

> You must not feel that I am simply aping you if I say that I feel exactly the same. I am very unhappy when I have to be with people for long at a time and to talk to them unofficially, as it were. I don't mind speaking to them when I can give orders, when I can say "do this" or "do that," "take such and such a post." But the things they call "worries" when they talk to me privately always bore me. They none of them know what they are living for. At most they have an *idée fixe*—one is always talking about his dentist, another about his family's bad luck, and a third about the job he didn't get. When I compare our contemporaries with the people whose biographies I have read, I realize all the more how petty everything is nowadays.

Kreuger, of course, had his own *idée fixe*, his dream of domination, and if he pursued his pleasure privately and socialized to a minimum, he took special delight in matching his wits in the conference room with some of the same persons he claimed bored him so much outside it. He was very clever at picking the brains of prominent visitors who came to see him out of curiosity or in the hope of getting something from him. First he would give them a few laconic comments and then start off on a series of his own "by the way" questions, as a result of which more than one man left the Match Palace feeling he had been mesmerized into revelations he should never have made.

In the highest financial circles Kreuger became known as *"L'Oiseleur,"* the bird charmer. One day early in 1927 he sat for eight hours at a table in Berlin with a group of Germany's foremost bankers who had come to appraise him prior to the introduction of some big new stock issues on Continental exchanges. The financiers wanted to know all sorts of things about his match properties and his other corporate and real-estate holdings. The gentlemen arrived in a skeptical mood, but Kreuger parried their questions so brilliantly, pleading secrecy in some cases and revealing tantalizing bits of information in others, that they all left with a highly favorable impression and within a fortnight he was besieged by requests from banks throughout Europe to be included among his sponsors.

CHAPTER 6

The Match King's Greatest Years

THE PERIOD from 1927 to 1930 was the most successful in Kreuger's life. It was during these years that he dazzled layman and expert alike with a swift succession of expansive and daring financial exploits, all of which he executed with an air of complete assurance. For the first time he seemed to enjoy the fruits of his reputation as a public benefactor, and more and more he took to hobnobbing with prominent statesmen on the Continent and attending important financial conferences.

Among other accomplishments, he arranged a vital merger of the various English match concerns such as Bryant & May, in which he held interests. In Asia he eliminated his greatest competition by secretly buying a number of Japanese factories that provided him with a dominant position in the industry there. In Italy, he bought himself quietly into a position of strength. His greatest coup, however, and one that brought him wide acclaim, occurred in France.

As a result of the prolonged post-war inflation and consequent political and financial instability, the Poincaré government, trying to stem the fall of the franc, had sought a large loan in the United States to supplement one for a hundred million dollars which the Morgan interests had granted in 1920 at eight-per-cent interest. However, Morgan and others in America now, in the mid-twenties, said they would do no more. The pendulum had turned, and both the American government and private sources were unwilling to invest heavily in Europe. Kreuger, alone among the world's prominent financiers, still had faith in the franc and in France, and he stepped in. First he bought about a quarter of a million francs' worth of French bonds, thereby giving Poincaré a small lift. Then, over a period of months, as one government after another fell and was replaced by a new rickety coalition, Kreuger conducted secret negotiations with Poincaré, seeking a partial match monopoly. When news of the deliberations leaked out, the Communists and Socialists bitterly assailed Poincaré, calling him "Ivar Poincaré." On the eve of the defeat of the monopoly contract in the Chamber of Deputies, Léon Blum wrote: "The Napoleon of matches has found his Waterloo in the financial committees."

But Kreuger promptly offered Poincaré seventy-five millions dollars at five per cent in return for the right to import unlimited luxury matches into France and also some machinery and raw materials. In October 1927, after Kreuger had bribed a number of influential politicians to a degree thought excessive by some of his staff, this lesser deal was approved for twenty years. IMCO in America took over fifty million dollars of the loan and Swedish Match the rest, and the French issued bonds for the amount at 93½ per cent of par. The transaction undoubtedly helped stabilize the franc at a critical time and encouraged the government to regain its financial strength, while Kreuger made a good profit on his imports. Though a portion of the vituperative

French press continued to attack him, he was awarded the Grand Cross of the French Legion of Honor. In one sense this big success in France was also his misfortune. Though he won the grudging admiration of Morgan and other international bankers, he simultaneously aroused their bitterness, for not only was it felt that his bold and easy terms had "spoiled the market" for future loans, if any were to be made, but his money enabled the French to pay off in advance the remainder of the more expensive 1920 Morgan loan, two thirds of which was still outstanding. This saved the French several million dollars in interest accruals, but didn't especially endear Kreuger to the proud house of Morgan.

Kreuger's prestige in Europe was now enormous. Feeling himself and his methods vindicated, he went ahead with some other big loans that eventually would prove part of his undoing. During 1928 and 1929 he obtained match monopolies in Estonia, Latvia, Yugoslavia, and Rumania, as well as in far-off Ecuador, and the money he lent to attain them raised the total he had dispersed to one hundred and eighty-five million dollars. He was like a fairy godmother. The optimistic atmosphere of the Locarno Treaty period, when it seemed that the broad political declarations for peace would be followed by a general settlement of other great issues, including the knottiest one of making Germany a going concern once more, had soon deteriorated. Trade imbalances, confused and critical currency conditions, and political animosities still flourished as recovery lagged. And as the United States continued to turn its back on Europe and refused to furnish enough working capital to restore the Continent's economy, Kreuger kept stepping into the breach. In the case of Rumania, for example, he came to that country's rescue after both America and England had turned down Queen Marie's requests for financial assistance.

Using the money of American investors, who apparently

placed more trust in him than their own government did in the future of Europe, Kreuger now concentrated on seeking a new mechanism for relations between the old and the fledgling nations. In almost every case, the money he lent, at an average rate of only six and a half per cent, was used to good advantage—the Rumanians achieved a degree of economic stabilization with the proceeds of their Kreuger loan, and the Yugoslavs built some much-needed public works with theirs. As one of Kreuger's defenders, Anders Byttner, a Swedish author, later wrote: "Ivar Kreuger realized more clearly than most of his contemporaries among statesmen and financiers that the first conditions for a real economic reconstruction of the war-devastated world was for an ample flow of capital to be directed to the European countries." After one big Kreuger loan, the *Journal of Commerce* in New York commented that his activities "call to mind the histories of the great merchant and trading companies of the Middle Ages and of early modern times which, in addition to their regular operations, financed wars and supported or overthrew dynasties." Something was wrong, the paper admonished, "when a private company is able to approach the world's markets more successfully than States that are presumably stable and in possession of sources of monopolistic income which might be pledged directly for loans instead of being farmed out to private capitalists."

More and more Kreuger seemed to bask in his glory. He let it be known that he foresaw a sort of international organism that would be beyond and above all nations, with a special monetary unit regulating international exchange and supervising the disposition of all currencies, and he thought of this new structure, with himself as the head of it, as a means also of regulating politics and averting war. In these respects he was undoubtedly ahead of his time, and many of today's mechanisms of international co-operation embrace his ideas, but he also obviously was allowing his generosity and his bold business aims to carry him too far too fast. In the first place, despite his belief in the future of Europe, he was oversanguine in appraising the economic and financial realities of the post-Versailles period. On one of those train rides across the Continent during which he liked to theorize, he told Jacob Wallenberg, the Swedish banker: "You know, I've come to the conclusion that government bonds are the safest thing to have because no government has failed on its obligations since 1815." He was wrong, of course, for Russia had defaulted, but, more importantly, his remark demonstrates his failure to realize how shaky some of the new hybrid governments were, and how likely it was that they would default once the going got rough. Secondly, Kreuger's growing sense of power, his desire to be more than just a match monopolist and to control as many industries as possible, was approaching megalomania, and, as one of the outside accountants observed after the crash, he had begun to engage in "financial dabbling at any cost."

It was expensive dabbling, too. Not only, for instance, did he greatly extend his iron-ore holdings in 1928-9, buying properties in Africa and South America, but he took over a whole new enterprise, the Swedish pulp industry. This consisted of about ten pulp factories in northern Sweden which had foundered during the post-war depression and had become entirely dependent on a large Swedish bank that was itself shaky. Kreuger was regarded as the great magician who alone could salvage the wreck. Having begun quietly to purchase some of the mills, as he had done before with match factories, he consolidated them in 1929 in a new trust called the Swedish Pulp Company, Inc., with a capital valuation of fifty million kroner—the shares being held by Kreuger & Toll.

Kreuger had in mind a vast control not only over the paper-and-pulp business but also over newspapers as a result of this move—about this time he and his brother Torsten bought three of Sweden's foremost papers. He seems also to have believed that the more he diversified his holdings, the better off he would be in a fluctuating market and the sounder his position when the match monopolies ran out. Accordingly, he also began to buy into the successful L. M. Ericsson Telephone Company, and he wrote enthusiastically to a German friend: "The telephone, as far as I am concerned, has the same qualities as matches. With the arrangement and management of telephone organizations, I can get State concessions and monopolies just as I can with my little wooden soldiers." He bought a sizable chunk of Sweden's famous ball-bearing business, and, perhaps reaching for his final destiny, bought a Swedish gold mine that promised to be a bonanza.

Many of these transactions were conducted secretly, as were some of his biggest match deals. One of these was the purchase of three hundred and fifty thousand shares of the newly recapitalized Diamond Match Company for thirteen and a half million dollars—Kreuger arranged this through an agent in Wall Street, in whose name the stock was bought and held. He also obtained partial or majority control of various other American match concerns, including half of the Ohio Match Company. Openly, Kreuger now controlled about two hundred and fifty match factories in every country of Europe except Spain, Russia and France, and in sixteen non-European countries, and he was selling three fourths of all the matches in the world. The world consumption of matches was about forty billion boxes a year, and the public paid about half a cent a box. The factories' profit was about half of that. As public corporations, Swedish Match and IMCO together were reporting net profits of some thirty million dollars on gross receipts of eighty million, and this was a far greater return than seemed feasible out of any match business, though few persons ever dared say so to Kreuger. "Such huge profits were just not logical," Wallenberg, who had had some experience in matches himself, later commented. "But when the question came up, the answer was always the same—the difference was made in speculations." Indeed, the books of Kreuger's ever more numerous companies were reporting the most amazing profits on transactions no one knew anything about, profits which he simply listed under his own name or under headings such as "sundry returns" or "cash in banks."

As one of his final fronts, he created something rosily called the International Financial Syndicate, which was supposed to work closely with Dutch Kreuger & Toll, the chief investment branch of the empire. In one year alone the Syndicate reported a profit of fifteen million dollars on three transactions in Europe. The accountant in Amsterdam, a typically pliable fellow named Victor Holm, listed the gains on Kreuger's orders and took Kreuger's word that the stock certificates were being held by Kreuger & Toll in Stockholm; as the Stockholm parent and the Dutch daughter had joint balance sheets, this seemed all right to Holm. In a number of other cases where Kreuger had bought valuable stocks and bonds, such as shares in General Electric and I. G. Farben and French bonds, he listed them by name but in amounts far above what he actually had, or as double entries, and all of this exaggerated hocus-pocus was designed to continue to inflate his total position so the public would go on buying new Kreuger issues.

The really huge issues began in 1927, when, in one fell swoop, Kreuger decided to sell as many new shares in Kreuger & Toll as already existed and to offer another third in Swedish Match. Simultaneously, in America, whose market Kreuger had recently described as "the greatest in the world and the one to which concerns of international scope must turn for future issues," IMCO offered fifty million dollars' worth of sinking-fund convertible debentures; they were promptly oversubscribed, and most of the proceeds were used to finance the big loan to France. In 1928 he came up with his own version of the participating debenture. It was devised with the help of no less a personage than the Foreign Minister of Sweden, Eliel Löfgren, who was also a crack lawyer, and its purpose was to avoid the heavy taxation on shares of stock in Sweden that even non-Swedish holders of securities had to pay. The new debenture was more like a bond that paid interest but was not subject to taxation. The idea worked splendidly, and, with the help of thirty-seven banks in seven countries, Kreuger & Toll put out sixteen million dollars' worth of new debentures in 1928 and another whopping eighteen million dollars' worth the next year. Many were sold in America, where they were deemed gilt-edged, in contrast to England, where they were considered highly speculative and where Kreuger wisely pushed his much safer Swedish Match issues instead. By this time he was engaging in widespread "supporting operations," paying various agents bonuses or giving them rebates to push the sales of all his stocks, and he took up an increasing amount of them himself, giving only his notes or pledges, which meant that money reported as having been received was not, in fact, on hand.

Yet the quotations kept soaring. At the start of 1929, when Kreuger & Toll's securities were the most widely distributed securities in the world, its common shares were selling at 730 per cent of par (100) and convertible debentures at 863 per cent, and the company's dividends were at 30 per cent while those of Swedish Match were at 16 per cent. Kreuger seemed to be of two minds about these astronomical figures. With a mixture of pride and cynicism, he remarked: "I've built my enterprise on the firmest ground that can be found—the foolishness of people." One afternoon in Paris Cederschïold found him smilingly shaking his head over the day's stock sheets and softly murmuring:

"They're crazy, completely crazy." But when Cederschiöld asked: "Do you think we should sell?" Kreuger looked up and answered: "No, they'll be more crazy." At the same time, however, he was getting a little uneasy. Privately he had begun to refer to the American financiers as "unsteady" and "careless," and, changing his earlier tune, he predicted that they would soon be overtaken again by their more conservative and canny counterparts in England. "It is risky," he said early in 1929, "to introduce securities in Wall Street, because once the New York operators start working on paper their quotations lose all relationship to real value."

It was typical of Kreuger, and scarcely anything for the Americans to look back on with pride, that at the same time he was twitting them and becoming a little fearful, too, of their wild and woolly methods, he kept trying to get as much out of America as he could while the getting was still good. The climax of his operations came, as did the climax of so many others, in that historic month of October 1929. His response was unique. Formidable advertisements appeared on October 23 in New York announcing a vast new Kreuger issue at twenty-four dollars per American certificate. The next day was Black Thursday, the first day of the big crash, when thirteen million shares changed hands. Two days later, on October 26, Kreuger astonished the whole world of finance. He announced that he would go ahead with previously disclosed plans to lend Germany one hundred and twenty-five million dollars at six per cent in return for a monopoly on both the manufacture and distribution of matches in the Reich for a period of from thirty-two to fifty years.

Kreuger was as sanguine about the economic future of Germany as he had been about France's. The political outlook didn't faze him—in New York he played up the need to grant the loan as a means of defeating Hitler and avoiding war, while in Europe he let it be known that he thought

Hitler might be a stabilizing influence. But his real reason for offering Germany so much money for a simple match monopoly was fear of new Russian competition, which now loomed as the only block to his complete control of the world's match markets.

: 2 :

The story of Kreuger's relations with the Russians forms an intriguing subplot that runs all though his remarkable history. He had always been fascinated by the opportunities in Russia—it will be recalled that as early as 1912, a year after he incorporated Kreuger & Toll as a contracting concern, he had set up a building subsidiary in Leningrad; he had also bought some Russian real estate. The Revolution had interrupted his plan to establish a Russian branch of his new match business. After selling the Bolsheviks some cheap surplus matches and some matchmaking machinery in the immediate post-war period, he had had little to do with the Russians. When Lenin abandoned his policy of militant Communism and made overtures for foreign economic and technical help, Kreuger had been among those approached, and he could have either shared in Russian match production and distribution in return for a loan, supervised the industry for a fee, or operated the Russian export business in matches for a profit. But he had had more pressing business elsewhere, and had chosen to wait and confine his Russian activity, for the moment, to obtaining aspen wood in that country and trying to sell more Swedish matches there.

By the beginning of 1926, however, Russian competition in matches had grown and Kreuger had begun to be disturbed about it. Through the Soviet ambassador in Paris, Krassin, with whom he had become quite friendly, he let it be known that he was ready to give Russia a loan in return for a match monopoly. Long-range dickering proved inconclusive, and he decided to go to Moscow himself. Traveling as an ordinary tourist, he entered via Finland and soon found that he was being followed by agents of the OGPU, the secret police. The terms offered him in Moscow were much tougher than he had been led to expect, so he remained in Russia only seven days and afterward described his mission as "a tourist trip for my birthday." He visited Christ Cathedral in Moscow and dropped a thousand-ruble note in the collection box, charmed the hotel folk with his generosity, and joked with minor bureaucrats—"It's a shame, Comrade Kreuger, that you're not on our side," one of them remarked—but the higher-ups, it appeared, wanted no part of him. Maxim Litvinov, then Foreign Minister, declared privately: "I cannot see how in any way he can be of use to us. He represents those American circles with which we can hardly be in agreement."

After Kreuger's loan operations were stepped up in Europe, and especially after the Russians got wind of his negotiations for a big, bolstering loan to France, which naturally was a threat to the French Communists, they reversed their field and tried to lure him back into direct negotiations with them as an alternative. Early in 1927, after some conversations with Russian agents in Paris—"It was like buying a rug in a bazaar," one of Kreuger's Paris aides noted—new negotiations came to a head in Berlin. The Russians, needing money for machinery, expressed willingness to give Kreuger what was tantamount to a match monopoly under certain conditions for forty million dollars, but again it was his turn to waver. In effect, he had, at this delicate point, to choose between Russia and France, and he chose France. The English, as well as the French politicians, objected to his making any arrangement with the Communists, while the attitude in America was that no deal with Moscow should even be considered which was not accompanied by an agreement to settle the outstanding debts to the West inherited from the Tsarist regime. (It is interesting to note that Kreuger made a successful speculation in Tsarist bonds at this time, under the impetus of the stir he had himself created.)

The sessions in Berlin marked the end of actual negotiations between Kreuger and the Communists, and then began an ulterior effort on the part of the Russians to lure him into a position of financial embarrassment. Wherever Kreuger sought to obtain new concessions and monopolies, as in Estonia and Latvia, Russian competition made him pay heavily for them. Following the successful execution of his French loan, the Russians sent one of their cleverest international agents, A. M. Fuschman, to see him, with instructions to offer control of the whole Russian match industry as security against an eighty-million-dollar Kreuger loan; Kreuger was also to be offered the match export business of the country, so that there would be a division of spoils amounting to a world monopoly. But the real purpose of the Communists now was to get Kreuger deep in debt on the eve of the depression they were predicting.

As Kreuger already dominated the world market in matches, he rejected the partnership suggestion. Fuschman was reportedly so taken with Kreuger, however, that he later tried to get Stalin to change his tactics. Stalin bluntly refused and—according to the former Russian Counselor of Legation in Stockholm, S. Dmitrievsky—said to Fuschman: "It is not in our interest to encourage and favor the Swede. On the contrary, we must bind him and make him harmless. He is a danger for us." In what amounted to a broad retaliatory gesture, Kreuger grandly offered to lend the Russians as much as a billion dollars if they would grant him monopolies in sugar, tea, and tobacco as well as matches, plus some mining rights—and acknowledgment of the Tsarist debts. Kreuger could never have raised the money if this bluff had been called, but it was not. Stalin snorted back the expected answer—that he was being asked to surrender to capitalism. The gauntlet had been thrown, and picked up.

The Germans had been worried about both the Russians and Kreuger for some time. They had been curtailing their match production for a number of years because it outstripped demand, but the Russians had kept shipping cheaper matches of fairly good quality into Germany. A monopoly and an import ban seemed the only solution, even though it would put Kreuger, who already controlled two thirds of the German match factories, in a more dominant position than ever. When he offered the Germans as much as one hundred and twenty-five million dollars, they decided to go ahead and establish a sales-and-trade monopoly in which they and Kreuger shared equally. They would let him keep his factories, and try to control him through the administration of the monopoly. Kreuger was more than satisfied to achieve this degree of state protection against the encroaching Russians, and he was also intrigued by the idea of "rationalizing" the industry of yet another major country and thereby adding to his own power.

At the same time, it is undeniable that, even though he believed firmly that the Continent's economic welfare depended on a strong Reich, whether under the Nazis or the Social Democrats, he would not have made so large a loan had he not been so afraid of Moscow. To the degree that the loan helped break Kreuger's back by forcing him henceforth to search desperately for funds to pay off the bankers in Sweden and America who helped finance it, the Russians would achieve their aim. Though the German monopoly contract closed the Reich's match business to the Russians, they kept pushing the sale of matches wherever they could, at about half the price of Kreuger's, and often at no profit to them. It was an economic war to the finish.

In the campaign to destroy Kreuger, who now became

the capitalist ogre personified, the Communists brought out their biggest propaganda weapons. Even the muses were called in. Ilya Ehrenburg, the novelist, who had been in poor standing with Moscow in the late twenties, was given a chance to redeem himself by writing what amounted to a fictional tract about Kreuger. He responded nobly, though with more prescience than style. After visiting Stockholm to study the picture at first hand, he wrote a novel called *The United Front* in Russian, which was translated into Swedish and then into English as *The Most Sacred Belongings.* Its protagonist, a Swedish capitalist named Sven Olsson, a match king and world financier, has no thought for the welfare of mankind but only for money-making and power. One section of a chapter entitled "Intermezzo" reads, in part:

> Olsson walked across the Kurfürstendamm and everyone smiled at him. The people strolling here were in a leisurely mood, the more so since the hour was propitious—the banks were closed, the cocottes had not yet begun to work. Only the matchsellers were busy, giving a little variety to the crowd. There went a blind man, walking straight ahead and gently tapping the pavement with the iron ferrule of his stick. His milky blue eyes were ghastly, no one dared look at them. He strode among ladies and fox terriers like a terrible warning. Yet he attacked nobody. He did not threaten reprisals. He only cried in a piteous voice:
> "Matches, matches . . ."
> In a doorway yonder—a lump of flesh. Instead of legs, short stumps. Who had planted him down so oddly—Mother Nature or the great god Mars? He lay in the mud like the stump of a cigar. This clod too cried out in a nasal tone:
> "Matches, matches . . ."

Additional beggars accost Olsson, who "listened involuntarily as though he were being called by name; matches and himself—were they not one and the same thing? He mused —he was linked with all these miserable wretches—a preposterous connection—for did not he, as they, live only on matches?" Olsson continues—"the wretched creatures would not let him alone"—and finally accepts a few matchboxes and hands out coins in return. "With professional interest" he tries a match. "It was only made with poplar wood, indeed, but was not any worse than the Russian aspen. The future might be faced with confidence. Resolutely and self-assuredly, Olsson continued his walk. Today he had contended not with Moscow, but with death, and, as always, he had conquered."

No one who read the novel could possibly have had any doubts as to whom the protagonist was intended to represent. What makes the quoted passage astonishing is a paragraph in a letter Kreuger wrote to a friend some time before the book's publication—there was absolutely no way Ehrenburg could have found out about it—in which Kreuger describes leaving a cabaret in Berlin late one night. "On the way home we were accosted by a lot of beggars," he says. "There have never been so many beggars in Germany. And it is going to be worse. It was really rather horrible—they all offered me matches—and I gave each of them money for my own goods. . . . As a matter of fact, I had never thought of these people before, selling my matches. . . ." Ehrenburg's Olsson, at the end of the novel, has a breakdown in a resort near Stockholm, returns to Paris, and dies there alone in his apartment from a heart attack. Even in this respect, life—and death—would imitate art.

Kreuger had always been fond of quoting Napoleon's definition of happiness—"the ability to see the difficulties gather at the same time that you can conquer them"—and he must have thought of it even as he was playing to the hilt his role as a European benefactor. His sole condition to giving Germany the money was that she ratify the Young Plan on Reparations before May 30, 1930. The possibility of a prolonged depression didn't seem to worry him unduly, and when Cederschiöld visited him in Stockholm in November 1929 he predicted that "the crisis" might last nine months. When Cederschiöld inquired: "Don't you think it will be difficult to get all the money for the German loan?" Kreuger replied, with his usual bland smile: "There's plenty of time—a lot will happen before then."

A lot would happen—Kreuger would go further out on a limb and prepare his doom, but first Germany would get the promised sum, and even more, from the remarkable Swede. As infatuated with him as ever, the American bankers had already agreed to take over fifty million dollars of the big loan, and the worshipful Donald Durant had even declared that the Lee, Higginson partners had "high hopes, some time in the future, of using the German loan as a brilliant excuse for [another] secured debenture issue." The rest of the loan was to be the responsibility of Kreuger & Toll and Swedish Match. The payments were to be made in two installments, one of seventy-five million at the end of August 1930 and the rest at the end of May 1931, but the Germans were so anxious to get the money to pay unemployment benefits that an international banking syndicate headed by Lee, Higginson discounted the total amount and paid it in the spring of 1930. Kreuger, of course, still had the responsibility of raising the money on schedule.

For the moment, Kreuger was the hero of heroes, and his reputation soared to its topmost point early in 1930, when he was invited to come to the second Hague Conference to arrange with the creditor powers and Germany the relationship between reparations payments and the servicing of the big new match loan. In his grandest gesture, one that for the first time made his lieutenants wonder if he had lost his sanity,

Kreuger not only agreed to refrain from financing a new capital issue of his own until after the floating of the Young Loan—a two-hundred-million-dollar advance to Germany from governments and banking houses in Europe and America—but also promised to take a thirty-million-dollar share of that loan himself. French leaders, led by Paul Reynaud and André Tardieu, declared rapturously that he had saved Europe from collapse. More importantly for Kreuger, the French prematurely redeemed their seventy-five-million-dollar loan in April 1930 at the callable rate of 110, which meant a large capital gain for him and enough cash to meet his first payment to Germany. Even in the staid financial circles of London the Swedish financier was praised to the skies by men such as Keynes and Sir Arthur Salter, while in New York the gentlemen who had supported him for so long were certain he would weather the storm; with pride they pointed out that Kreuger stocks had reacted much less sharply than most others to the original impact of the market crash.

This is one of the rare times in Kreuger's life when success seems to have made him actually heady. As usual, however, he celebrated in his own peculiar fashion. One night during the final loan negotiations he left his Berlin apartment about eight o'clock and went across to the Hotel Adlon nearby. Momentarily disregarding his dietary proscriptions. he ordered a collection of his favorite dishes—a chocolate soufflé, caviar and crackers, bouillon and ice cream, in that order. Then he went back to the apartment, telephoned Inge Hässler in Stockholm, and asked his old-time mistress to play the piano to him over the phone. At his request, she rendered several thousand kroner' worth of Russian melodies. The evening after the successful Hague meeting he hastened back to Paris and solemnized the event more tangibly with one of his newer girls there. If he had any private fears of what was to come, he didn't show it. Undoubtedly he knew that he had gone much too far to turn back. Embarked on the greatest bluff of his career, he now had to risk an attempt to raise more money in a collapsing world to pay off his pledges. As long as the Americans continued to help, he thought he could save himself. If he failed, another way out was always available. Years ago, walking through a park in Stockholm with Inge, he had told her that the day he knew his life work was destroyed he would put a bullet through his heart.

CHAPTER 7

The Beginning
of the End

ECONOMISTS have summarized the practices and institutions
of the twenties which built up to inevitable collapse and led
to the long depression of the thirties. Among the many con-
tributing factors were an uneven distribution of income; an
uncohesive banking structure that created a disastrous chain
effect of failures once the crisis began; an imbalance of international trade which, on top of the burden of war debts
and other obligations due America, forced European nations
to disgorge their gold and then, when that ran out, to default
on a large scale; and a loose and flagrantly uncontrolled corporate system that proliferated wildly and was easily plun-
dered. When the boom broke, however, what specifically
destroyed most men was the lack of liquidity. Beyond fixed
capital assets, liquidity represents financial fuel. Its attributes
are temporal, and the time concept is as vital in the realms
of finance and economics as in physics.

In the case of Ivar Kreuger, liquidity was basic to his very
structure. Through his loans to countries in distress, he in-

curred steady long-term obligations, and the rate of repayment to him was spread out over many years. While the getting was good, he was obtaining the money for his loans by borrowing, in effect, from investors in America, and what he did not use for his big match deals he reinvested generally on an optimistic schedule. When the crash took place and the crisis was prolonged, he was trapped by the collapse of the whole structure of international payments. The effect was that of the proverbial rolling snowball. Banks in America found themselves with unpaid short-term debts owed them in Europe. The lack of an adequate tax reserve that might have compensated for the general shortage of funds aggravated the tight money situation in the United States. As the liquidity of the banks diminished, they denied funds to their customers, large and small; in the summer of 1929 brokers' loans, about half of which came from banks, exceeded seven billion dollars, so the denial of fresh funds had an immediate catastrophic effect on the millions of investors who had plunged in the market on margin—buying, among other stocks, the seemingly sound and attractive issues of Kreuger & Toll and IMCO. The brokers raised the margin levels and the whole false picture began to crack. In time, of course, having liquidated their customers, many of the banks would be liquidated themselves.

While prosperity had lasted and money was readily available, Kreuger's system had worked beautifully and, as we have seen, he had consistently bewitched and bewildered his friends and supporters in New York with personal charm and glowing declarations, backed up by constant fresh outpourings of dividends. Through 1930 he more or less sat tight and managed to hold his own, predicting, as did many others, that the crisis would soon end. By the spring of 1931, however, his far-flung group of companies was feeling the impact of the world financial collapse. Such assets as Kreuger owned were, for the most part, in countries whose currency was weak and sometimes blocked, whereas he owed *dollars* to these same nations. His predicament could no longer be hidden from his associates, among whom he had for so long cultivated his reputation as a man of mystery who perforce had to keep his accounts to himself and his affairs in his head.

A number of his co-workers began to fear that he had lent out too much and borrowed too much. To them his continued expansion in a period of rapidly declining values seemed dangerous. Kreuger knew, however, that to pull in his horns, even to cut his dividends, was impossible—it would start rumors that could lead to embarrassing inquiries —so, instead of retrenching, he determined to push ahead harder than ever. As the response to his newest stock issues lagged, he supported them himself in what investigators afterward said "can only be described as 'bucket shop' conditions," and at the same time he kept expanding and engaging in "an orgy of financial ventures" that included the secret purchase of more stock in American match companies, of real estate in Paris, and of various European brokerage houses. Through undercover representatives he increased his speculations in an effort to get his hands on some ready cash.

His chief problem was to find enough money to pay back the bankers who had raised the millions for the loan to Germany and to cover another loan of thirty-two million dollars to Poland, which he had reluctantly made in 1930 to maintain his ten-year hold on a monopoly there. Though not a Nazi sympathizer, he now let it be openly known in financial circles that he felt the election of Hitler might stabilize conditions all over Europe. As the economic and political outlook grew more uncertain each week, however, Kreuger's plight worsened, and soon it became common knowledge that the Match King was feeling the pinch. Several astute bankers in Europe who had followed his career closely began to have real qualms about his general financial condition. "I had never quite understood where he made all his money anyway," Jacob Wallenberg recalls, in looking back over this period, "but even though I hadn't been able to make sense out of his profit-and-loss statements, he apparently had been quite liquid around 1927, before the over-lending and overborrowing began. By 1931, however, when it was pretty obvious he needed money, I was particularly puzzled by the fact that he still showed a big cash reserve in some of his companies and in some banks, including a bank in Danzig."

What Wallenberg did not know, any more than did Kreuger's own accountants, was that this private Danzig bank, like a number of others he owned, had no cash at all and was just a dummy. Kreuger was now using it as part of his scheme to free real funds for speculation, taking them out of bona-fide accounts and pretending to deposit them in Danzig and elsewhere. Even though Wallenberg and his family had seldom dealt with Kreuger, they still respected him as a compatriot who had helped put Sweden on the map of big-time finance, but some non-Swedish banking experts were by now less charitable in their opinions. The German financial expert Hjalmar Schacht thought Kreuger was "too much of a visionary." In Holland the directors of Mahler's Bank, who had had some dealings with Kreuger, suddenly announced that they were breaking with him because they had not received a satisfactory reply to an inquiry. And in Switzerland the well-known banker and theoretician Felix Somary predicted privately to a prominent German official at the start of the year that the world crisis would not end until three major events took place: a banking collapse in Austria and Germany, the renunciation by England of the gold standard, and the bankruptcy of Ivar Kreuger.

Such a prophecy of doom, if it had been voiced publicly,

would surely have dismayed and frightened millions, from Bangkok to Brooklyn. It would also have been tantamount to slandering Kreuger personally, though he could scarcely have dared contest it. His mounting indebtedness alone might have started a panic had it been generally known. In Sweden, at the end of 1930, he owed his chief supporters, the Scandinaviska bank in Stockholm, more than two hundred million kroner (about fifty million dollars). In France, where he had been on friendly terms for years with a number of banks and where his credit had been progressively renewed, the stop sign had now gone out and no longer was money flowing. Faced with such a situation, Kreuger began to use any and all collateral he could get hold of, including government bonds issued on some of his earlier match loans which, by agreement, were supposed to stay put in certain banks or companies and not be pledged away unless replaced by something of equal value. He now took these and other securities, replaced them with lesser values or with none at all, and used them to get cash elsewhere. Fully aware of the danger and illegality of what he was doing, he saw no alternative. And, having operated for years on the principle that he was privileged and inviolate, that whatever he did today which wasn't quite legal could be fixed up tomorrow with no one knowing the difference, he thought he could still get away with it while he rode out the storm.

Despite his large debt to it, his main source of funds continued to be the Scandinaviska bank, of which he now himself owned about ten per cent. The bank's officers, having gone along with him so far, concluded that they must go on helping him in the face of adversity because the bank's own security depended so largely on his solvency. His chief bulwark there remained Oscar Rydbeck, the old admiring friend he had carefully cultivated for nearly two decades. Rydbeck, beyond doubt, had a brilliant financial mind, but it was unfortunately handicapped by a weak and overgenerous nature. His chief virtue, from Kreuger's viewpoint, was his penchant for dreaming of great projects and leaving the details to others. He had continued to idolize Kreuger and loved to appear at important financial conferences on the Continent as the possessor of arcane knowledge of what Kreuger was up to. This suited Kreuger perfectly because the ever popular and esteemed Rydbeck was excellent window dressing, both at home and abroad. In a typical maneuver, Kreuger had made him a member of the Kreuger & Toll board without even getting his consent. They had discussed the matter and, while Rydbeck had liked the idea, he had hesitated in view of what he deemed a proper relationship between a banker and a speculative finance company. A decision had been left in abeyance, or so Rydbeck had surmised, but Kreuger suddenly confronted him one day with a *fait accompli* by announcing that he had just been elected. When Rydbeck demurred, Kreuger murmured apologies about the "misunderstanding." As it would have been embarrassing all around for Rydbeck to resign, he stayed on the board, though he attended very few meetings because Kreuger developed a habit of calling them when Rydbeck was traveling. The banker's consummate faith in his idol remained staunch until the very end, however, and it was primarily Rydbeck's urging that had led Scandinaviska to support the steady flow of stock issues in Kreuger's companies and to accept some of the fresh shares each time as collateral for more loans. By the end of March 1931, with the help of more than twenty-five million dollars obtained in America by the issuance of new debentures in Wall Street, Kreuger had managed to bring his debt to the bank down about two fifths, to thirty million dollars. Even so, the decline in the value of his collateral, especially of the shares in the Kreuger concerns, worried Rydbeck's fellow bank directors. For the first time it seemed that

Rydbeck's great faith in his man might not be enough to bolster that of the others, and Kreuger probably sensed it.

: 2 :

While Kreuger's predilection for adding a few zeroes to figures had scarcely bothered his conscience, he had never stooped to anything that could be called criminal *per se*. He had often signed the name of someone in the office to a document—in fact, he kept the signatures of his principal associates handily filed on ink stamps on his desk. Now, faced by the need to raise cash somehow, he performed a crude private counterfeiting drama involving outsiders.

Summoning the assistant director of the Stockholm firm that had always prepared his stock certificates, and pledging the man to secrecy on the grounds of political expediency, Kreuger ordered the lithographing of forty-two Italian government bonds with a face value of five hundred thousand English pounds each, and of five additional promissory notes representing interest of a million and a half pounds each— a total of a hundred and forty-two million dollars' worth of bonds and notes. Each bill and note was to bear the Italian coat of arms, and as a model Kreuger produced a small envelope on which the coat of arms was embossed. The bonds, when delivered to him, had the imprint of the coat of arms on top, the name of the Italian Monopoly Administration below it, followed by a few lines in English that represented them to be six-per-cent "treasury bills," with the interest payable at Barclay's Bank, Ltd., in London. Then came "Rome 15 August 1930," and the words "General Director." In the lower left-hand corner was printed "Guaranted [*sic*] as to principal and interest by the Kingdom of Italy," and, after a space, "Minister of Finance."

As soon as he had received the bills, Kreuger locked himself in his private office on the top floor of the Match Palace in Stockholm and, working from genuine signatures he had obtained, forged in ink the names of "G. Boselli" as the "General Director" of the monopoly administration and of "A. Mosconi" as the "Minister of Finance." On the promissory notes he forged Boselli's name alone. These forgeries provide perhaps the first indication that, despite his outward calm, Kreuger was already a nervous and despairing man—or it may have been that the flagrancy of his act nudged some buried kernel of guilt; in any event, he did something astonishingly careless for him: he spelled *Boselli* three different ways on the forty-seven documents. After he had finished his forgery, he locked the bills and notes in his private safe with a certificate of deposit which he drew up. Under the terms set forth in the certificate, the International Match Corporation in New York was to acquire ninety per cent of the shares of the Italian match monopoly by the end of 1935. The bonds were then to stand as security against a large loan to Italy—though no definite figure was mentioned, it was later rumored to be somewhere between seventy-five and a hundred and twenty-five million dollars.

Despite Kreuger's brazen manufacture of these bonds, the history of his dealings with Italy was at least partially legitimate, and the forgeries later became a much-debated issue. He had started buying up Italian match factories in 1925, and by the end of 1926 he had collected fifteen of them. Thereupon he had offered Mussolini a sizable loan in return for an official monopoly, but the Italians had said they didn't need the money. Rebuffed, Kreuger had begun to buy into the government monopoly, which controlled sales but not production, and he had ultimately purchased a third of the shares of its component factories. Simultaneously, working through a secret agent in Italy, he had bought up more manufacturing plants. He was then ready to make a fresh pitch at Mussolini. In October 1930 he left Paris, ostensibly to do some business in Hungary, and only his personal secretary in France, Baron Kurt von Drachenfels, who arranged the visas, knew that he intended also to go to Italy. "I had never heard him be so secretive about anything," Drachenfels afterward said.

Kreuger entered Italy unobtrusively from the north and went directly to Florence, where he stayed at the home of a friend, Count Constantini. Giovanni Boselli, the Italian monopoly director, and Antonio Mosconi, the finance minister, met him there to discuss a loan in return for a combined match-and-telephone monopoly. The Italians needed money at this time to finance a naval rearmament program, but, according to their subsequent statements, they could not agree with Kreuger on specific terms. After his death they produced a copy of a letter Boselli had supposedly written to Kreuger on December 23, 1930 (the original was never found in Kreuger's files, and some of Kreuger's aides maintained that the Italian version was a fake), that read:

> Sir: I am in receipt of your letter of the 12th inst. I note that you prefer to wait on account of the present financial situation. In view of this and also in view of the mendacious talk that has occurred, I am compelled to inform you that we do not wish to continue the negotiations. These are therefore terminated. I am, Sir, your humble servant, G. Boselli.

The "mendacious talk" ostensibly referred to gossip in France, with whom Italy was engaged in a bitter rearmament dispute, that Kreuger was arranging large French credits and planned to use them for his Italian venture. As Mussolini himself afterward put it in firmly denying that Italy ever got any Kreuger money, "Even if we were dying of starvation, we'd never take a lira as a loan from France."

Whether or not this proud belated declaration was the whole truth and nothing but the truth never was settled. Kreuger's defenders, when he was no longer around to testify himself, insisted that he had indeed given Mussolini some money secretly. Some neutral observers, including a British naval source, also believed that this was likely, for the Italians did do some expensive naval building in 1931, apparently with outside funds. The records of international payments do not indicate that there were any large transfers at the time, but Kreuger could have handed the money to Mussolini clandestinely, or he could have turned back some of his lira profits from the Italian match business. In any event, no one denied that negotiations had taken place in the fall of 1930. Nor was there any denying that the bonds *were* forged.

On previous occasions, as part of his effort to inflate his position, Kreuger had calmly chosen to assume that an unconcluded deal, or even one that had proved abortive, was as good as sealed, and he had gone ahead and extrapolated its value freely. His friends later argued that the Italian deal was a valid projection and that the bonds, even if fabricated, were simply "a kind of bookkeeping voucher for a claim he actually had," but, as no one offered proof that terms had been agreed on or that any money had changed hands, this was at best presumptive. Kreuger's purpose in forging the bonds, it would appear, was threefold: he wanted to manufacture collateral that he could use for raising the cash he so desperately needed; he wanted to tell his American associates that they had just obtained another huge "secret" monopoly; and he wanted evidence to convince his own bankers and accountants that he was better off than they had begun to suspect.

For the moment, the last of these reasons was the most important. Late in the hectic spring of 1931 Kreuger's assistants were trying to close the 1930 books of the Swedish Match Company, of Kreuger & Toll, and of various subsidiaries. Sigurd Hennig, the chief Swedish Match accountant, was vainly seeking to trace Kreuger's shifts of assets and collateral among his many concerns. He was especially confused about the constant transfer of assets from Kreuger & Toll to Kreuger's personal account, and he was disturbed by the fact that Kreuger now owed his own company more than one hundred million dollars. Kreuger had been evasive and vague whenever Hennig had brought the subject up, and Hennig mentioned his predicament to one of the top directors of Kreuger & Toll, Erik Sjöström. When he showed Sjöström a preliminary list of intercompany claims and debts, that very worried, nervous man, who later went totally crazy, cried out hysterically: "Well, I have always said we're all heading for hell!" That scarcely quieted Hennig's fears, but after they had talked the matter over further and figured that Kreuger owned a number of things that weren't listed on the books yet, including a gold mine in northern Sweden, Hennig felt a little better. However, he again approached Kreuger with questions about the constant shifting of assets, and this time Kreuger became testy.

"There must be something wrong here, Hennig," he said. "The money can't have run away, can it?"

He then explained that during 1930 he had invested in many new enterprises, and he mentioned French real estate and his secret match holdings in America, which now included more than five million dollars' worth of Diamond Match Company stock and six million worth of the Ohio Match Company's.

Hennig, with more nerve than either he or anyone else in the organization had ever demonstrated before in addressing Kreuger, suggested that there were still some untraceable assets in the books. Why, he wondered, had a claimed item of no less than four hundred million francs' worth of French bonds been deposited in a small and seemingly insignificant Dutch bank that Kreuger owned?

Kreuger flushed. "That bank is a good bank," he declared heatedly. "Besides, the French bonds have been sold."

Hennig had no way of knowing that they had never even been deposited in the bank, which was just about as "good" as the phony one in Danzig. Kreuger had simply obtained a deposit slip from the bank's director, whom he had of course appointed, to substantiate his claim that he owned a lot more of the bonds than he had ever had. Politely, Hennig added that some of the other accountants were also worried about the disposition of assets, and now, for one of the few times in his life, Kreuger really lost his temper.

"Is this a conspiracy against me?" he shouted. "Have you all joined in an attack against me?" Then, calming himself, he fixed Hennig with a long, hard stare.

The stare worked. Hennig placatingly explained that he simply wanted to help Kreuger out in every way he could and that of course there was no thought of a plot.

Kreuger thereupon threw out his new trump card. With a great air of mystery, he confided that he also owned "twenty-one million pounds of Italian state bonds" representing "a big secret deal" with Mussolini. He did not actually show the bonds to the shrewd Hennig, who might have caught on to them, but a few days later he did bring them out when Anton Wendler, the far less sharp auditor for Kreuger & Toll, visited him to determine how to arrange Kreuger's private debts so as to put the Kreuger & Toll statement "in a decent and good position." Wendler figured that some seven million pounds were needed to balance the company books, and Kreuger went to his safe, took out the Italian bonds, and let Wendler count them in order to prove that he had the necessary money, and more. Kreuger then locked the bonds away again, and Wendler went away happy and wrote seven million pounds' worth of "foreign bonds" into his books.

For the moment, Kreuger could breathe more easily. He had mollified his own staff by means of his brazen forgery, and in extreme confidence he told Rydbeck that he had just made one of the largest deals of his life. When an English match director suggested that, in view of some disturbing rumors going around, it might be wise to submit the inter-company books to an independent audit, Kreuger stared him down, as he had done Hennig, and asked blandly: "Do you think I'm a crook?"

Serious problems still remained, but Rydbeck, despite his fellow directors' doubts about Kreuger, managed to arrange another thirty-five-million-dollar loan from the Scandinaviska bank in April. The other directors' hesitancy was dissipated when the Swedish Riksbank, the government bank which had been disinclined to lend money to Kreuger directly because he was a private person, agreed to rediscount the loan. Kreuger's next big problem was to raise enough cash to pay interest due in July on Kreuger & Toll debentures, and for this he was now prepared to make a highly unusual and, as it turned out, fatal deal in New York.

: 3 :

Unlike the handful of bankers in Sweden and on the Continent who had begun to voice private fears about Kreuger's solvency, no one in America in the dark spring of 1931 had any idea how shaky his foundation already was and how frantic his efforts to repair it were becoming. He was still regarded so highly in New York that his quoted words of confidence were like a tonic amid the prevailing gloom.

Early in May, while Kreuger was bluffing his accountants in Stockholm with his fabricated Italian bonds, he had sent a laconic cablegram to Sosthenes Behn, the president of the International Telephone & Telegraph Company, that had caused a quick stir of excitement in the offices of the big private communications firm at 67 Broad Street. The unexpected message declared that if I.T.T. still wanted to make a deal it had broached two or three times during the past year or so, Kreuger, who had not been interested before, was now prepared to come to New York to discuss it. What was involved was a possible partial merger of I.T.T. with the L. M. Ericsson Telephone Company of Sweden, the large phone organization that Kreuger had begun buying into in 1927 and whose remaining stock he had purchased in 1930, looking ahead to creating a European telephone monopoly to correspond to his match empire.

Though the depression had thoroughly settled in, Behn and his associates were anxious to expand their operations abroad, looking to the future, and after they had talked the matter over with some partners of J. P. Morgan & Co., their bankers since 1925, Kreuger's suggestion for further discussion was accepted. He, in turn, had let it be known that he would come to New York as soon as he could.

Certain circumstances affecting the prospective merger serve to underline Kreuger's predicament and indicate that he must have sensed danger even in broaching it. A long-time exception to the host of his adulators in the United States had been the staid house of Morgan, some of whose cautious members regarded him with skepticism and with mild disapprobation that was partly pique. They felt that too little was known about him, that while his profits had steadily risen, and with them his dividends, which had remained high even after the 1929 crash, his vastly ramified organization was too secret in its methods of operation and too much of a one-man show. Their annoyance had sprung from the fact that he had continued to lend some governments money at rates of interest much lower than they, or any private bankers, had done previously—and what particularly rankled was the case of France, where Kreuger's loan had enabled the French to pay off their earlier loan from Morgan ahead of schedule, which had been tantamount to twisting the tail of the tough old Morgan tiger.

Nothing has ever prevented bankers and businessmen, even if they have been standoffish about each other, from getting together on a worth-while deal. Nevertheless, in the light of this special background, and as Morgan's close relationship with I.T.T. was further demonstrated by the presence of two Morgan senior partners on the I.T.T. board, Kreuger's cable to Behn may seem rather surprising. Reversing his decision to keep complete control of the phone company in Sweden, it reveals that in his search for fresh cash here, instead of resorting to his usual source, Lee, Higginson & Co., he was willing to approach tough-minded strangers who were sure to ask sharp questions about certain phases of his operation which no one had dared ask before. The depression, however, was making many a man compromise, and, whatever they had thought of Kreuger before, Behn and Morgan did not suspect that he was having real difficulties—if they had, they would undoubtedly have refrained from dealing with him.

Kreuger showed up in New York late in May. The city, as always, had a salutary effect on him, and from the moment of his arrival he seemed to be his old suave and imperturbable self. He discussed the world situation coolly, and pointed out the importance of improving the international credit structure and of stimulating new investments. He traveled down to Washington and talked over these and other matters with a fellow engineer, President Herbert Hoover. Back in New York, he confidentially told Donald Durant at Lee, Higginson & Co. about the Italian affair, emphasizing that it would redound to the advantage of the International Match Corporation. The deal could not be pub-

licly revealed yet because of the touchiness between Italy
and France, Kreuger said, but he suggested that for the time
being it should be listed by IMCO as an asset deriving from
business with "Country X"—one of the three countries referred to in his earlier "XYZ Memorandum."

Privately, working through a number of his own people
and outside agents, Kreuger stepped up his stock-market
gambles. He had already lost about four million dollars in
five months, most of which he had taken from a savings account maintained at the Chase Bank and dispersed among
five different brokers. Now he opened new accounts with
other brokers, putting up some of his own stock as security
for loans and margin purchases. When one of his secret
agents in Switzerland, who was playing the Wall Street
market for Kreuger through a dummy company in Zurich,
asked him if he didn't think enough of a loss had been sus-
tained and the account shouldn't be closed, Kreuger told
him to "keep right on, because I expect conditions to
change." Whether he really thought they would change or
whether he was whistling in the dark, he was caught up by
now in a wild speculative euphoria, and he seemed to enjoy
the game he was playing, though it was frightening the wits
out of his employees in New York who knew about it.

The negotiations with Behn and the board of the International Telephone and Telegraph Company lasted a fortnight or more. Throughout the intricate discussions of terms
Kreuger was represented solely by himself, and he astonished the I.T.T. people with his consummate ability as a
hard, canny negotiator who combined stubbornness and patience to an inordinate degree. The fact that Kreuger
wanted partly cash and partly I.T.T. stock for his Ericsson
stock, so that he could present the affair publicly as a merger
rather than a sell-out on his part, made the transaction a
difficult one to arrange. A few months before his death in
1960, Edwin F. Chinlund, who at the time of the merger

talks had been controller and vice-president of I.T.T., gave the author a personal account of the prolonged sessions and the arguments over details of the contract, and recalled particularly some of Kreuger's tactics.

"We were anxious to make the deal, even though some felt we shouldn't push it through in bad times with short-term borrowed money," Chinlund said. "The Swedes were tough competitors for us—they were using equipment, for example, that weighed less than ours and could be readily replaced when it wore out, and we admired some of their research techniques. All in all, it seemed a good idea to pool our resources with theirs. We all had great respect for Kreuger's intelligence. I didn't realize then, as I found out later, that part of our admiration was prompted by one of his cleverest tricks. As the negotiations went on, Behn had to make certain from time to time that his bankers and board members who weren't present would go along with him, and he sometimes left our meetings with Kreuger for as much as an hour at a time. When he did that, Kreuger would stay and sit around, or maybe have lunch with us, and he'd invariably talk at length about some subject that he would unobtrusively bring up or pick up from what someone else had said and expound on so thoroughly, and with such an obvious wealth of information, that we would be astonished at the knowledge he had in his head and his great memory for facts and statistics. I decided one day that I'd check him on details—I think it had to do with Hungary's economic and financial condition—and I was amazed to find out that he had been right about every last decimal point and conclusion. Less than a year later, in Stockholm, I discovered from one of his business associates how he did it. The night before an important meeting, he would look up a lot of information on a specific subject and then simply make sure the subject came up the next day. I'm positive he used the same trick when he spoke with President Hoover and other statesmen, as well as with his American banker friends.

"He had another neat trick too. When we reached a point in our contract discussions when it was apparent the next word should be up to him, he would slowly take out a cigarette, tap the end of it on the table for several minutes, slowly light it, then twirl it around in his fingers and squeeze the tobacco out of the unlit end before he finally tore the end off or crunched the cigarette out. The whole process might take five minutes or more, and then he might repeat it. Nine times out of ten, someone else would break the silence by saying something that would somehow modify the type of answer Kreuger gave. His poise was tremendous. Toward the end of the negotiations there were six contractual points that one of our directors brought up on which we wanted his consent to make changes. There he was, in really desperate need of the money we were to give him—though we didn't know at the time how desperate he was, of course—and yet, when Behn sent me to see him, he remained adamant and held his ground firmly on the most important point until we finally made some changes in the language of it that satisfied him. The whole transaction could easily have fallen apart, even at that last moment, yet he stuck to what he wanted."

In the middle of June, Behn and Kreuger signed the contract whereby six hundred thousand shares of L. M. Ericsson were deposited in Swedish banks in the name of I.T.T. in return for a check for eleven million dollars made out to Kreuger & Toll. The moment he got the money, Kreuger shot it by cable to Stockholm to cover the large Kreuger & Toll interest payments on bonds due July 1, which otherwise he would have had to omit for the first time. As I.T.T. wanted to obtain more complete control of Ericsson, a second part of the transaction, to be completed by June 1932, provided that the American firm was to get another four hundred and ten thousand Ericsson shares in exchange for a number of its shares, the exact amount to be determined, upon Chinlund's insistence, only after an examination of Ericsson's earnings for 1931 had been conducted by the well-known accounting firm of Price, Waterhouse & Co.

Handling his own accountants was one thing, but the sudden prospect of having outside auditors come to Stockholm, especially those of Behn and inferentially those of Morgan, was something Kreuger scarcely welcomed. "I'm sure he didn't like it," Chinlund recollected, "but he needed those eleven million dollars and he probably figured he had enough time before the deal was wrapped up to get over whatever hurdles there were and handle the inspection matter himself."

Kreuger put up his usual brazen front. Jean Monnet, the French financial expert, happened to be in New York at the time, and he congratulated Kreuger on the deal. "Yes," said Kreuger, "it's fine, but can I trust the I.T.T. balance sheet?" Privately, he must have realized that an examination of the Ericsson books could be extremely dangerous to him. Unlike the occasional American or British accountants who had visited Stockholm or asked him questions from afar, Behn's auditors would refuse to be fended off by pleas of lack of time, the need for secrecy, or the sensitivity of Swedish feelings.

Ernst & Ernst had remained the auditors in New York for the International Match Corporation, and young A. D. Berning was still the accountant who certified the books in America—after Kreuger dictated them to the pliant IMCO treasurer here. Tied down as he was by the lack of requests from IMCO's directors to do anything beyond checking Kreuger's arithmetic, Berning declared in a typical statement at the end of the 1930 IMCO report: "We hereby certify that we have examined the books of account and record of IMCO and its American subsidiary companies as of

December 31, 1930, and have received statements from abroad with respect to the foreign constituent companies as of the same date. Based upon our examination and information submitted to us, it is our opinion that the annexed consolidated balance sheet sets forth the financial condition of the combined companies at the date stated, and that related consolidated income and surplus account is correct. . . ."

As the twenties had marched on, Berning had been in the habit of visiting Stockholm for a week or so each year, and when he was afterward asked if this had not at least given him "an opportunity for a casual inspection of the situation over there," he replied that he had simply picked up a few supplementary reports he thought the directors in New York might want to look at, but "in no case were these reports or memoranda the results of any auditing or accounting work. . . ." On the few occasions when he had wanted to check something before signing the IMCO audits, Berning had cabled Kreuger in Stockholm and had always got a quick, reassuring answer. In 1926, for instance, he had wanted to know if Garanta, the Amsterdam subsidiary supposedly operating a secret Polish sales monopoly for matches and owing IMCO seventeen million dollars, had enough money on hand to meet that obligation. Kreuger had shot back a cable stating that Garanta (which was completely phony and didn't have a red cent) had forty-six million Dutch gulden—conveniently enough, just a million gulden more than its debt to IMCO. The following year, in Stockholm, Berning had asked about the Spanish match monopoly Kreuger had claimed to have, and Kreuger, as he did with his own inquiring accountants, had quickly flashed the agreement that he pretended had been signed by Primo de Rivera and then tucked it away in his safe again. Neither Berning nor anyone else was in a position to push Kreuger further on these matters.

In the spring of 1929, after he had taken a trip around

the Continent to inspect several Kreuger concerns—a rare treat indeed—Berning returned to New York "very enthusiastic" about what he had seen, according to Donald Durant, who thereupon asked him to write a letter about the trip for Lee, Higginson to file. Berning wrote, in part: "The operations of the three larger companies, namely A. B. Kreuger & Toll, Swedish Match Company, and the International Match Corporation, are closely related, as you well know, and the inter-company transactions are quite large. All of those transactions which have come under my notice have always been handled with the highest degree of fairness. During none of the many examinations which we have made of the affairs of International Match Corporation have we ever had occasion to question the fairness of any transaction which this company has had with any of its affiliates. I thought you would be interested in this observation." The gentlemen of Lee, Higginson most assuredly were.

Though Berning had established a regular if rather frustrating association with Kreuger, the man who perhaps came closest to putting his finger on the financier's position was another young accountant named F. Gordon Blackstone, who had been hired by Lee, Higginson & Co. in the spring of 1927 to conduct an independent audit of IMCO and its Stockholm parent, Swedish Match. Kreuger was riding at his highest then, and there wasn't the slightest suspicion about him, but the investment bankers thought it would be a good idea to find out more about how their golden goose laid its eggs. Blackstone mapped out a detailed plan for himself that naïvely included a thorough inspection of the balance sheets of Swedish Match and of the companies with which it did business in various countries, and, if he had miraculously succeeded in carrying out his plan, he would undoubtedly have uncovered a lot of hocus-pocus. Kreuger, however, soon sensed what he was up against and went out of the way to be polite to his young American visitor.

He first invited Blackstone to come with him to Poland to look over some factories there, but the accountant demurred. "I wasn't there to watch wheels go around," he afterward recalled. "Kreuger went off on his tour, and for two months I sat and waited in Stockholm and read published statements and documents. I saw his top aides in the match company, but none of his accountants. Apparently he had taken care of that. Then one day, shortly after he returned, he came to see me in great consternation, waving a letter or a cable he had ostensibly just received. He said it was a request from some other outside accountants to come to Stockholm to do a job like mine, and he insisted that this all implied a lack of confidence and that it would disturb the atmosphere around the company and in Sweden generally. He took the wind right out of my sails. I've never been sure the message he got wasn't made up, but at any rate it meant the end of my assignment. Kreuger said he would discuss the problem with the Lee, Higginson people in New York and that maybe a year later I could come back, but nothing more was ever done about the matter."

Kreuger had obviously thwarted him, and Blackstone now has the impression that if it hadn't been done one way it would have been done another. When the lid blew off the Kreuger scandal, Blackstone emphasized that he had seen nothing suspicious and said he was "flabbergasted," but, as he looked back years later to his odd experience in Stockholm, he felt that something should have happened as a result of his having opened the door, even so slightly. "Why wasn't my mission followed up a year later and carried out at the insistence of the people here?" he asked. "Five years should never have been allowed to go by. The pity of it, the pity of it."

After Blackstone had been warded off, Kreuger had undoubtedly persuaded his friends at Lee, Higginson that sending that young man or anyone else to Stockholm would serve no useful purpose. If for his admirers his wish had been virtually their command, this was not to be the case with Sosthenes Behn and the International Telephone & Telegraph Company. Behn's auditors were not due in Sweden until early in 1932, though, and Kreuger realized that in the meantime he had to go on pretending his structure was strong enough to withstand the earthquake of the depression. Only he knew that it was riddled by the termites he had introduced, and he kept hoping the world situation would improve so that he could repair his house before Behn or anyone else became aware of its condition.

: 4 :

Up to a point, at least, hope engendered belief, and Kreuger became a dedicated, almost demonic man. He had always been a fine actor, but now, as the curtain went up upon his ultimate life-and-death struggle, he did more than act out a role: he completely identified himself and his personal fortune of some forty million dollars with his work. As he poured increasing amounts into one breach after another, he became more and more isolated within himself. Never much of a mixer, he now sought no companionship beyond the female variety that he regarded as simply an outlet and had always carefully separated from the rest of his existence. One of his old friends asked him one day in Paris: "Why aren't you with us as before?" and Kreuger replied: "I don't dare to be together with people any more. I'm scared to be influenced by their wrong opinions."

Though he had been unemotional all his life, he began to show some of the strain in his shifting moods, but the revelations were fleeting. Per Jacobsson, who worked for Kreuger briefly during the late twenties, remembers having lunch one day with him and Leon Fraser, the banker, in Basle,

Switzerland. A quick, almost frightening change came over Kreuger immediately afterward. "He had been animated and optimistic while we ate and talked about the decline and what to do," Jacobsson recalls. "Then, when lunch was over, I went with him to the hotel and saw him there alone. He fell suddenly into deep despair. Perhaps it was the burden of all his past sins that he could no longer carry."

If his sins were a burden, it was not Kreuger's nature to dwell upon it. His ability to inspire trust in other men had always been the keynote of his amazing success, and he depended on it, and on luck, to see him through. He could also seek inspiration in the knowledge that there was more at stake than just his own salvation and wealth—there was the validity of the broad theories he had so brilliantly put into practice, despite his concomitant falsifications. If he had been a crook, he could, at the same time, fully relish his role as a private broker to Europe in distress. As the House of Rothschild had acted as England's agents in Europe after the Napoleonic wars and had worked for peace and stability by helping keep Austria afloat and Metternich in power and by saving the Prussian financial structure, so Kreuger in this post-Versailles period had applied his help dramatically at a crucial moment. But as events now mounted beyond his control, he saw all of his work coming to naught.

While he was traveling to America, the situation in Europe had worsened perceptibly with the collapse of the Austrian Creditanstalt, the largest bank in the country and one of the most important on the Continent. By the time Kreuger got back to Europe in July, the banking crisis was causing grave difficulties in Germany and throughout the Balkans. In that month all German banks were suddenly shut down in the face of the demand from abroad for repayment of short-term loans; when they reopened after a few days, new currency regulations protected them against any withdrawal of foreign funds. During Kreuger's absence the directors of the Scandinaviska bank had held a private meeting at which they had once more taken uneasy note of "the greatly deteriorated liquidity" of their prize customer. It had been decided, finally, that as soon as Kreuger got back Rydbeck should have a most serious talk with him. "There was to be plain speaking, no mistake about that," another officer of the bank later recounted, and Rydbeck was to "tell him not to let things go but to act immediately in this situation."

When Rydbeck approached him, Kreuger pulled a typical trick on his old friend and foil. Pierre Laval, President of the Council of France, had just invited Prime Minister Ramsay MacDonald, of England, and Dr. Heinrich Brüning, the German Chancellor, to a meeting in Paris to discuss the general banking crisis. Like an old confidence man, Kreuger saw his chance. As afterward described by the above bank official: "When Rydbeck came in to me after his talk with Kreuger, he was almost crestfallen. Ivar Kreuger had in deepest confidence informed him that he had been invited by Dr. Brüning to accompany the latter and his staff on the trip to Paris in the capacity of a private adviser. How was it possible to treat a man too harshly who in this way was permitted to take part in the big, decisive conferences of the world? The liquidity problems of the Kreuger group—and also those of our own, as far as that goes—were suddenly reduced in importance quite considerably." Four years later, when this official was in a position to check directly, he learned that Kreuger had never been invited to Paris by the German Chancellor or by anyone else. He had told an outright lie, and it had worked, for he had momentarily evaded the bank's pressure.

His need for money, however, was as great as ever. In August 1931 he asked his friends at Lee, Higginson & Co. in New York to try to raise eight or ten million dollars for him in America. The best they could do was get four million from four commercial banks for six months. As fast as Kreuger acted, events continued to catch up with him. England went off the gold standard at the end of September, and a week later Sweden followed suit. Publicly, Kreuger hailed the move, and, aware as always of his capacities as a financial barometer, he put up a fresh show of optimism. He expressed gratification over the devaluation of the pound and the krona and hoped that one result would be a general increase of monetary movements among nations—in his case, that would mean that some of the profits from his match operations would be unfrozen and hence available for him to withdraw. But his hopes proved empty, and the freeze continued. In September, Germany was granted a moratorium on its debts; the announcement was made by President Hoover, and it was afterward charged in Congress that Kreuger, when he had seen Hoover in June, had asked for exemption of Germany's debts to private individuals. Whether this was true or not, the announcement sent Kreuger's debentures up more than a hundred points in Wall Street, from 353 to 458—they had been as high as 863 before the crash—but his satisfaction was short-lived, for they quickly tumbled again.

Two of the bold predictions of Felix Somary, the Swiss banker, had now come true—the Austro-German banking crisis *had* taken place and the British *had* gone off gold—and Somary was saying privately that his third condition for recovery was also a fact, though it remained to be proved: Ivar Kreuger *was* bankrupt. Somary was not completely right, though the stage was indeed set for the final act that would bring about Kreuger's destruction.

: 5 :

Much would afterward be said and written by Kreuger's defenders about the role his enemies played in his defeat. If their deeds and influence were exaggerated in the attempt to exonerate Kreuger, there is no denying that a ruthless opposition to him did exist in financial circles. This opposition was concentrated in France, where a group of stock-market bears had sought constantly, once the depression started, to drive down the prices on Kreuger's many securities and to encourage his collapse by forcing him to go deeper into debt supporting his own stocks and bonds. By the fall of 1931 these bears were well organized around the Continent, and were stepping up their operations. Early in the year the attacks against the Match King had begun in a series of small forays on Kreuger issues. The front was soon widened to include the buzzing Amsterdam exchange, and the objective was to drive down the prices of the most recent Kreuger securities, which he had pushed in order, among other reasons, to help finance the German and Polish loans.

Counterattacking swiftly, he bought large quantities of bonds and shares himself and managed to back the bears against a wall by demanding prompt delivery of some shares they had sold short—that is, for future delivery. They responded by launching a more dangerous flank attack on the various government bonds issued as security for Kreuger's foreign loans, and by driving down these quotations they forced him to write down the value of the bonds in his balance sheets. Speculators were bribed and blackmailed into co-operating with the scheme. A veritable rumor factory was also started, and the venal French press was solicited. The Paris papers, never particularly fond of Kreuger, now attacked him mercilessly wherever they could. Among other things, they picked up one of the Russians' pet propaganda themes, the "eternal match," an invention of Dr. Ferdinand Ringer, a Viennese research chemist. Dr. Ringer's device, a three-inch flint-like mechanism, was prematurely praised and hailed as the successor to the ordinary match. Though it afterward achieved a measure of success, it has never, any more than the mechanical lighter, supplanted matches. Dr. Ringer himself said a number of years ago: "I showed my invention to Mr. Kreuger in Paris in 1931, and, though it was too expensive for commercial manufacture, the news of it got around and caused Kreuger shares to go down." Dr. Ringer even claimed, perhaps facetiously, that he was responsible for Kreuger's ultimate undoing, but it wasn't as simple as that.

The attacks against Kreuger gained in strength, and when they began to influence conservative British brokers, he issued a brimming, self-laudatory statement which he distributed globally with much hoopla. It gave a completely bogus account of his liquidity and expected profits for 1931, in order to show that the decline of his stocks was unjustified. The drop was attributed to "the present monetary conditions in different European countries and to the general market situation," which, Kreuger added, "has been taken advantage of by an internationally organized bear syndicate that does not seem to hesitate to spread unfounded tales regarding the concern." The statement failed to halt the downward plunge, led by the Kreuger & Toll debentures, which at the end of October hit a low of 138.

As all his properties, new and old, fell in value and the void of bankruptcy loomed ever closer, Kreuger must have seen the handwriting on the wall, but he remained remarkably self-possessed. Dr. Bjerre, the psychoanalyst, later wrote: "One can imagine that he suffered a loneliness unto death, fighting like a drowning man to get a grip on a piece of wreckage and yet knowing even then that he was sinking together with thousands who had trusted him." Even so, Dr. Bjerre noted, the loneliness was more the result of outer circumstances than of any "conflict at the bottom of the soul," and because Kreuger was as adaptable as he was amoral—"a horizontal man," without permanent roots, who had always been able to adjust himself to any psychological and emotional climate—he was able, despite occasional lapses, to play out his role until events impinged upon him so forcibly that his whole being crumbled.

During these last months of 1931 Kreuger spun back and forth like a top from Stockholm to Paris, London, and Berlin in unceasing efforts to raise money. All of his top associates had now placed their personal fortunes at his disposal, and he was employing their cash and stocks as if he were deploying soldiers. On the one hand, he continued to take up the unsold shares of his own issues; these cost him nothing, for he simply debited what he owed for them to his personal account, but the maneuver made it appear that the issues had been fully subscribed and paid for in cash. Then, while he was quietly selling some old shares on various exchanges to raise money, he told his closest friends, such as Krister Littorin, to go on buying all the stock they could. Although he knew full well how sick his securities were, he advised his Paris physician, Dr. Charles Bove, to buy some, promising that Bove would triple his investment. He talked so convincingly that Bove, disinclined to speculate before, went out and bought twice as much as he had intended; eventually he lost one hundred and thirteen thousand dollars, so it is scarcely surprising that he has retained mixed feelings about Kreuger. "Altogether he was unprepossessing, and one would scarcely suspect upon a blind meeting that this fellow was the owner of one of the largest industrial empires of modern times," the doctor wrote in his memoirs, twenty-five years later. Nevertheless, Bove had considerable respect for the manner in which Kreuger conducted himself, especially toward the end. "I knew him for an indefatigable worker who put in long hours at his business, keeping awake by plunging into ice-cold baths," he added.

Gunnar Cederschïold, in Paris, has recalled how steadfastly Kreuger pushed ahead during these months, giving no outward manifestation of his peril. During the autumn of 1931, for example, he personally supervised the construction of his new twenty-room apartment in the Place Vendôme, the terrace of which was planned to look out upon the square at exactly the same height as the pedestaled statue of Napoleon. "He knew he had to keep up his associates' optimism as well as his own," Cederschïold afterward observed, "for in order to allay the rumors going around we had to make an impression on others. It must have taken great strength to be confident when he was in a hell of an anxiety. He alone suffered for all of us, without any need to share the burden."

Cederschïold and Baron von Drachenfels, the personal secretary, sought to shield Kreuger from the strangers who wanted to see him, for many of these proved to be crackpots soliciting bribes, or individuals with ridiculous schemes to foment Balkan revolutions or kill Stalin; one man, a science bug—with an irony Kreuger may have privately appreciated—submitted an elaborate plan for a machine that could run entirely on air. Occasionally, however, Kreuger could not help showing the effects of his tenseness, and there were plenty of extenuating circumstances. He came into Cederschïold's office one morning, particularly nervous, and inquired if Cederschïold knew anyone at the Sûreté. Kiddingly, Cederschïold asked if he wanted to get a ticket fixed, but Kreuger, with a frown, explained that at a restaurant the night before he had run into a nephew of Alfred Nobel, the inventor of dynamite and a fellow Swede. "He told me I was being followed by the police," Kreuger said, almost ingenuously. "What do you think it means?" Cederschïold replied that it was undoubtedly just protective. "Maybe they're afraid the Bolsheviks will kidnap you," he said. "Are you sure that's it?" Kreuger said, somewhat relieved. A few days later Cederschïold ascertained that Kreuger was indeed being followed as a general precaution.

In the odd atmosphere of suspense which characterized this period, Kreuger's aides, even the heretofore worried accountants, reflected his attitude of hope. In a sense, he had mesmerized them. "We all lived under an illusion, calm and content in our absolute faith in Kreuger," Cederschïold said. "We had known a lack of cash in the organization before, in 1920 and again in 1926, and we were not pessimistic because we had heard of a number of tremendous reserves and hidden assets." Only Kreuger knew that many of these, notably his vast "reserves" in Dutch Kreuger & Toll, the Amsterdam offshoot of the Stockholm company, were either completely false or highly exaggerated. He did have one genuine ace up his sleeve, however, and it was perhaps fitting that he who had been credited for years with an almost magic gift for making gold should, in his last-ditch fight, have depended on a gold mine to save himself.

The mine was named Boliden, and it had been discovered in 1924 in the Norlaand district of Sweden. Reputed to be the third-largest gold deposit in the world, with twenty grams of gold per ton, the mine was also rich in silver, arsenic, sulphur, copper, zinc, and lead. Kreuger had bought eighty per cent of it in 1929 from the Scandinaviska bank for fourteen million dollars, part of which he paid in cash and the rest by a personal draft on his credit at the bank. As security against the draft and partly to secure his general debt to Scandinaviska, he had left the Boliden shares with the bank.

Only a few of his closest associates knew about his interest in Boliden, the development of which had proceeded slowly because of the mine's great depth and because of smelting problems. Not long after he had bought it, Kreuger had offered the Guggenheims in America a half-interest if they would help him develop it, but they had turned him down, after looking it over, on the theory that it wasn't worth their time and investment unless they could get all of it. New electrical drilling methods, however, now promised to make the mine a real bonanza, and the output of gold alone, Kreuger predicted, would soon be worth nearly seven hundred thousand dollars a month. For more than two years Kreuger had looked upon the mine as his greatest secret treasure. "It nourished his optimism above all else," Cederschiöld said, "and he used it to nourish ours. He was saving it for the right moment, when the market turned, and then he wanted to play it so that everyone would rush out and buy and the whole market would soar." When the economic clouds grew darker and darker, however, he had to bring out his ace sooner than he wished.

Late in October 1931, back in Stockholm after trying to thwart the bears in Paris, he went again to Sweden's government bank, the Riksbank, and requested a loan of forty million kroner, or about ten million dollars. As security, he offered to put up some of his German bonds, issued to him by the Reich to secure his big loan, but the bank wouldn't take them. Kreuger then mentioned his Boliden holdings, and the government authorities pricked up their ears. They agreed to accept the mine stock as security for the loan; but the trouble was, Kreuger didn't have the stock—the Scandinaviska bank did. As usual, he found a way out. Fifty million dollars' worth of German bonds owned by the International Match Corporation in America had never been transferred to New York and had been reposing in IMCO's name in the vaults of the Deutsche Union Bank in Berlin, one of the bona-fide banks Kreuger owned. Early in September, however, in order to satisfy the demands of the

Scandinaviska bank for firmer collateral against his private debt there, he had ordered the Berlin bank quietly to transfer the German bonds to a small bank in Copenhagen. For the moment, he had substituted nothing at all in Berlin in IMCO's behalf, as he was supposed to do. Ten days later he had told the Copenhagen bank to list thirty million dollars' worth of the German bonds in Scandinaviska's name. Now, at the end of October, following his conference with the Swedish Riksbank officials, another twelve million dollars' worth of the bonds was assigned to Scandinaviska, in return for which he obtained the release of the Boliden shares, and he promptly pledged these with the Riksbank for the new ten-million-dollar loan. But Kreuger did not stop there; he was determined to get everything he could out of Boliden. A few weeks later he "sold" his stock in the mine, pledged away though it was, to Kreuger & Toll for fresh debentures worth about twenty million dollars, which he intended to put on the New York stock market eventually. Some of these debentures, still unregistered, leaked out in Paris and New York through an unscrupulous broker, and angry cries of "bad delivery"—unauthorized securities being circulated—went up, which played right into the hands of the anti-Kreuger bears.

On November 23, 1931, with his new loan in hand, Kreuger left Stockholm for the last time. To most of his associates he appeared to be under less strain than he had been for several weeks. Only one person afterward gave any clue that he knew he might never come back. This was Inge Hässler, the financier's former mistress, whom he had not seen for the last three years—in fact, he hadn't even talked to her since she had helped him celebrate his German loan arrangements by playing Russian music for him over the long-distance phone. Kreuger still felt a sense of responsibility toward her, however, and the fact that he now visited her was indicative of what must have been his true state of mind. "I was scared when I saw how he had changed," she later wrote. "He was nervous, there was a jerky movement in his shoulder, and I wondered if he had had a stroke. He smoked constantly, something he had seldom done before." Most significantly, Kreuger told Inge he had arranged a will and planned to leave her a hundred and twenty-five thousand dollars in cash. (The testament—as it turned out, the only one Kreuger ever wrote—had been prepared in April 1930, but he had never mentioned it before.) Then, without saying any special good-byes to his elderly parents, his four sisters, and his brother, Kreuger entrained for Berlin for a series of conferences.

Those who saw him there thought he was in good spirits. When Sigurd Hennig, the match-company accountant who had asked the embarrassing questions about intercompany accounts back in March, came down from Stockholm to see him, the financier was full of renewed confidence, Hennig thought. Time had enabled him to straighten things out, Kreuger said, and he showed Hennig a joint balance sheet for Kreuger & Toll and Dutch Kreuger & Toll which appeared quite sound to the accountant. Previously Hennig had talked about some "holes" in these books, but now, with the Boliden mine available for listing as an asset and the German bonds pledged to secure his bank loans—he told Hennig an outright lie when he said his bankers in New York had consented to the bonds' transfer—Kreuger said: "You see, Hennig, the holes are not as big as you seem to think."

Although it appeared that Kreuger had overcome his immediate emergency, the problem of raising additional cash and collateral as other loans soon fell due and new obligations arose remained pressing. "He hoped to get more money in New York, where he was going after stopping in Paris," an old friend who saw him in Berlin said. "We had dinner together at his flat the night before he left, and in spite of a new panic on the Stockholm exchange, he seemed unusually optimistic." In Paris his associates had the same feeling. He talked like his former self, and when a crisis developed over some Belgian match factories that were trying to muscle in on Kreuger's French match business, he boldly ordered his Belgian representatives to "buy them out." The price was ten million francs, and when he was reminded that cash was still low, Kreuger calmly replied, with one of his old, soft smiles: "That's not much. Go ahead."

He stayed in Paris a fortnight, conferring constantly on various matters but also finding time to check on his new Place Vendôme apartment, which he found so satisfactory that he commissioned the architect to enlarge his place on Park Avenue in New York too. Whether all this was bluff was hard to tell, but the consensus of the Paris staff members, as well as those in Stockholm, was that everything would soon be all right. Not only would he successfully complete his big telephone merger, they thought, but now he could also make a deal for his big gold mine, and both were calculated to bring fresh sources of revenue into the organization. It would not take long for this rosy prognosis to be sadly disproved. In a matter of weeks, all his schemes would blow sky-high.

CHAPTER 8

Walpurgisnacht

WHEN THE North German Lloyd liner *Bremen,* guided by a bevy of tugs, slid gingerly through a thick fog into her Brooklyn berth in midafternoon on December 22, 1931, Kreuger, traveling incognito as usual, debarked quietly without being recognized and was whisked away by two friends and his housekeeper to his nine-room penthouse apartment on Park Avenue. His presence in New York was not publicly noted until two days later, when the financial section of the New York *Herald Tribune* carried a short columnar item under the subheading "Coincidence:"

> Ivar Kreuger . . . came to town late Tuesday and yesterday Kreuger & Toll was the only stock among the fifteen most active that closed with a net gain (it went up from 4¼ to 4⅝; the high for the year, much earlier, had been 27¾). It is understood that Mr. Kreuger will inspect his match properties and certain other interests while here. It is also expected that he will confer with

officials of the International Telephone & Telegraph Company in regard to the I.T.T.-Ericsson Telephone deal, but little other than details of the transaction will be discussed, the major points having been settled some months ago.

Thus, unobtrusively, began the final fateful visit to America of the man who had been regarded as the greatest financial figure of his own time and perhaps of all time. If Kreuger's magic, for the moment, seemed reduced to causing so fractional a stock rise, his wondrous ability to make millions for his stockholders in happier days had not been forgotten, and his every word and action were examined for some token of encouragement at the end of the depression's second abysmal year. Among those who awaited his optimism was President Hoover, and when Kreuger again visited the White House early in January, the President was indeed enheartened. Coming out of the meeting, Kreuger summed up his views to reporters: "I don't feel that there is any reason for the American people to feel nervous over the situation in Europe. As a matter of fact, I do not think the European people take to heart their problems as much as you do in America. European problems will be solved, and there is no reason why the American people should become hysterical about them."

If there was hysteria underlying the preponderant gloom here—breakdowns and suicides were commonplace by this time—Kreuger was practicing what he preached by demonstrating his customary suavity and self-assurance. During his first fortnight in the country he maneuvered behind the scenes, directing his initial efforts as much to the creation of confidence as anything else. Though, like almost everyone, he was looking for money, no one had any suspicion that he was in serious trouble. Quietly, he was making a point of meeting some bankers in America he had not dealt with before, to see if he could borrow from them. One of the first banks he approached was the Bank of America, which was itself having trouble, and subsequently it became apparent that, beyond borrowing from the bank, Kreuger had entertained some hopes of taking it over. The previous September, when Elisha Walker had won control of Transamerica, whose greatest asset was the Bank of America N.T. and S.A., and its founder, A. P. Giannini, had been forced out, two officers of Lee, Higginson & Co.—Frederic W. Allen and H. O. Havemeyer —had been made Transamerica directors. Now there was a new struggle for control of the bank, and within a month Giannini was to wrest it back from Walker and begin a dramatic door-to-door campaign among depositors which eventually put it back on its feet. Because of this continuing struggle, and despite the presence of the two Lee, Higginson men on Transamerica's board, Kreuger was unable to borrow any money from the bank. Giannini always maintained, however, that it had had a close call at Kreuger's hands, almost becoming his heavy creditor, and that, furthermore, Kreuger came close to gaining a dominant voice in the bank's reorganization at a critical time, working through Lee, Higginson.

As other banks around the country as well as in New York proved unable or unwilling to lend Kreuger money, he devoted himself more assiduously to his general campaign of raising confidence, undoubtedly hoping to talk his way into a position where renewed faith would open a few fresh bank vaults to him. In addition to traveling to Washington to see Hoover, he went to Boston and Philadephia and Chicago, and in the Midwestern financial capital he appeared before a private meeting of bankers and brokers at Lee, Higginson's offices there. Delivering one of his rare formal addresses, he decried the "terrible pessimism" in the country and said: "The most essential thing is to get a different spirit in America. If that comes, I am absolutely certain Europe will react very quickly. . . ." Quotations of securities, especially of foreign bonds, were ridiculously and inexcusably low here, Kreuger added, and this was all the more unpardonable because America was still on the gold standard.

He then gave an elaborate analysis of his own companies, full of subtle half-truths, to demonstrate that they were all in fine shape. The world match business was booming despite the depression, he said, and though the International Match Corporation might have slightly reduced total earnings for 1931, they would still be well above dividend requirements. In what amounted to an outright lie, he declared that the profits of Kreuger & Toll "have not been touched very much," though he admitted that the company's stocks and bonds had suffered as a result of bear attacks and a bitter propaganda campaign launched against the concern by the Russians. One by one, Kreuger went down the list of his other investments—in pulp, iron, banking, real estate, and telephones—and the only one he was at all momentarily disappointed about was iron. Finally, he brought forth, for the first time, his ace in the hole: the Boliden gold mine. After reciting its history, he boldly announced: "I think it is quite certain that it is the most important gold mine outside of South Africa. . . . The first day I arrived in New York, I received a cable saying they had found a new deposit . . . but I think it would be better if nothing about it came into print at the present time. It is not the right moment to give out good news."

By the time Kreuger got back to New York a few days later, the news of course was all over Wall Street, but he delivered another "confidential" chat about the mine. He was dangling it adroitly, both to impress the Americans and to bolster the confidence of his supporters in Sweden that his standing in this country was as good as ever. On Janu-

ary 19 he sent a private wire to Felix Hamrin, the Swedish
Finance Minister, in Stockholm. The atmosphere in New
York had been "pure panic" when he had arrived and conditions generally were much worse than when he had been
here in the spring, he told Hamrin, but, even so, "the
prospects are good" for making a deal to sell some shares
in Boliden "to a big American industry which is financially
interested in mines." If the deal came through, Kreuger
added, it "would not in any way reduce our freedom to
collaborate with the Swedish state if the Swedish government should desire such collaboration."

As soon as he thought it feasible, Kreuger intended offering twenty million dollars' worth of new Kreuger & Toll
participating debentures to the public—the issue that, in
effect, represented the Boliden value, following his "sale"
of the mine to the company. That he also had in mind offering a separate share issue in Boliden, possibly in an ex-
ploration-and-development company, is attested by Jacques
Coe, a well-known New York broker. A few days after
Kreuger sent up his second trial balloon on Boliden, Coe,
who was generally optimistic about the future of gold as
an investment, was invited to visit Kreuger by Sune
Schéle, a Swede who was acting as the financier's private
stock-market agent in New York and who, in his own
name but actually on Kreuger's behalf, was speculating
with a million-dollar margin account in Coe's firm. "You
know, the boss is very interested in gold, and he's going to
have the biggest gold mine in Europe in production soon,"
Schéle told Coe. "He'd like to see you." Coe and his lawyer
went up to Kreuger's penthouse. He remembers being
ushered into Kreuger's study and seeing a number of boxes
on a long table, each of which was stacked with cables
from a different European city. Presently Kreuger, "looking astonishingly like an undertaker, in a dark suit," came
in. Never one to lose an opportunity to impress a stranger

with a bit of dramatics, the financier asked to be excused a moment while he looked over the contents of the boxes. Picking a cable out of the Paris container, he smiled and remarked in a confidential tone: "Ah, ha—you know, some of my enemies have been depressing my stock in a completely unwarranted fashion, and I'm going to pull a big squeeze on them." After this aside they got down to business, and Kreuger asked Coe what it would take to put a public Boliden issue on the curb exchange. Coe, after examining the facts, told Kreuger, among other things, that there would have to be evidence of wider distribution of the mine shares, and he suggested the formation of a private syndicate to bring that about. "When he asked me how long that would take, and I told him probably several months, Kreuger lost interest immediately," Coe recalls. "It was later obvious to me, of course, that he needed the money the day before yesterday."

Kreuger was apparently loath to offer the Kreuger & Toll participating debentures, backed by the Boliden value, on the market at this time for fear they would further depress the demand for other Kreuger & Toll securities and incite fresh bear attacks. But he could still go on promoting Boliden for all it was worth and also use the new debentures privately as collateral to get more loans. Accordingly, during the last week of January he persuaded Herbert L. Dillon, senior partner in Eastman, Dillon & Co., investment bankers, to give him a loan of a million dollars, and for security he put up six hundred and fifty thousand shares of mixed Kreuger & Toll stock. Then, a few days later, he made a big public announcement about his mine. The news was released simultaneously in other capitals, and in Paris, where the bears, as Kreuger had told Coe, were still exceedingly active, the information about Boliden was given out amid much fanfare and pouring of cocktails by the Swedish Minister to France.

Kreuger had depended on Boliden so completely that he was now in for a rude shock. In his announcement he had admitted, notwithstanding what he had said earlier, that Kreuger & Toll's net profits for 1931 were down from about thirty-three to twenty-one million dollars, and he had also written down the value of foreign government bonds held by the company. His obvious hope was that Boliden would become the basis for fresh financing as soon as the general situation improved a bit. But the news caused no upturn in Kreuger & Toll securities, and the bears immediately began to spread stories that Kreuger had vastly overrated the mine. While Boliden eventually was to prove extremely valuable, more for its other ore deposits than for its heralded gold, Kreuger had absolutely no knowledge yet of what the proved reserves were to come to or of how much its development would cost. He had been forced to jump the gun on the mine because of his financial plight, and he had depended on the glitter of his own name as much as on the buried gold to put the project across. When his announcement failed to create the sudden stir he had hoped for, and no deals were forthcoming, he was in the position of a man whose ace has been trumped.

With Boliden in abeyance, the financier turned his full attention to stock-market speculation. It was costing him more and more, and he was getting poor results there also. Kreuger now dealt with a score of brokerage houses, but seldom in his own name. His principal Wall Street agents were three of his most trusted employees: his old friend, Anders Jordahl; Alexis Aminoff, a young Swede who acted as his general representative in New York and had a private office adjoining Lee, Higginson & Co. at 41 Broad Street; and Schéle, who was busily engaged in trying to raise money from banking sources in addition to carrying on speculating activities in Kreuger's behalf.

Jacques Coe at this point figures further in what may be considered a typical Kreuger investment maneuver. A few days after he had discussed the Boliden affair with Kreuger, Coe got a call from Schéle, who told him: "The boss liked you and wants to do you a favor. He has a business associate, a very wealthy man named Lange, who wants to open an account with you, and arrangements have been made for Lee, Higginson & Co. to send fifty thousand shares of Kreuger & Toll stock to your office to use as collateral for whatever Lange wants to buy." Coe said that was fine so long as the collateral would not be used to buy more Kreuger & Toll, as that would be against the policy of his house. Schéle seemed disappointed to hear that, but nothing further was said about it. Coe, naturally curious about Lange, asked Bishop Service, Inc., a financial checking house, to find out about him. In a week or so the word came back from Stockholm that a man named Karl Lange (who was none other than Kreuger's lower-level dupe and front for several shadow companies, including the Dutch one, Garanta, though Bishop Service didn't find that out) was listed as the operator of a restaurant in the Swedish capital and appeared to have only modest means. Coe was thoroughly taken aback by this information and went at once to see Donald Durant at Lee, Higginson. In Coe's presence, Durant telephoned Kreuger, who happened to be in the building. "Ivar, do you know a man named Karl Lange?" Durant inquired. When Kreuger replied that he did, Durant asked: "Is he responsible?" Kreuger replied firmly that he was, and Durant thanked him. "You see, Jacques," Durant said, turning back to Coe, "you have nothing at all to worry about!" Coe wasn't happy about the matter, but he got off the hook a few days later when Lange cabled him instructions to buy some Kreuger & Toll stock. He replied that he could buy anything else, but not that, and in another few days got a cable requesting him to please return the fifty thousand collateral shares to Lee, Higginson, which he did at once.

In addition to Schéle and his other major henchmen here, at least half a dozen additional friends and agents were playing the market for Kreuger feverishly. Almost all the orders were given privately by Kreuger himself—he was on the phone virtually all day, talking from his Park Avenue apartment, from his private office at 522 Fifth Avenue, from the office of the International Match Corporation at 25 West Forty-third Street, or from Aminoff's office downtown. No one was ever able to figure how much Kreuger lost in stock-market gambling, but the total was probably somewhere between fifty and a hundred million dollars. As long as the world's exchanges were booming, he had done well enough, but once the depression took hold he was in so deep that he couldn't extricate himself even if he wanted to—which he didn't—and he kept piling margin upon margin and throwing whatever cash he could muster into the brokers' hoppers in vain efforts to recover his losses and get the market to turn.

Among other things, Kreuger was trying to prevent his own stocks from dropping further in the face of the organized bear attacks against him abroad, and as a result of the general depressing trend in Wall Street. A particularly bizarre turn of events now made his task more difficult. A thirty-year-old Texan-born speculator and investment counselor named Jackson Martindell, who subsequently became the majority owner of *Who's Who* and head of the American Institute of Management, was in the unique— and, as far as Kreuger was concerned, detrimental—position of controlling nearly a million of the seven and a half million outstanding American certificates of Kreuger & Toll. Toward Kreuger, Martindell was as bearish as a bear can be. The young man had made a fortune in the market before the 1929 crash, and he was still trading successfully, buying stocks on downturns and selling short on rallies. As the operator of an investment firm named Fiduciary Counsel, Inc., he was handling the portfolios of nine of the country's wealthiest men, among them Joseph T. Ryerson of Inland Steel, some members of the Armour and Swift meat-packing families, Marshall Field, Powell Crosley, Andrew Jurgens, and Edwin M. Herr of the Westinghouse Electric Manufacturing Company. Collectively, these men owned the Kreuger & Toll shares on which Martindell was sitting.

Over the last six months Martindell had felt as if he were on top of a keg of dynamite instead of a large number of highly regarded securities. In May 1931, when Kreuger & Toll was still selling at about twenty-one dollars a share, he had realized that he held about twenty million dollars' worth of stock and yet knew virtually nothing about it. (A similar lack of knowledge had scarcely bothered the gentlemen of Lee, Higginson or any other stockholders before.) He had made several efforts to obtain some certified accountants' statements from Lee, Higginson and other sources, but had got nowhere, and had slowly begun to sell the stock, disposing of some two hundred thousand shares during the rest of the year. Prorating his sales on a daily basis, Martindell had had little or no trouble getting rid of the securities. Although the quotation on Kreuger & Toll had dropped to a low of $4.25 in the third week of December, when Kreuger had arrived from Europe, it had moved back up to nine dollars a share in early January, when Kreuger had gone out to Chicago to make his optimistic speech and his first disclosure about Boliden. The meeting arranged there by Lee, Higginson had been partly inspired by Ryerson, upon whom Martindell had urged it beforehand. Martindell had insisted that Ryerson place a stenographer in an adjoining room to take down in full what Kreuger said. Immediately after the meeting Ryerson had telephoned Martindell and had told him he was all wrong about Kreuger, that the Swede had made a tremendous impression, and that Martindell ought to stop selling so much Kreuger & Toll—the young broker by then was moving as much as a thousand shares a minute. Strangely enough, everything he had offered had been quickly bought, and he had begun to suspect what he soon confirmed: a large group of brokers were banded together in a supporting operation. The following day Ryerson had called back. He had an odd confession to make, he had said, having carefully read the stenographer's transcript of the Kreuger speech. "It's the damnedest thing," Ryerson had told Martindell. "I suddenly realize that he said nothing new at all. It adds up to a lot of double-talk."

Martindell, with about half of his supply of Kreuger & Toll shares still left, promptly decided to get rid of the rest at around nine dollars a share, if he could, and he gave orders to step up his sales. A day or so later, toward the end of January, he received a visit from a vice president of a well-known New York bank, who bluntly asked him what he thought he was doing and accused him of "trying to ruin the country." The banker admitted that a brokerage syndicate was indeed buying Martindell's shares as they were put on the market and told him that the syndicate had been formed "to support the Stock Exchange itself, because we're all trying to save a very damaging situation." When Martindell remained adamant and refused to cancel his selling orders, the banker asked him what he wanted. Martindell said he had been trying for months to get reliable figures on Kreuger & Toll, but without success. "If I see that the stock is really worth nine dollars a share, I'll stop my orders," he added. The banker promised that he'd get some figures the next morning. Later that same afternoon one of Martindell's big clients, Herr, of Westinghouse, called to say that he was pulling out of Fiduciary Counsel, Inc., and wanted Martindell to stop selling his Kreuger & Toll stock. "I've just talked to Lee, Higginson and some bankers, and they tell me you don't know what you're doing," Herr said. Martindell did his best to dissuade Herr, who had invested almost all of his savings in Kreuger & Toll, but to no avail.

By now, of course, Kreuger himself knew what was going on, and he sent one of his own agents to see Martindell with two typewritten pages of what Martindell regarded as financial gobbledygook purporting to show that Kreuger & Toll was really worth thirty dollars a share. Martindell was naturally unsatisfied and kept on selling. He next received a visit from the secretary of the Stock Exchange, who repeated what the banker had said about the great disservice he was rendering the country and threatened to have him ostracized from the Exchange. At worst, Martindell realized, he would lose his private wires to brokerage houses, but he replied that he could always use the public phones. He continued to sell Kreuger & Toll stock until he got rid of everything except fifty thousand shares of Herr's. "I don't know how many millions I saved for my other clients," he recalls, "but I know that Philip Armour built himself a million-dollar home with what he managed to recover just in time on his Kreuger and Insull holdings. I disposed of most of what I still held at between nine and seven dollars a share, and I was later told that fifteen million dollars had been put up by the syndicate in Wall Street to support the stock. I've always wondered how a house such as Lee, Higginson could have got itself into such a position, but I realize, too, that the ramifications had become a lot wider toward the end."

: 2 :

The nerve-racking Martindell affair was only one facet of Kreuger's increasingly desperate situation. He had now stepped up his own gambling in the market in a feverish effort to improve his cash shortage. Between the end of January and February 15 he called in every bit of cash he could lay his hands on abroad and ordered it transferred to New York. His personal deposits at the Chase National Bank during the three-week period came to just over three million dollars, and all of it quickly went out to brokers. To meet his pending obligations, Kreuger needed huge profits in a hurry, and nothing in his life more clearly showed his innate gambler's instinct than his wild speculations during this eleventh hour. Between the last part of February and the beginning of March 1932 he had several major payments to make. In New York a two-million-dollar loan that had been granted the Swedish Match Company was coming up for repayment. Four million dollars lent by four big banks to the International Match Corporation was also due. He needed $1,200,000 to meet scheduled Kreuger & Toll dividends, and, finally, he owed two million dollars to Turkey and more than a million to Lithuania as installments on match loans.

At the end of January, Kreuger had cabled Krister Littorin in Stockholm that he expected to borrow seven million dollars from the Drexel family in Philadelphia, but on February 19 he informed Littorin that the loan had fallen through. He did not tell Littorin—or anybody else immediately—that on the same day he had received much worse news: his big telephone deal with the International Telephone & Telegraph Company was suddenly off.

Kreuger had certainly not forgotten his agreement of

the previous June to let I.T.T. accountants examine the books of the L. M. Ericsson Telephone Company, but he may already have been so inwardly disturbed that he failed to realize that the collapse of the transaction was imminent. Back in mid-December, Chinlund, the perspicacious I.T.T. controller, had decided that he ought to go to Sweden himself and take a look at the Ericsson books before the Price, Waterhouse inspectors arrived to make their formal inspection of Ericsson's 1931 earnings. Sosthenes Behn had thereupon suggested this to Kreuger, and Kreuger had demurred, saying he wanted to be in Stockholm himself "to introduce Chinlund around." In Chinlund's words: "When Behn came back and told me that, I had an instinctive reaction—my auditor's nerve was struck. I wasn't suspicious, but I was more than ever determined to go. Behn told me to go see Kreuger myself, which I did. I told him I couldn't wait, that it fitted into my own plans to go soon because I had other business to do in Europe too, and I suggested that he simply let the Ericsson people know I was coming. Kreuger gave me one of his long pauses, and then he asked me if I might arrange things so that I could go to the other places I had in mind first—Berlin, Paris, and London. I said I would do that, and that I would let him know the date of my arrival in Stockholm."

In the back of Kreuger's mind there had undoubtedly been the hope that he might yet be able to get over to Sweden during Chinlund's mission there; but when his cash-raising efforts in America had struck a snag, he had been forced to remain where he was. Had he been able to get back in time, he might have avoided, or at least postponed, what happened; as it was, his failure to take some precautionary steps from New York can only be set down as a costly product of the overstrain that was soon to break him down.

Chinlund left New York in mid-January and, after making his other stops, reached Stockholm on January 28, the day Kreuger was making his public announcement in America about the Boliden mine. As Chinlund told the story: "I wired Kreuger, as I had promised, but got no answer. Traveling with me were the Price, Waterhouse accountants from New York, but I told them I wanted to have a talk alone first with the Ericsson officers, and the next day I met the two top men, Nils Ahlström and Axel Grönberg. I explained my mission to them and said I would like to have the Ericsson balance sheet through November, and a supporting statement. They brought a balance sheet out at once. It was in Swedish. I didn't know much Swedish, but I did know accounting, and the principles of course were pretty much the same. I saw immediately that some things in the statement were unclear to me and that it needed more study. I returned to my hotel and wrote up a series of questions to put to the two Ericsson men the next day. When I went back the next morning, I thought the two were somewhat evasive, but I kept plugging. Finally, Grönberg said to Ahlström, in Swedish: 'This man isn't going to let go of this, and we might as well tell him the whole story'—my Swedish was good enough to understand that. They then gave me correct and thorough answers, and I became convinced that, as far as the terms of the contract between I.T.T. and Ericsson were concerned, there were several substantial errors from an accounting point of view. Both Ericsson men made it clear to me that they knew Kreuger had done the wrong thing when he gave us an outline of the Ericsson balance sheet in New York. It was obvious to me that erroneous statements had been made about Ericsson's cash position, on the basis of which I.T.T. had purchased its original six hundred thousand shares."

The confusion could hardly have been unintentional on Kreuger's part. In the English version of the merger contract he and Behn had drawn up in June, Ericsson's liquidity had been defined as "cash in hand and in banks." The Swedish translation, Chinlund discovered, read "cash, bankings and *on deposit*." He quickly noted that about six million dollars which I.T.T. had assumed was in the Ericsson treasury had been placed "on deposit" with Kreuger & Toll. As security, Ericsson had been given some German match-monopoly bonds. While they were good bonds, Chinlund realized that their market value was no longer so high as it had been and might well go down further. There were also four or five other discrepancies between the Stockholm statement and what Kreuger had claimed in New York.

Chinlund immediately told the two Ericsson officers that the situation was to be regarded as serious, and he wrote a cable, which they initialed, to send to Behn. Several days later Chinlund received a telephone call from Behn, who told him what a bombshell he had thrown and suggested that he hurry back home. Behn had already shown Chinlund's cable to Kreuger, who dismissed it as "an accountant's brainstorm." The mix-up about "on deposit" was the result of an error in translation, he maintained, not mentioning that he himself had done the translating. Having employed the Ericsson money for speculative purposes, he knew that it was too late now to cover up and was determined to brazen the thing through, if he could. The money had been used by Kreuger & Toll, he calmly explained, to buy two French telephone companies that Ericsson would later take over. Behn and his directors were unimpressed. No matter what Kreuger said, "on deposit" and "cash receivable" and French phone companies were not the same as cash. Following Chinlund's return to New York, the I.T.T. directors agreed that the contract must be rescinded and I.T.T. must be given back its eleven million dollars—the money paid to Kreuger the previous June in return for the first block of Ericsson shares. The bad news was given to Kreuger by Behn and his attorney on the morning of Friday, February 19, at the I.T.T. offices at 67 Broad Street.

Kreuger, of course, didn't have even part of the eleven million dollars to pay back to I.T.T., but he quietly agreed to the rescision of the merger contract and at first seemed hardly perturbed. "He never lost his equanimity," Chinlund said, "not even when we asked him to tell the facts at once to his American and Swedish bankers. He simply kept on insisting, in his soft voice, that I had been wrong, and that the confusion was all due to a simple matter of translation." Consummate actor though he was, his calmness at this time was not altogether an act. He was in fact totally stunned. The bottom of his world had suddenly dropped out. He requested, and was accorded, a few days' delay, and returned at once to his penthouse, where he sat alone most of the afternoon and evening. At some point he apparently decided to kill himself and dragged out of the closet a hunting rifle he had purchased some time before. After examining it, he placed it in an umbrella stand in the hallway.

About eleven o'clock the next morning he went to his Wall Street office and then uptown to the one on Fifth Avenue. His choice made, he had regained his inner poise. Politely, as always, he told the office staff to leave early for the long week end (Washington's birthday fell on Monday), setting out some stamps and stationery that he wanted to take home. Around noon he returned to his apartment, and an hour or so later he received an unexpected visit from, of all people, Chinlund.

Following the Friday session at the I.T.T. offices, Charles Mitchell, the banker, who was on the I.T.T. board, had called his associate Gordon Rentschler, of the National City Bank, and told him that Kreuger had been requested to inform Lee, Higginson and his other bankers of the I.T.T. decision by Tuesday at the latest. Rentschler had a date to play golf with one of the Lee, Higginson directors on Sunday, and he felt that he could hardly go through that pleasant occasion with the secret knowledge that two days later his golf partner would get the awful news about Kreuger. Rentschler thereupon called Behn and requested that he be allowed to disclose the cancellation of the telephone contract to his golfing friend in advance of the Tuesday deadline, and Behn asked Chinlund to find Kreuger and see if that was all right with him. Chinlund went to Kreuger's office and, upon being told that the financier had gone home, he taxied up Park Avenue to Kreuger's apartment.

"On my way up I rehearsed what I'd do if Kreuger pulled his cigarette stunt on me," Chinlund recalled, "and I resolved to grit my teeth and let him be the one to talk first. I put my question to him almost as soon as I got there. Out came the customary cigarette. He lit it, twirled it, squeezed it, broke it, as always, and then he said: 'Well' and stopped, and went through the whole procedure again. I sat tight. Finally, he said: 'Well' again and then: 'Sunday or Monday or Tuesday, I don't suppose it makes any difference.' There was another long pause, and he looked at me gravely and said: 'Mr. Chinlund, you are committing the worst mistake anyone ever made. Up to now, you have had a fine career, and now you'll be ruined.' I replied that if that were so, if a mistake had been made, I was already ruined, and nothing I could do would alter that. Kreuger then said: 'Think about it. You still have until tomorrow morning to change your mind'—by which he apparently meant Rentschler's golf date. I again said there was nothing I could do about it, the facts were all there. I started for the elevator and he accompanied me, asking me about my relatives in Sweden. As I walked through the hall, I noticed the gun in the umbrella stand, and I asked him if he got any chance to do any shooting in this country. 'Yes, occasionally,' he answered, and then I shook hands with him and left. As I thought about it on the way home, it was apparent that he was making a last desperate gamble with me. He knew he couldn't offer me a bribe, but he undoubtedly thought that he could bring his great influence to bear on me, a young man, by alluding to my career."

∶ 3 ∶

When Chinlund left, Kreuger began a hectic afternoon and night of writing letters, sending cables, and making transatlantic phone calls. Everything he did bore the mark of a man at the end of his rope. Although his motivations and innermost thoughts had been carefully hidden from even his best friends, he had been a generous man and had often gone out of his way to help others, even strangers, with gifts of money and favors of one kind or another. He had not dared to forewarn his friends, such as Littorin, about his true financial state so that they could save some of their fortunes, but he had taken quiet steps to protect his mother and father and sisters and brother, and now, penultimately, he concluded these arrangements. Before he had left Stockholm, he had transferred some valuable securities, mostly shares in iron and ball-bearing companies and in a Swedish newspaper he owned, from his office safe to his private apartment, where he had placed them in a secret cupboard next to his bed. At the end of January he had cabled one of his brothers-in-law, Gunnar Ekström, to get the newspaper shares and give them to Ernst Kreuger, Ivar's aged father. Now, on the dark night of February 20, he wrote to Ekström and instructed him how to divide the rest of the securities among members of the family, himself included. He also sent a cable to Erik Sjöström, the Kreuger & Toll director, ordering the transfer of some valuable Greek bonds to Torsten Kreuger, and he then telephoned a Stockholm broker and told him to deliver a large cash balance to Torsten. A telephone call to Karin Bökman, Kreuger's attractive red-haired secretary, ordered her to give some other securities in the office safe to Torsten. After he had hung up, Kreuger wrote a letter to Miss Bökman, for whom he had a close personal attachment, saying that things didn't look too bright and that he wanted to leave her something while he still could. "Therefore, please accept the enclosure," he added, and he slid three ten-thousand-dollar bills into the envelope. The letter ended with the words: "Farewell, and thank you."

Sometime in the early hours of the morning, having finished his macabre chores, utterly fatigued and beginning to suffer from a cold, Kreuger showed symptoms of a complete physical and psychological breakdown. He muttered financial figures incoherently, started to make phone calls and then stopped. His housekeeper, Hilda Aberg, finally prevailed upon him to lie down. The next morning, though he had slept several hours, Kreuger seemed worse, and Miss Aberg didn't know what to do. He wandered around the apartment, muttering, and refused to eat. Late in the afternoon, to Miss Aberg's immense relief, Donald Durant and George Murnane, another Lee, Higginson partner, appeared. During the morning Gordon Rentschler, released from his obligation to keep silent about the I.T.T. deal being off, and apparently even in advance of his golf date, had called Murnane in Brookville, Long Island, and said he had something very important to discuss. "I was on my way to mass, with the holy mantle wrapped around me, but afterward I went right over to Rentschler's house nearby," Murnane recalls. After telling Murnane what had happened, Rentschler advised him to get hold of Kreuger at once, so Murnane called Durant in Cornwall-on-Hudson and they agreed to go to Kreuger's apartment at five o'clock that afternoon.

"When we got there," Murnane says, "we found him in a terrible state. He was almost unrecognizable as he sat huddled in a chair in front of the fireplace. He talked in jumps, with his hand to his head, and then paused for minutes at a time. It seemed unreasonable to discuss anything with him. 'I'm so tired that I just can't seem to get down to anything,' he said. He was in a very nervous state. That is what alarmed us so—it was not like him." Durant added that he had never seen anyone in quite that condition and that "it was very pathetic to see him like that, a man who had been so brilliant, so tireless before."

Realizing it was no time to ask him about the telephone matter—Murnane was inclined to look upon it anyway as "just a financial question . . . a thing that could be straightened out"—the two Lee, Higginson men summoned a physician, Dr. Joseph Wheelwright (a man whose patients, ironically, included some top Morgan partners), and he diagnosed the case as one of cardiac fatigue and complete "brain fag" and warned that any further pressure on Kreuger might drive him out of his mind. The doctor ordered the phone in Kreuger's room turned off, and the financier lay down in his clothes and slept sporadically. Paris called three times during the night, and Miss Aberg, who answered the phone in another part of the house, said he could not be disturbed. When he awoke at six the next morning, Kreuger was furious and tried to trace the call. Despite his earlier resolve to kill himself, his gambling instinct and his pride—and, undoubtedly, the would-be suicide's instinctive fear of not being able to go through with the act—created a new and phrenetic force in him that led him to resume his desperate efforts to raise money.

Beyond the bad news about the telephone deal, this was the big week of decision, with his various other obligations coming due. Between fitful bouts of sleep, almost always reclining in his clothes in the soft chair at his desk, he placed and received dozens of emergency transatlantic calls and sent a stream of cables to Paris, Berlin, Warsaw, Amsterdam, and, of course, Stockholm. Aminoff, the young Swedish assistant, came to the house late Monday to stay with him overnight, and he later recalled the ordeal. "Kreuger began answering the telephone without its ringing," he said, "and he would also get up and ask somebody to come in, imagining he had heard a knock at the door. Then he would fall back in his chair and drift off for a few minutes, and get up and start all over again. At one point he roved around the drawing room and shouted: 'I'm losing my mind, Aminoff, I can't remember, I can't think.' "

This went on for three days. When the sedation he was under was working, Kreuger would spend hours just sitting and staring, and when Miss Aberg told him: "You can't go on like this," he would mutter: "I must wait for a call" and remain where he was, dazed. Durant came by a few times and joined Miss Aberg in trying to console him by telling him everything would be all right if he would only rest, but he kept crying out: "I don't see how. You don't understand. I don't see how it will ever be right." These were his low and disconnected periods, but when he could marshal his thoughts he seemed fairly lucid. He sent a cable to Oscar Rydbeck, telling the banker, as he had been requested to do, what had happened to the telephone transaction and inquiring if Rydbeck could come to New York to help out in case there were difficulties over the contract cancellation. Rydbeck replied that he would come if it were absolutely necessary, but thought he ought to remain in Europe—which he did.

The more Kreuger brooded about the I.T.T. deal, the madder he became, and he began to accuse I.T.T. of wanting to welsh because the depression was getting worse, and of "blackmailing" him into staying in New York until he had signed the rescission agreement. Throughout the week of February 22, while I.T.T. and Lee, Higginson sought to work out an arrangement whereby the transaction could formally be called off without Kreuger being accused of having done anything improper, the matter of his departure remained in abeyance. Meanwhile, there were the other debts to be dealt with.

The first, falling due on February 23, was the two-million-dollar obligation of the Swedish Match Company, which was to reduce a larger loan the company had received here. Some time on the 22nd Kreuger spoke on the phone with Krister Littorin in Stockholm, but the connection was bad and Kreuger was apparently quite incoherent besides. Littorin consequently queried Durant by cable and received the following reply,

> Friend you talked to remembers nothing of the conversation stop Doctor says only terribly tired and needs rest. . . .

A short time later Littorin got a relatively clear, though still somewhat odd, cable from Kreuger:

> Arrangements I thought would produce amount necessary for acceptance credit fell through stop It is vital avoid default tomorrow stop This should be made clear to banks stop If absolutely impossible have funds telegraphed tomorrow then company should cable a statement explaining delay and stating that money will be wired following day stop If nothing is possible then wish company to cable a statement explaining how it proposes to meet the obligations stop

Either because of his illness or because he knew he had exhausted his own good will in Sweden, Kreuger seemed to be depending more than ever before on his aides. With Carl Bergman, another of Kreuger's oldest friends and associates in the match company, and Sigurd Hennig, the trusted accountant, Littorin immediately set out to raise money in Stockholm. February 23 became a day and a night that none of the three men ever forgot. During the morning they held prolonged conferences with officers of the top three Swedish banks in an effort to establish a consortium that would extend more credit to Kreuger. The results were negative. Around noon Littorin and Bergman went to the Finance Ministry, and a meeting was arranged for midafternoon at the Riksbank, the state bank. Conferences went on there until eight o'clock in the evening, and most of the top bankers in Stockholm as well as several government representatives were in attendance. Littorin dashed in and out all day to talk on the transatlantic phone to Kreuger or Durant, who kept reminding him how short the time was.

While trying to get the banks to agree provisionally to make some credit available, Littorin and the others were searching for acceptable collateral, and at one point during the long afternoon they decided to open Kreuger's private safe. In three loose envelopes the astonished Littorin found seven million pounds' worth of Italian government bonds. He had never heard of them before. "For Heaven's sake, boys," he exclaimed, "here are four hundred million kroner' worth of securities that are not pledged! Just think of it! This solves the question. . . ." It scarcely solved it. Hennig repeated what Kreuger had told him in the spring about circumstances that made it necessary to keep the bonds secret, and Littorin quickly decided they ought not to be used for collateral after all.

During the evening Prime Minister Karl Gustav Ekman,

hurriedly summoned from his dinner to the marathon meeting at the Riksbank, made what amounted to a personal decision: to allow the bank, already a Kreuger creditor to the tune of more than ten million dollars, to give him another million if the three big private banks in Stockholm would jointly provide another million. One of the three immediately refused, but the state bank agreed to supply a third of the extra million too. The decision was to prove a tragic one for Ekman, a thoroughly admired statesman who had previously accepted a twelve-thousand-dollar political donation from Kreuger. Ekman would soon be forced out of office because of that donation and because of his show of generosity; in defending himself, he told Parliament he had decided that Kreuger should have the money, no matter what the momentary collateral situation, because the financial responsibility of Sweden as well as that of Ivar Kreuger personally had seemed to be at stake. Referring to the session at the Riksbank that evening, Ekman said: "It was a difficult meeting. I was startled by the utter lack of knowledge shown by representatives of the Swedish Match Company, especially concerning the co-ordination of subsidiary concerns and affiliated industries. Others present got the same impression. I therefore told the representatives of the Riksbank that it was my conviction that no further demands for credit should be considered during present negotiations. And it was resolved that the Riksbank should take the initiative for a thorough investigation of the business of the Kreuger concerns."

Ekman's impression was, of course, completely justified. It was all but impossible for anyone other than Kreuger to figure out where various bonds and cash holdings were and whether or not they had been pledged with banks, or sold, or exchanged. The best the harried aides could do was meet each emergency as it arose. The moment Littorin received the good news of the new Riksbank loan, he sent cables to both Kreuger and Durant saying that the required two million dollars would be on deposit at the Guaranty Trust Company in downtown Manhattan the next morning, to the account of Lee, Higginson & Co. He was thanked and reminded that another crisis was close at hand. On the coming Saturday, the 27th, the four-million-dollar loan that four American banks had granted Kreuger in August through the International Match Corporation in New York was due, and he had to get it renewed somehow. He had told Durant that he had been expecting an interest payment of $4,700,000 from Spain, which he had wanted to use to pay off the banks, but that the Spaniards had failed to deliver the money on time. The truth was, no money was due from Spain. The "Spanish match monopoly" was, like the Italian one, a fake that Kreuger had invented to make the International Match directors in America think they were doing a profitable business that was nonexistent.

As soon as Durant got the news about the Spanish "delay," both he and Berning, the Ernst & Ernst accountant, began bombarding Littorin with cables, seeking information about the disposition and whereabouts of certain match bonds and other IMCO assets in Europe which might be used as collateral to continue the bank loans here. Durant was becoming increasingly puzzled by the inability of Littorin or anyone else in Stockholm to give him definite answers. Late on February 23 he sent Littorin the following cable:

> We will of course have to plan immediately on our approach to the participants in the loan maturing Saturday stop. . . . In order that we may be in as good a position as possible under the circumstances please cable us information on the following points stop *One* is the difficulty which is arising on these payments due

primarily to restrictions being imposed by the government or Riksbank on the banks or the company because of the general exchange position stop *Second* has the failure to provide these funds been due primarily to failure to receive expected amounts from a certain country and can efforts continue through the week to accomplish that payment stop *Third* what proceeds can reasonably be counted upon from minor sources through the week in order to make as great a down payment as possible stop *Fourth* please list various bonds or other collateral that might be made available as collateral security for the loans as unquestionably banks will demand collateral

Dondurant

The following day Littorin replied at length, using the familiar letter-like form that Kreuger usually employed in sending cables. He said:

Dear Donald in reply to your telegram with the four points we are frightfully sorry to be obliged to say that these arrangements we reached late yesterday night after continual conferences from early morning with the government the Riksbank and the private banks were the limit of our efforts and of what we can do at present stop Several times during the conferences any further discussion seemed useless and we emphatically assure you that the reason why the credit was finally given was solely to prevent an immediate crisis and to give time to look over the situation and make up a program for the future stop I ask you earnestly to understand and also to make your partners and others interested understand . . . there is no possibility whatever of arranging a credit on this side for assisting in the payment of the four million dollars payable Saturday especially as this payment concerns IMCO which is here looked upon as an American company stop. . . . Dear Donald we are awfully sorry to have to send you a telegram of this tenor but that was one of the conditions last night for obtaining the credit

Littorin Bergman

In subsequent testimony Littorin said plaintively: "When they asked all these questions from New York we came together and conferred and got nowhere. . . . Everybody thought it was only the liquidity that was wrong and that the solidity was all right, so it only meant getting funds to get out of the difficulty until all the money should come in on the different bonds where we had monopolies, and from other sources." Bergman, at Littorin's side throughout the crisis, added: "We all still had absolute confidence in Kreuger. All we wanted was that he come home and get everything straightened out."

The news of the Riksbank credit seemed to cheer Kreuger immeasurably as he wandered in his bathrobe around his penthouse, and on February 24 Durant informed Littorin:

Friend is better today stop We are much encouraged stop Doctor says question of rest and a little time stop

Donald

The second loan crisis, though it involved twice as much money as the first, seemed easier to handle. About two weeks before, Kreuger had prepared some ammunition, which was now brought out. It later proved to be his last big hoax. As those in Stockholm seemed unable to figure out where all the assets were, Durant had suggested that Kreuger should try to make some presentation of what the financial position of the International Match Corporation was. A secretary named Mrs. Greta Gluydes had been called to the penthouse, and Kreuger had rapidly dictated to her a most glowing and altogether phony statement. After listing a number of expenditures and expected receipts —the latter had included the payment expected from Spain —he had "forecast" that there would be between five million and eight million dollars in cash on hand at the end of February. Mrs. Gluydes was later asked if she had not thought it strange that Kreuger had rattled off the figures without consulting any books or memoranda. "Yes, I thought it strange," she testified, "but I accounted for it because I had been told that Mr. Kreuger was a genius." She had been so impressed, as a matter of fact, that she had immediately drawn two thousand dollars out of her bank and, to her everlasting chagrin, had invested it in Kreuger & Toll stock.

In retrospect, it should perhaps have appeared odd that a company such as IMCO, with one hundred and fifty million dollars in listed assets, should have had practically no cash in its till, but, as several bankers pointed out afterward, this was not unusual, especially in 1931. At any rate, now that the four-million-dollar loan was due, Murnane, armed with Kreuger's "forecast," went to see S. Sloan Colt, president of the Bankers Trust Company, one of the four creditor banks. Murnane suggested that the loan be reduced by ten per cent and then renewed, with collateral provided. Casting a quick glance over the "forecast," Colt seemed agreeable, and Rentschler, of the National City Bank, another of the four creditors, also agreed, even though he knew all about Kreuger's troubles with the International Telephone & Telegraph Company. Murnane and Durant were further encouraged when the other two banks, one in Chicago and the other in Pittsburgh, also came around. The two Lee, Higginson men then went back to see Kreuger. There had been rumors for some time that Kreuger, in his efforts to obtain control of American match companies, had secretly bought a lot of Diamond Match Company shares, and now Murnane asked him, point blank: "Do you own any, or does the International Match Corporation own any Diamond Match stock?"

"Yes, they do," Kreuger said.

Murnane suggested that three hundred and fifty thousand shares would be enough to provide collateral, and Kreuger said he could round up that much, but added: "I dislike to have the Diamond Match stock talked about a great deal." Murnane promised that the matter would be treated confidentially, and these shares were then quietly pledged with the four banks as collateral for the loan renewal. Kreuger had bought the shares, worth more than five million dollars at current prices, in 1929 and had deposited them with a small financial house in Paris. He now cabled orders to Paris that the securities be delivered to Lee, Higginson's representative there, to be held for the American banks. In Stockholm, with this new evidence of faith in Kreuger to cite, Littorin was able to prevail upon the Riksbank to come to the rescue once more and provide another credit of one and a quarter million dollars to take care of the dividend payments Kreuger & Toll was obligated to make in America on March 1.

Things seemed to be brightening, but only Kreuger knew how serious his plight still was, especially now that everyone had begun to ask where all his bonds and other securities were. The most persistent questioner was Berning, the now aroused young accountant. Among IMCO's most valuable holdings were fifty million dollars' worth of German government bonds. They were supposedly still held, in IMCO's name, at the Kreuger-owned Deutsche Union Bank in Berlin, but shortly before leaving for America, as we know, Kreuger had secretly transferred them to Copenhagen, and from there had pledged most of them as collateral for his large private debt to the Scandinaviska bank in Stockholm. Obligated to replace them in Berlin with something of corresponding value for IMCO, he suddenly realized, on February 25, during one of his more lucid moments in New York, that he must do something before the inquisitive Berning found out that the Berlin cupboard was bare. That afternoon he telephoned Littorin and ordered that a cable be sent to him in New York stating that a meeting of the IMCO executive committee—ordinarily consisting of Kreuger, Littorin, and Carl Bergman—had been held on February 5 despite Kreuger's absence, at which it had been duly noted that all the German bonds owned by IMCO had been transferred to its daughter company, Continental, and had been replaced in Berlin by bonds of "equal value" issued by Country X, which was supposed to be Italy. This was, of course, an outright lie, but Littorin, who regarded it simply as a retroactive bookkeeping shift, did not know that the German bonds had already been pledged elsewhere by Kreuger, any more than he knew that the Italian bonds were forgeries. During this same week Kreuger ordered his accountants back home to list two thirds of the Italian bonds as an asset in the Continental books.

With Littorin and the Stockholm accountants as confused as ever about the hide-and-go-seek game they were playing, Kreuger's friends in New York had to turn to him for help in clarifying the financial picture. On February 27 he seemed to have perked up considerably, and Durant wired Littorin: "We are delighted at the very marked improvement of our friend," adding reassuringly that the original "thorough brain fag" had only been the "very natural result of carrying too many problems without sharing them." That same day Berning received permission to visit Kreuger, and they spent several hours together in the evening in the Park Avenue apartment. Berning was especially curious about the German bonds, and, as he afterward told the story, "Mr. Kreuger explained to me that these bonds had been transferred from IMCO to its wholly owned subsidiary company abroad, which meant, in other words, putting them from one pocket into another. The ownership was still in the group, but just once removed. I questioned him as to why that had been done, and the explanations he attempted were most peculiar. The more I pressed him for an understandable answer, the more confused he became and the more he fumbled. His efforts were either those of a sick man or of someone not entirely in his right mind. It concerned me a great deal, and I left with a feeling of great uneasiness." Berning told Durant about Kreuger's vagueness, and Durant spoke to Kreuger, who promised to "reverse" the switch of bonds at once. Several days later Kreuger showed Berning a cable from Berlin stating that the bonds were back at the Deutsche Union Bank there. Kreuger had pulled off a simple ruse: he had cabled a woman friend of his, a hat-check girl in a Berlin night club, and asked her to send him the desired message signed by the bank. The trick worked just long enough to help Kreuger get on a boat back to Europe.

He was scheduled to leave on the *Ile de France* at midnight on Friday, March 4. The fact that he continued to feel better cheered his cohorts in Europe immensely, and they were more eager than ever to get him home for consultations. Littorin had answered Durant's last report by cabling:

> A thousand thanks for your thoughtfulness to send that encouraging and kind cable about friend's health stop My heart has been aching for the poor boy . . . amidst all unpleasantness and humiliation bestowed upon us last week from certain quarters. . . .

But it was still not clear sailing for Kreuger. There remained the particularly nasty problem of signing the agreement that would legally rescind his telephone merger with the International Telephone & Telegraph Company and commit him to returning the eleven million dollars I.T.T. had given him. Above all his other troubles, this seems to have continued to aggravate Kreuger most and to have exacerbated his mental breakdown. He felt that he had been betrayed by leaders in Wall Street who all through the last decade had thrown themselves and their money at his feet, though he seems to have forgotten that the powerful partners of J. P. Morgan, so close to I.T.T., had never been among those supplicants. Except perhaps to a few intimate friends in New York, Kreuger did not express his bitterness openly, but on one of his last evenings here he wrote an angry and rather disconnected letter to the woman he had become closest to in recent years, the pseudonymous Itta Sandt. The letter read in part:

> I can't understand why you bother so much about people. . . . If you depend on them they only make use of you, and you keep finding out that you haven't any real friends. At most one has accomplices, and then one is a lost man. I have had very bad headaches for several days. I'm not really fit at all. Worst of all, I sleep so badly. Not that that is anything new. But it is extra bad just now. The lights in this town worry me. Before they always used to thrill me. But there is a terrible piercing red—I can't bear to look at it. Everybody here is a gangster, from the City Hall to the police and the bankers. I wish I'd never been near this country. . . .

By now he must indeed have wished that he had never seen this rich and gullible nation that, by tempting him to overreach his cleverness, had made him first a world success and now a bankrupt. Undoubtedly he knew, if his

American friends did not, that he was leaving here for the last time.

On the afternoon of March 4 he finally signed the rescission of the telephone deal. In effect, having been virtually held here by the threat of legal action until some settlement was reached, Kreuger was being allowed to go back to Sweden only because Lee, Higginson & Co. agreed to vouch for him on the eleven-million-dollar obligation. Kreuger promised, in the signed statement, to return the money with six per cent interest before the first of September. Durant happily cabled Littorin:

> After two weeks most intensive effort glad to report all accusations have been kept out of final document which we consider to be of transcendent importance
> Dondurant

"From our standpoint, the whole thing was simply being transferred back to Stockholm," Murnane later said, "and it was decided that two of our officers, Durant and N. Penrose Hallowell, should go back on the boat with Ivar to determine in Europe if there had been anything queer going on." Despite their doubts about the wisdom of some of Kreuger's recent actions, the Lee, Higginson partners retained their high opinion of him, and some of them by now were downright mad at and suspicious of I.T.T. According to Murnane, "We thought he had been taken for a ride and we also still believed I.T.T. was just looking for a better trade." Even so, but only because his breakdown had given them such a scare that they were worried about his future mental condition, Kreuger was asked by Lee, Higginson on the eve of his departure to sign a unique statement in which he declared that "I am entirely willing to cause to be brought about changes in the corporate practices and bookkeeping methods of the International Match Corporation,

Kreuger & Toll and the Swedish Match Company and their subsidiaries, to the end that more definite information will be correctly available and to the further end that these corporate practices will approach more nearly the methods understood in the United States." It was, unfortunately, somewhat late for such a precaution. The barn doors were at long last being closed, but the horse had long since been stolen.

Undoubtedly, during his last frenzied ten days in New York, while alternately lucid and incoherent, Kreuger had veered back and forth between two alternatives: should he kill himself as he had previously intended, or should he go back to Europe to face the consequences or try to brazen things out? At the last moment, having warded off or at least postponed the worst here, he nevertheless reverted to complete pessimism and gloom. At two thirty in the early morning of the 4th, Hilda Aberg had found the lights burning in Kreuger's room but Kreuger was gone. An hour or so later, apparently, he had come back and gone to sleep on the bed in his clothes. After he had shaved and gone out again around ten, Miss Aberg had found some matches from an all-night Lexington Avenue restaurant on his dresser, and alongside them a note that read: "I am too tired to continue."

That he was still dwelling on suicide is further shown by a letter he wrote that afternoon, following the telephone settlement, to his old Norwegian friend and companion of three decades, Anders Jordahl:

> Bäste [My dear] Jordahl: I hope that things will develop in such a way that you will be getting as little trouble as possible from the present situation. Please remember that the apartment, 791 Park Avenue, is in this name and I hope it follows that all the house property really serves as security for any engagements I

may have toward you. Regarding the apartment in
Paris, it is possible you will get a letter from Miss
——, of Helsingfors, Finland, for some help in connec-
tion with it [this referred to a place in Paris which
Kreuger had rented for the girl, one of his mistresses].
If you do not hear from her before three months
from now, please write her a letter offering your help.
Regarding the shares in Jordahl & Co., I consider that
they belong to you. Goodbye now, and thanks.
Yours, Ivar Kreuger.

Jordahl, not yet in receipt of the letter, had dinner with
Kreuger on the evening of departure, and sometime after
eleven they took a cab to the dock. The theater traffic delayed them and Kreuger almost missed the boat—Jordahl
had to tell the driver to go through all the red lights and
promise him that any fines would be taken care of later,
and this bit of corner-cutting was the ironic conclusion of
Ivar Kreuger's long career of chicanery in America. His
two Lee, Higginson shepherds, Durant and Hallowell, were
waiting for him on deck, along with an attorney for
Sosthenes Behn, the I.T.T. president, who was being sent
to Europe in case any details of the rescission agreement
needed to be re-negotiated. It was a cold *bon voyage, sans*
champagne, Kreuger's favorite drink. He just shook hands
all around and retired quickly to his cabin. Privately, Jordahl asked the captain to keep an eye on his famous passenger because of the great strain he had been under. This
last trip would not be one that Ivar Kreuger could take incognito.

CHAPTER 9

Götterdämmerung

THE CROSSING was relatively calm. Kreuger seemed to be in a reflective and almost benign mood, and though he kept to himself a good part of the time, playing solitaire and writing letters, he also mixed with the other passengers and drank and played shipboard games with them. He told Durant he felt better than he had for two months, and Durant thought he seemed "almost one hundred per cent normal" and was like the man "we had known and believed in and liked . . . not afraid of any problem." Camille Gutt, the Belgian banker, who knew Kreuger slightly, had been asked by the captain to entertain him, and he found nothing strained in Kreuger's conduct. A woman who remembers the trip says: "I talked with Mr. Kreuger a good deal, or rather listened to him. He seemed well informed on practically every subject. Everything he said carried complete conviction." And Sonja Henie, the figure skater, who sat at the table next to his in the dining salon, said afterward that "he seemed to be in good spirits and I definitely did not get the impression he knew this voyage was his last."

On the second day out, Kreuger sent a cable to his Stockholm secretary, Karin Bökman, in which he told her to ignore the contents of the "farewell" letter he had mailed her from New York on February 20. (Miss Bökman thereupon put the letter, and the three ten-thousand-dollar bills he had enclosed, in a safe-deposit box.) However, perhaps the best indication of his mood—a sign that, if he was trying to fight off the idea of suicide, he was also already looking upon himself as a historical figure who had moved into a kind of predestined limbo—appeared in a self-revealing and clairvoyant letter he wrote to Itta Sandt. Referring to his recent troubles in New York, he said:

Very little more, and they would have called me a rogue and a cheat. So far they haven't dared to do so; but they may at any time now. I was in such a state of nerves that I certainly should not have been capable of standing up for myself very satisfactorily. But you will remember what I have often told you when we have been discussing the basis of capitalism—that what one capitalist should always say to another who accuses him of speculation is: "And what about you— aren't you a speculator?"

Once we begin to go into deep water we soon get out of our depth. What sort of a foundation does this world rest on? Forests draw their nourishment from roots and earth, the seed grows in the corn, man springs from man. All that is certain. But what certainty is there about money, which after all holds the whole world together? It depends on the good will of a few capitalists mutually to keep to the agreement that one metal is worth more than another. . . .

If you hear people abusing me just now you must

laugh, and must not believe that those who grow in-
dignant have any right to do so. Only those who did
not know what I was have that right. The Russians,
for instance, might. In fact, they certainly will, for
they have no sense of humor. . . .

Kreuger's enemies, especially the stock-market bears in
France and elsewhere who had been stepping up their attacks on him all during the long crisis in New York, were
apparently also on the minds of some of his close associates.
Littorin, in his cables to Durant, had referred to the "organized slander" of the bears and had announced his intention to sue them, and an executive of Kreuger's telephone company in Stockholm had sent him a cable that
hardly seemed calculated to soothe his soul: "Be very careful when you talk to people on board. Your enemies want
to take your life. Don't make any business decisions before you return to Europe." But there was not very much
business to be discussed on board the ship, and neither Durant nor Hallowell pressed him. Everything now depended
on meetings in Paris with Kreuger's own staff and on a
meeting in Berlin, scheduled for March 13, at which he was
to confront his Swedish bankers collectively and try to explain what his true situation was. The only disturbing item
that came up during the trip concerned those pesky German bonds. Back in New York, the indefatigable accountant Berning, still not satisfied even after Kreuger had
shown him the wire from Berlin stating that the bonds
were there, had privately commissioned a Berlin accountant to make an independent check. Two days after the *Ile
de France* had sailed came the answer that verified Berning's fears: the bonds were *not* in Berlin, and were still
recorded at the bank there as having been transferred to
Copenhagen. Berning cabled Durant, who asked Kreuger
about the matter, but Kreuger muttered something about

the arrangements not yet having been completed for the bonds to be brought back physically to Berlin. Now thoroughly alerted, Berning got on a ship for Europe himself. On the last night out, the customary ship's banquet and ball took place, and Kreuger participated with considerable verve. He gave a small party of his own at which, according to at least one woman's recollection, "champagne flowed freely and he danced with all the ladies"—one of whom, Miss Henie, said later that the financier made a date to take her to lunch in Paris the next day. The ship docked at Le Havre on the morning of March 11 and Kreuger, Durant, and Hallowell traveled to Paris together on the boat train. From the station Kreuger took a cab alone to his apartment at No. 5 Avenue Victor Emmanuel III (now Avenue Franklin Roosevelt). There, waiting for him in front at eleven o'clock, was his old friend Krister Littorin, down from Stockholm. "He did not seem very cheerful," Littorin afterward said. "He looked very tired. I had known him since 1897, and I had been working with him for eighteen years and was tremendously fond of him. So when I saw him I went up and put my arms around his shoulders and said: 'By Jove, old man, it's good to see you again,' and he said: 'The same thing here, Krister.' "

They went upstairs to Kreuger's seven-room flat on the third floor, where Jeanette Barrault, the housekeeper, had prepared lunch (if Kreuger had made a date with Miss Henie, he apparently forgot about it), and in a few moments another old friend, Sune Schéle, joined them. Ever since he had left America a fortnight ahead of Kreuger, Schéle had been futilely trying to raise money in London; not having seen Kreuger during the period of crisis in New York, he was now shocked. "He looked terrible," Schéle recalls. "He hadn't cut his hair for ages, and he seemed broken down." The three talked in desultory fashion for two hours, with Littorin doing his best to cheer up Kreuger.

Once, while Littorin was out of the room, Kreuger pulled out his wallet and suddenly handed Schéle a ten-thousand-dollar bill. "I was flabbergasted," Schéle says. "I needed perhaps two hundred thousand to take care of the stock-market obligations I had assumed for him in London. I suppose he meant it as a gift. 'You keep it, Ivar, you'll need it more than I will,' I said, and he put it back."

Phone calls started to come in, first one from Kreuger's secret agent in Rome, and then another from Torsten Kreuger in Stockholm. Torsten wanted to know if he should come down to Paris, but Ivar said it wasn't necessary. "We've ridden out the worst of the storm," he replied, and he added that, except for a cold he had caught aboard ship, he felt all right and was planning to go to Berlin, thence to Stockholm, and subsequently back to New York. Durant, who, with Hallowell, had gone to the Hotel du Rhin on the Place Vendôme, rang up to say that Rydback had dropped in and that it had been suggested they all get together with Kreuger the next morning at eleven o'clock at the Du Rhin "to clear up the situation" before Kreuger's session with all his bankers in Berlin.

At two thirty in the afternoon, after Schéle had left, three of Kreuger's accountants and one of his directors, Gunnar Bergenstråhle, came to the apartment. The thirty-year-old Bergenstråhle, regarded as the organization's boy wonder and Kreuger's favorite, had been asked by the Riksbank to help unravel the mystery of where Kreuger's securities were, so that something could be provided at once for collateral. The accountants, led by Sigurd Hennig, had come on a similar mission, Hennig having suggested to Kreuger that it would be a good idea to try to get all the balance sheets straightened out before the Berlin meeting. "We have come here to help you," he announced as soon as they had all sat down. Kreuger did not seem altogether pleased, especially by Bergenstråhle's new dual role.

First, Victor Holm, the accountant for both the Continental Investment Corporation and Dutch Kreuger & Toll —the two major European companies through which Kreuger had for so many years drained off the millions he had raised in America—took the floor. As Holm recited the list of assets and liabilities as he understood them, Bergenstråhle interrupted whenever anything sounded vague or implausible to him. "Kreuger was very nervous," he has recalled. "He hardly talked, and just walked back and forth, looking at himself in the long mirror, which was a habit of his. He seemed utterly dejected and was no help at all in giving us information. Not yet knowing the real truth, I didn't have the impression we were putting him under attack, but we all felt the picture had to be clarified. Maybe, since I was trying to help both Kreuger and the Riksbank, I was becoming desperate, and I bluntly said, at one point, that we just had to get the facts."

Now and then Kreuger would disappear into the bedroom, once remaining there for fifteen minutes on the pretext of looking up some papers. Toward the middle of the painful hour-and-a-half session Hennig brought up the question of the Italian bonds, which no one yet knew Kreuger had forged. He wanted to know how Kreuger had raised so much money to lend Italy, and he asked if some interest coupons on the bonds, which had also been found in Kreuger's safe in Stockholm, had been cashed in yet, as they had fallen due. These were also forgeries, but Kreuger affirmed that he had received the interest, even though the notes had not been stamped "paid," as they would ordinarily have been. He was altogether evasive as to just how the money had come in. Finally, Hennig stared at him fixedly.

"Are they genuine?" he asked, referring to both the bonds and the notes.

Kreuger stopped walking and looked up at the rococo

ceiling, where golden cherubs and cupids were engaged in plaster byplay. Hennig, now in his eighties, still remembers the moment clearly. "He finally looked back at me, with those cow-eyes of his, and replied: 'Yes,' and then he went inside," he says.

Littorin, who had been suffering silently throughout, said to Hennig: "You pressed him very hard," and Hennig thereupon followed Kreuger into the bedroom to apologize and suggest that they all come back the next afternoon and complete the balance sheets then. Kreuger agreed, and the three accountants and Bergenstråhle left. "Seeing him had aroused the greatest suspicion of my life," Bergenstråhle says. "I thought he was in a state of shock. My hero was a beaten man. I had only recently seen a certain person when he was contemplating suicide—the hopeless, frightened, hunted look in the eyes—and Kreuger had that look. I went out to dinner and had several stiff cocktails."

Bergenstråhle was not alone in his suspicions. The earlier fears of Hennig, by far the smartest accountant in Kreuger's entourage, had been fully revived, and he spent his cocktail hour at Kreuger's local bank, the Banque de Suède et de Paris, reading some recent statements. They quickly convinced him that, among other things, Kreuger had vastly overrated the value of his French real estate. Matching this growing suspicion of insiders was a purely intuitive sense of doom on the part of a number of prominent Swedes who happened to be in Paris on personal missions. As the symbol of Sweden's position as a new economic power, Kreuger was still a source of national pride, not least as a result of his popularity and prowess in America. Reports of his current difficulties there had, of course, spread back across the ocean and had provoked some talk and worry. Now, overnight, a feeling of foreboding set in. Joseph Sachs, owner of Stockholm's biggest department store and one of Kreuger's good friends, remarked to

Björn Prytz, who had become Sweden's leading ball-bearing manufacturer: "I feel worried, as if something awful is going to happen," and Prytz replied: "I'm worried too, Joe." Sachs, who was famous for his intuitions, put a call in to London to Jacob Wallenberg, whose bank had particularly encouraged the forthcoming general investigation of Kreuger's affairs. Wallenberg, too, had been feeling apprehensive, and after talking to Sachs he called his brother, Marcus, in Stockholm, and said: "I'm sure things are bad."

Watching and listening, desperately trying to sort things out in his mind, as he had tried in New York, Kreuger alone knew how bad they really were. Heretofore, dealing separately with his various associates and accountants, he had managed to keep everything neatly compartmented, to shield himself by keeping his key employees apart, and to avoid letting one falsehood impinge on another. Now, for the first time, everything was coming together, everybody was making demands of him, and it was no longer possible to hide his falsifications and exaggerations. Those who wished him well could not help doing him ill by their mere collective presence, let alone their solicitous inquiry. He must have accepted this bitter reality on the afternoon of March 11 after the accountants had gone. Littorin noticed how terribly tired he seemed, but he reluctantly told Kreuger that he had made a four-o'clock date at the Hotel Meurice for the two of them to talk things over informally with Rydbeck.

Rydbeck, almost single-handedly responsible for Kreuger's huge credits at the Scandinaviska bank, had admired and revered the financier as much and as long as had Littorin. He had seen in him his own clear image of grandeur, and now the image was starting to tarnish. Durant and Hallowell had brought him up to date on the touchy events in New York, and he was now determined to make Kreuger realize the absolute seriousness of the situation as it concerned all of the Swedish bankers, not least himself.

When Kreuger walked into Rydbeck's hotel room—in contrast to some of the others, Rydbeck thought he "was more or less his usual self, somewhat pale, perhaps"—the banker said bluntly that, as everyone in Sweden was doing everything possible in the difficult circumstances, Kreuger owed it to his friends and supporters to co-operate by giving complete information about his financial condition so that "he could return to America as soon as possible, which we assumed was necessary for the continuation of the discussions with I.T.T. concerning L. M. Ericsson." Rydbeck wanted to leave for Berlin the next day, but Littorin demurred, insisting that the books could not be put in shape so quickly. "On my emphatic statement that the meeting in Berlin must take place, since all the participants had made their plans, we agreed to postpone our departure from Paris until Sunday," Rydbeck later said. Kreuger told Rydbeck that if it had not been for his illness in New York and the bear attacks against him centered in Paris, he would have been able to handle the crisis better. "But he seemed to take the situation that had now developed very calmly," Rydbeck added. While Kreuger had been in America, Rydbeck, like Littorin, had for the first time learned of the existence of the Italian bonds, though previously he had known that Kreuger had been negotiating a big deal with Italy. Now he suggested that, as cash was needed in a hurry, Kreuger should try to sell the bonds back to the Italians at a price advantageous to them. "I suggest that the sooner negotiations are started, the better," Rydbeck said, firmly.

Summoning up his last reserves of aplomb, Kreuger murmured: "I must go to Rome myself and negotiate."

"Yes, of course," agreed the persistent Rydbeck, "but then you should go there from Berlin."

Kreuger said he had to go to Stockholm first, and muttered something about the German bonds he had transferred as collateral to Rydbeck's bank having to be shifted back to Berlin. Rydbeck did not know that Kreuger had replaced them in Berlin, theoretically at least, with the Italian ones, and he raised his eyes at the suggestion that they be removed from the Scandinaviska vaults, but, as he subsequently put it, "I didn't bother to go further into detail at the time, since I would have an opportunity to return to the matter on our trip to Berlin."

Littorin afterward set the time of their departure from Rydbeck's room at the Meurice at five o'clock. Rydbeck put it at six—and the discrepancy was much debated. It was suggested that if Rydbeck's diary entry of the hour was correct, Kreuger would not have had time to purchase a revolver, which—according to evidence and testimony that would have been difficult if not impossible to have had fabricated—he now did.

Rydbeck's show of firmness, following that of the accountants earlier in the afternoon, was undoubtedly the factor that forced Kreuger's hand and made him decide, once and for all, to commit suicide as he had first resolved to do in New York in February. He knew that he could not possibly avoid a final showdown in Berlin, and the realization that his grossest crime, the forgery of bonds, was bound to come out was undoubtedly the ultimate blow to his pride.

Littorin accompanied him in a taxi back to his apartment and asked if Kreuger wanted to have dinner with him. Kreuger said no, he was tired, and suggested that Littorin have dinner with Durant and Hallowell at the Du Rhin and talk over the general situation. As soon as Littorin had left, Kreuger went back downstairs. The dusk was gathering now and a sharp wind had risen off the Seine River, a block away. From her loge opposite the elevator, Mme

Fermin Veron, the concierge, watching the switchboard, her children, her several canaries, and the comings and goings outside all at once, saw Kreuger move slowly through the swinging glass doors. According to her husband's subsequent testimony, "My wife noticed that he was not in his usual mood, since when he passed her together with our children he only greeted her by lifting his hat, whereas he usually said a few words and caressed the children, for he was a very kind man. My wife was so surprised at this that she looked to see where he was going. She was also surprised to see him walking . . . because he normally rode when he left the apartment."

Kreuger walked left about a block to No. 39 Avenue Victor Emmanuel III, the gun shop of Gastinne-Renette. The seventy-year-old salesman Antoine Bervillier, who waited on him, later set the time uncertainly as between four and five. Kreuger asked for a revolver, and Bervillier first showed him a small Browning automatic pistol. Kreuger said it was "too small." The next caliber size Bervillier brought out provoked only one word from the laconic customer: "Bigger." Bervillier then produced a nine-millimeter automatic Browning. "I'll take it," said Kreuger. He asked Bervillier to show him how to load it, and the salesman did so, using blank cartridges. Kreuger asked for four boxes of bullets—a hundred altogether—which he put in his pocket. The total price came to about three hundred and thirty francs, and, according to Bervillier's request, Kreuger's name and address were recorded in an order book. "I did not know the customer," Bervillier later said. "Nothing led me to believe that he intended to kill himself." Even so, he did not load the gun with real bullets because the owner of the store, "in the event that one is in the presence of a client who intends to commit suicide, desires that the latter be forced himself to load the gun, in which way he will have time to reconsider." All in all, Bervillier thought his customer was "calm but thoughtful."

Kreuger walked slowly back to his apartment—he had been gone about twenty minutes—and around seven o'clock told Mme Veron not to put through any more phone calls to his flat that evening. The housekeeper, Mlle Barrault, was off duty until the next morning. At eight o'clock Kreuger's doorbell rang and he received a young Finnish girl with whom he had been having relations for two years or more and who had accompanied him on trips to various places in Europe. This was the same girl he had referred to in the farewell letter he had written in New York to his friend Anders Jordahl, mentioning the apartment in Paris that he had rented for her. For this last tryst, as the housekeeper was away, he apparently preferred to have her come to his place. "Ivar was very happy that night," is all she has ever since said.

He was surely as happy as he ever would be again, and undoubtedly a lot happier than some other Swedes in Paris. At this last moment, even though they had all gathered there for a common purpose, Kreuger's men reverted to type and, betraying their long training, kept to themselves. Bergenstråhle, miserable over his cocktails, got through dinner with some friends and went to bed. Hennig dined alone with his burgeoning doubts and did the same. Gunnar Cederschiöld, though still Kreuger's chief Paris man, had been quietly staying on the sidelines, and he saw no one else in the organization, nor did Baron von Drachenfels, the social secretary. Rydbeck took a long walk and ate by himself at the Chatham Bar, reading in a Swedish newspaper about the dreadful murder of another friend of his, Hjalmar Sydow, a prominent industrialist who had been shot by his crazed son. Only Littorin, having been virtually ordered by Kreuger to dine with Durant and Hallowell, shared any further confidences, and what he was told simply upset him more. The Lee, Higginson men gave him full details of Kreuger's collapse in New York and of the difficult telephone negotiations, and then showed him the fancy "cash forecast" Kreuger had prepared to facilitate his loan renewals in America. One look at the prediction that a sizable cash reserve would shortly be available in various banks was enough to show Littorin that the statement was erroneous.

At eleven o'clock, when he got back to the Hotel Continental, Littorin found Sune Schéle waiting for him in the lobby. Schéle during the day had received more bad news from New York: a number of brokerage firms, including Eastman, Dillon & Co., had made claims for immediate cash repayments on large loans to Kreuger because the value of Kreuger & Toll debentures he had put up as collateral while in America had declined as a result of heavy short-selling by the bears in Paris. Schéle thought Rydbeck ought to be informed at once, so he and Littorin walked across the street to the Meurice. Rydbeck received the news philosophically, saying there was nothing he could do about it at the moment. The three sat around in gloom for an hour and, about midnight, parted and went sadly to bed with their separate thoughts.

The next morning, Saturday, March 12, was chilly, gray, and windy. It was a sad day for France, for Aristide Briand, one of her great statesmen, who had died six days before, was going to his grave. Crowds gathered early along the avenues to watch the funeral cortege, and when Kreuger awakened about eight, he could see them, dressed in black, as they lined the sidewalks. The Finnish girl left his apartment at eight thirty, and at nine he telephoned Karin Bökman, who had come to Paris from Stockholm. In view of her special relationship to Kreuger, Miss Bökman was hurt because he had failed to call her sooner, and Kreuger told her to drop by after ten. At nine fifteen, Littorin called, and Kreuger asked him to come over right away. It took Littorin half an hour to get through the funeral crowds, and when he arrived Kreuger was getting dressed. Mentioning the cash forecast Durant and Hallowell had shown him, he wondered aloud where Kreuger had got all the false figures. "It was probably not so good to give that statement," Kreuger replied. Littorin afterward testified: "As this told me that the figures were intentionally incorrect, I went up to him and, taking his arms, said: 'Whatever you have done, whatever you have said, and whatever you have written, you must realize that you are surrounded only by friends who wish you well and who want to help set everything straight.' "

Kreuger gave a vague nod and went into the bedroom to finish dressing. At ten twenty Miss Bökman arrived, and Littorin departed after asking her to remind Kreuger of the meeting scheduled for eleven at the Du Rhin with Durant, Hallowell, Rydbeck, and himself. Miss Bökman and Kreuger then went into the drawing room, and she asked him how things were. He replied that they were difficult, but he thought they would soon be better, and that the principal trouble had been his inability to collect his thoughts because he was so tired. All he felt like doing was playing solitaire, he added. Neither he nor she mentioned the good-by letter he had sent her from New York or the subsequent cable from the *Ile de France* telling her to disregard it. As he spoke, he kept pacing the floor without saying anything for minutes, but this was an old nervous habit of his and Miss Bökman was used to it. As she prepared to leave, about ten forty-five, he told her he would go to Berlin the next day and would then return to Stockholm, and he suggested that, as there was nothing for her to do in

Paris, she should go back to Stockholm right away. On her way out, she reminded him of his date in a quarter of an hour.

As Kreuger shut the door and turned back into the apartment, Mlle Barrault, about to go to market, asked if he would be home for lunch, and he first replied no, but then said he might be. Mlle Barrault left, and a few minutes later the doorbell rang. It was a messenger boy named Lucien, from the Paris office of the match company, come to deliver a routine telegram that had arrived from Istanbul. Taking it, Kreuger smiled and said: *"Merci bien,* Lucien." These were his last known words.

Seating himself at his desk, he prepared two letters—one to Littorin and one to his youngest sister, Britta, in Stockholm. He put Britta's into a large envelope marked for Littorin and, enclosing a third letter—the one he had written to Sune Schéle on February 22 in New York but hadn't mailed—placed the envelope on top of the blotter. During the past half-hour a number of calls had come in at the switchboard downstairs, including one from Anders Jordahl in America, who had wanted to talk about the stock-market situation. Kreuger had ignored the ringing extension phone alongside him. At eleven forty-five he went into the bedroom and took out the gun he had bought the day before, which he had kept in a corner of a large chiffonier. He lay down on the bed, fully dressed, unbuttoned the jacket and vest of the dark-blue, pin-stripe suit he was wearing, and moved aside a leather-covered coin that had been a favorite talisman. Holding the new, still-oiled Browning revolver close to his monogrammed silk shirt with his left hand, he shot himself just below the heart and died almost at once.

Mlle Barrault returned to the apartment at ten minutes after twelve. Noticing that Kreuger's hat and coat were still hanging in the vestibule, she assumed he had not yet gone out. When the phone rang a few moments later, she answered it and an unidentified man's voice asked for Kreuger. Mlle Barrault, laying down the receiver, opened the bedroom door and saw Kreuger lying on the bed. She thought he was sleeping and told the caller to ring back. Meanwhile, over at the Hotel du Rhin, the waiting conferees were growing nervous. At eleven thirty Rydbeck had telephoned the apartment and, when Kreuger failed to answer, had assumed he was on his way. Kreuger was known for his tardiness, and, in view of the Briand funeral, it was thought he might have been held up in traffic, but when he had not shown up by twelve thirty there was genuine alarm. Littorin and Miss Bökman, who had been upstairs in her room packing after buying a ticket to Stockholm, returned to the apartment by taxi. "I fear the worst," Littorin said, and Miss Bökman, who, oddly enough, seems to have told no one about Kreuger's earlier suicidal note to her, remained silent. When they reached the flat, a little after one, Mlle Barrault said she had made two attempts to rouse Kreuger by knocking on the door but he seemed to be sleeping very soundly. Littorin went into the darkened bedroom alone. He saw the immobile body of his friend, then the gun lying to the left on the bed, and a small stain of blood on Kreuger's shirt. "He is not sleeping, he is dead!" he cried.

Some ten minutes later, when he and the two women had got over their initial shock, Littorin found the letter in the outer room and opened it. The note to him, written in English, which was the language Kreuger and he had mostly used together in recent years, read:

Dear Krister: I have made such a mess of everything that I believe this is the best solution for all concerned. Please take care of these two letters. Please also see to it that two letters, sent to me a few days ago by Jordahl to 5 Victor Emmanuel, are returned to Jordahl. The letters were sent on the *Majestic*. Good-bye now, and thanks. I.K.

Instead of telephoning the Du Rhin or the police, Littorin went right back to the hotel with Miss Bökman, where he told the others in person what had happened. When the consternation had subsided, Rydbeck took charge, and placed a number of long-distance phone calls. He spoke first with Ekström, Kreuger's brother-in-law in Stockholm, and asked him to tell Kreuger's parents what had happened and to keep the news from the public. Rydbeck's idea, which everyone had quickly concurred in, was to avoid the panic that might result if European holders of Kreuger securities placed selling orders on the New York market, which in 1932 was open until noon on Saturday— five P.M. Paris time.

In that connection, Durant immediately sent a cablegram to Lee, Higginson in New York which said cryptically: "For partners only Oak [a code name for Kreuger] died very suddenly today not public yet please say nothing until announced here." Durant was later criticized for failing to let it be known at once that Kreuger had killed himself, and he was asked, during the ensuing Senate investigation into banking and currency practices, if he had not regarded it as "a moral duty" to tell the full facts at once that unhappy Saturday so that investors could protect themselves. He claimed, rather unconvincingly, that he thought it was up to the police to make any announcement of suicide, as "I did not know it, I was not there."

His cable was received by Lee, Higginson about ten o'clock, and when George Murnane, the senior partner on hand, opened it, he felt, as he later said, "as if I had no wind left." Having gone to so much trouble to re-establish Kreuger's position, he added, "I suddenly knew we had all been idiots." Lee, Higginson, however, although its partners as well as its customers had invested heavily in Kreuger stock, did no trading in Kreuger securities that morning, except that it canceled some buying orders. Even so, one hundred and sixty-five thousand Kreuger & Toll shares were sold in Wall Street between ten o'clock and noon, and nearly all the orders emanated from Paris. Unwitting investors here gobbled them quickly, so that at one time the price had risen thirty-seven cents, and the stock closed at the opening figure of five dollars a share.

The Saturday trading in New York, the manner in which the suicide was handled by the Paris police, and the known hostility toward Kreuger in certain quarters led some of his partisans to maintain later that he had been murdered. Kreuger being Kreuger, it was probably inevitable that such stories would be spread, and they have been promoted through the years by a number of persons whose fate was closely tied to Kreuger's death. Though no one in his entourage who was in Paris at the time has ever expressed any doubt that it was suicide, Kreuger's enemies were certainly far from sorry to see him pass from the scene, and it was widely felt, even among those who had no suspicion of murder, that the case was ineptly investigated. The authorities were not informed of the death until three o'clock in the afternoon, when Littorin, Miss Bökman, and Veron, the concierge's husband, finally made their way through the crowds of Briand mourners to the nearest available police station, at No. 154 Faubourg St. Honoré. Police Commissioner Felix Mangaud went immediately to the apartment, followed by a police surgeon, who found the body "still semi-warm" at four o'clock and declared that "death appears to have occurred by suicide with a firearm." There were two cartridges remaining in the gun, and an empty cartridge case was on the floor alongside the bed. Mangaud, who seemed more impressed by the fact that the dead man was a Grand Officer of the French Legion of Honor than by anything else, interrogated Littorin and Miss Bökman. At Littorin's request, ostensibly to protect relatives, the news was withheld from the public until six o'clock Paris time, an hour after the close of the New York Stock Exchange.

The police never examined the gun for fingerprints, no effort was made to discover who tried to phone Kreuger in the hour before his death, and the activities of his financial enemies in Paris were not investigated. Within a week one of the chief speculators was arrested, and eventually was sentenced to five years in prison for illegal stock dealing, but the ramifications of the bear ring were not looked into, and hence the source of all the selling orders that flooded Wall Street that day was never identified. Kreuger's other enemies had been the Russians, and none of the stateless Russians living in Paris were questioned either, though they had occasionally acted as middlemen for Moscow in the long, abortive negotiations between Kreuger and the Communists. (An incidental macabre note was the discovery, at Kreuger's bedside, of the novel written two years before by Ilya Ehrenburg about the match king named Olsson, whose machinations and villainy end with his death from a heart attack in a Paris apartment.)

Although the police got the gun-shop salesman to identify a picture of Kreuger, he subsequently failed to recognize several other photographs of the dead financier which were shown him, and the murder theorists emphasized this fact. Beyond the disagreement about the time when Kreuger was supposed to have bought the gun, it was thought odd that he should have given his right name to the salesman, and it was suggested that the purchaser might have been someone else who looked like him—a specific Russian agent was mentioned. As the concierge and her husband had been uncertain on the morning of the 12th as to whether Kreuger was out or in, it was argued that they could have missed the comings and goings of others also. The most farfetched story, but one that was given considerable circulation, maintained that a man with the alias of John C. Brown, a "well-known agent of J. P. Morgan," visited Kreuger about ten thirty and told him that his fate was sealed and that he had no recourse but to kill himself.

There was so much talk about the case—including some really wild rumors that the corpse had been a fake and that Kreuger had escaped and was living in faraway seclusion —that the police released a report of sorts a year later. It recounted the events and included statements corroborating the suicide from Kreuger's associates who had been in Paris at the time, but it failed to satisfy everybody. Most damaging to the murder theory are the three letters Kreuger left. It would have been hard for anyone to force him to write so personal a note to Littorin—the handwriting was identified as his by an expert who noted "strong emotional tensions . . . signs of unrealistic hopes and desires, a pathos based on illusions which ended in tragedy and loneliness." The letter to Schéle, the one written originally in New York, included the ten-thousand-dollar note Kreuger had tried to give Schéle the day before—surely another firm indication that he was about to kill himself; the brief note, unaltered since he had prepared it, dealt with some stock-market matters, specifically with closing some accounts. The third letter, to Kreuger's sister Britta, was never made public by her. There is a strong suspicion that it was a clear and positive personal declaration of intention to commit suicide, and that she was persuaded to keep it secret by Torsten Kreuger, who for twenty years following his brother's death engaged in a costly and rather pathetic campaign to clear the Kreuger name.

CHAPTER 10

Truth and Consequences

THE DEATH of Ivar Kreuger proved to be the most disillusioning and shattering experience in the lives of many individuals, and the painful revelation that the genius was a swindler and a forger was probably the greatest blow the morale of the world of finance as a whole has ever suffered. It was all the more painful for the way in which the truth came to light, in the manner of a suspense story told in slowly unfolding installments.

While to the world at large the suicide at first appeared a compelling personal rather than public calamity, those close to the situation and aware of the fearful pressure of the financier's final weeks were quick to suspect the broader implications. Late on the day that Kreuger killed himself, practically everyone in Paris who had been importantly associated with him gathered in one room at the Hotel du Rhin—the visiting Americans, the bankers and Kreuger aides from France and Sweden, and the various accountants. The session quickly turned into a financial wake that took the form of a series of embarrassing confrontations. These proved especially discomfiting to Durant and Hallowell as the representatives of the Americans who had blindly supported Kreuger for so many years. Cederschïold, the Paris man, who had handled some inconclusive Spanish negotiations for him, revealed that Spain had never granted a match concession, though the Americans had been told by Kreuger that they had got the concession in return for a twenty-nine-million-dollar loan to Spain, on which Kreuger held bonds. "When I looked up, I saw staring eyes and harsh faces," Cederschïold said afterward, "and I remembered Kreuger's warning about the need for secrecy on Spain, that it should include Lee, Higginson & Co."

In turn, neither Cederschïold nor Littorin nor Rydbeck had ever heard of the Dutch company called Garanta, which was supposed to be doing millions of dollars' worth of match business as a distribution monopoly in Poland and was considered another of the Americans' major assets, but turned out to be phony. "Everyone was asking questions of everyone else, and no one knew too much about anything," Sune Schéle said. Cederschïold summed up his private feelings, which must have been general: "Kreuger's death was a great calamity, but these doubts were a thousand times worse. I had lost him twice that day."

The news of the suicide became generally known in Sweden between six and seven o'clock in the evening, and it caused an immediate sensation. Restaurants, cafés, and theaters were emptied, and people clustered on street corners to discuss the event in hushed and awed voices. King Gustav was vacationing on the Riviera, but his son, Crown Prince Gustav Adolf, serving as regent, rushed from a Masonic meeting to an emergency cabinet session called to consider a moratorium on payment of all debts to Kreuger & Toll—Prime Minister Ekman had wisely prepared such a measure in late February. The wheels turned quickly. At ten thirty the Riksdag—the Parliament—met, and at one o'clock in the morning the measure was passed. The cabinet, gathered at the Palace, voted at three to implement it immediately. That day, Sunday, was a day of national mourning, and flags were put at half-staff.

Everywhere in the world the news that the depression had now claimed the great Kreuger was received with a consummate sense of shock, and in the days that followed, while Kreuger's body lay in a white cloth on the bed in his flower-filled Paris apartment, awaiting embalming, the prevailing reaction continued to be one of tremendous sadness and of admiration for the dead financier. The only exceptions were the voices of the Communists and the Socialists, who decried the evils of capitalism as personified by Kreuger. Per Albin Hansson, the Socialist leader in Sweden, for example, who soon succeeded Ekman as Prime Minister in the wake of the scandal, wrote: "I think we can speak of another example of the danger of private enterprise and private initiative being allowed to run wild in the economic sector without any social control."

It would not take long for the spell to break and for Hansson's harsh words to be vindicated. The Swedish bankers who were to have met with Kreuger on March 13 in Berlin rushed back to Stockholm, where Finance Minister Hamrin made it clear that the planned investigation of Kreuger's affairs would not be delayed. Officials advised calmness and expressed the hope that the Kreuger concerns would all be found solvent; this was in part a successful effort to avoid runs on banks, though there were several suicides of small investors. A six-man commission of prominent persons was appointed on March 15, and it called in the Price, Waterhouse accountants at once to conduct the examination that was to be so prolonged. During that entire week of March 14 the stock exchange in Stockholm was closed, but there was considerable activity elsewhere in the world. In New York, on Monday alone, sales of Kreuger & Toll certificates, at five dollars or less a share, totaled six hundred and seventy-four thousand shares —a third of the total market volume for the day. With no voice of suspicion against Kreuger yet raised, long-believing investors rushed to pick up what they falsely hoped would be bargains. Back in 1929 the same stock had sold for forty-six dollars a share, and earlier in 1932 it had sold for twenty-seven, so it seemed a good enough buy now. Within weeks it would go down to five cents, and ultimately it would sell for as little as three cents a share.

In Paris, Bernard Lane, an embalmer from Cincinnati who was working abroad, had the distinction of preparing the remains of Ivar Kreuger, and on Tuesday the body was placed in a zinc coffin, which was then put into a heavy oak one. Each had a small window in the top so that the face of Kreuger could be seen—this was quite customary in France, and Kreuger's family in Stockholm had requested it. About twenty persons saw the body before it was sealed away, but the little windows served to encourage subsequent rumors that a wax figure had been substituted and that Kreuger was still alive somewhere. On the 17th the coffin was loaded onto a baggage car attached to the Nord Express. The only persons who came to the station were three White Russians, and the only accompanying flowers were some lilies of the valley contributed by an anonymous old lady who had read that they were Kreuger's favorites. When the train got to Stockholm a day and a half later, the coffin was taken to a small church for private viewing. The funeral was held on the 22nd at the Stockholm Crematory, on the northern side of the city. Thousands lined the way from the church—other thousands were demonstrating against unemployment that day —but only two hundred and seventy-five ticket holders were allowed to watch the brief services. There was another profusion of flowers, including a seventy-five-dollar wreath from Sosthenes Behn in New York. The pastor spoke of life's "instability" and asked rhetorically if it were nothing but "a gamble of blind powers without meaning and without goal." The coffin was lowered into the crematory flames to the playing of a Beethoven sonata, and all that was left of Ivar Kreuger was a three-and-a-half-liter box of ash, the usual amount for a man of his stature.

Three days later came the first indication that Kreuger would hardly rest in peace. The investigating commission, in its first pronouncement, declared that "the appraisal made so far . . . seems to show that the position of the company [Kreuger & Toll] is not tenable, and that its assets, in case of foreclosure at current values, would not with certainty be sufficient for the paying of all obligations." In New York, Lee, Higginson & Co. began to get nervous and issued a statement pointing out that "the conclusion reached . . . is strongly at variance with the company's published report for the year 1930" adding that Kreuger, while in New York, had indicated that everything was in good order. The next warning flag went up four days later when the Scandinaviska bank in Stockholm, which had claims on Kreuger and his companies amounting to approximately a hundred million dollars, was promised a supporting credit of some fifty million from the government and a loan of another ten million from private banks.

On the morning of April 6 the romantic image of Kreuger started to flicker out for good with the publication of Price, Waterhouse's first findings: that Kreuger had "grossly misrepresented the true financial position" of Kreuger & Toll and its affiliated concerns in his 1930 balance sheets, and that he had been doctoring his figures flagrantly. Lee, Higginson's sad admission of Kreuger's apparent hoodwinking of his American friends followed, and then, in mid-April, came the awful diclosure that Kreuger was a forger of bonds.

ITALIAN MILLIONS WERE JUST SWEDISH PAPER, the headlines blared. The miserable details were provided the next day by the Stockholm printer of the bonds, who had acted in complete good faith, and by former Foreign Minister Johannes Hellner, who had secretly been sent to Italy by the investigating commission to talk to Mussolini. Mussolini had immediately denounced the signatures of two officials on the bonds as forgeries. Hellner had replied that "it would be desirable for all concerned if clear proof could be brought out regarding the falsity of the documents," and a protocol to that effect was then prepared and signed by the two officials and by Mussolini himself. Hellner triumphantly brought it back to Stockholm. He was subsequently criticized for having approached the Italians in the manner of a man seeking proof for his worst preconceptions, instead of as a creditors' representative searching for information. There was no doubt that Kreuger had forged the bonds, but Hellner made it easy for Mussolini to attest to the fraud without going into the question of whether he had actually received secret payments from Kreuger, which still seems not altogether impossible. This would have been hard to prove—Mussolini certainly would have been loath to admit it—but the net effect of Hellner's fast trip was to wipe out overnight an asset of twenty-seven million dollars that the International Match Corporation in New York, supposedly owning the Italian match monopoly, was carrying on its books.

The disclosure of the forgeries, on top of what Price, Waterhouse had already found out, turned the Kreuger case into a full-fledged scandal with world-wide ramifications. In Stockholm a criminal investigation was begun, and during the summer a procession of strange Kreuger henchmen from all over Europe poured into Sweden. First to be apprehended, questioned, and indicted for conspiracy to commit fraud were the obscure dupes that the public had never heard of before, the shady accountants and undercover agents Kreuger had employed to falsify the books of his far-flung subsidiaries, many of which turned out to be empty shells pretending to do millions' worth of investment business. A white-bearded man named Lange admitted to running the books of the fictitious Garanta company in Holland. A footloose pair named Bredberg and Holm related how, at Kreuger's dictation, they had entered millions of dollars in stocks and bonds in the books of Dutch and Swiss and Liechtenstein companies without ever having seen any of the securities. A slick fellow named Huldt tried to explain how he had run one of Kreuger's dummy banks, passing fictitious investments in and out of it at Kreuger's behest. All these enterprises were revealed as parts of Kreuger's basic effort to inflate his total values so that investors would gobble up his successive stock issues.

As the investigation unfolded, it became apparent that the top directors and accountants in Stockholm, men such as Krister Littorin and Sigurd Hennig, must or should have known what was going on and that their failure to carry out their responsibilities amounted to criminal carelessness and neglect. They, too, were questioned and indicted, and the total testimony and evidence of the pre-trial police investigation alone comprised eight thousand pages gathered into fifty bulky volumes. The twenty persons eventually found guilty were sentenced to terms that varied from a few months, as in Littorin's case, to three years, as in Hennig's.

One of the most tragic figures in the scandal was the believing banker Oscar Rydbeck who had hitched his wagon so firmly to Kreuger's star. Rydbeck, highly esteemed everywhere for his abilities, resigned from the Scandinaviska bank three weeks after the suicide, and, while he still insisted that Kreuger could not have been "consciously dishonest," he ruefully admitted that "he evidently suffered from some kind of megalomania that made him feel like a superman whose superiority to all others entitled him to disregard ordinary ideas of right and wrong." Even as the evidence to the contrary began to come in, Rydbeck maintained that "all of Kreuger's reports were perfectly clear and logical and one could not suspect them," and he declared that the directors could not have been expected to follow all of Kreuger's operations because so much had been done secretly for seemingly good reason. After suffering a stroke and losing his fortune, Rydbeck went to jail for ten months for having failed to carry out his responsibilities as a Kreuger & Toll director. It is significant that the men who had been closest to Kreuger were the most willing to forgive him. "He wished good to all humans," Rydbeck insisted, and Littorin, whose life was surely shortened by the tragic affair, declared: "Ivar made me a big man, important and rich. I'm going to jail and I'm ruined, but my only regret is the way he finished, that my beloved friend is dead."

The man with the greatest legacy of bitterness was Kreuger's brother, Torsten, the only member of the immediate family who went to prison (Ernst Kreuger, the father, though a board member, was deemed too old). Torsten, at the time of this writing in his seventies, had never got along particularly well with his older brother, although they had been associated in business as far back as 1920. There were stories that he had been a devil's advocate, and contrary claims that he had tried unsuccessfully to restrain Ivar's wildest speculations. Whatever the truth was, Torsten served a year and a half as a result of a rather minor machination involving a pulp mill supported by Kreuger & Toll and the sale of its bonds to the public on the basis of fraudulent earnings statements. A number of intricate legal points in the case raised doubts in the minds of many as to Torsten's culpability, and he has spent a minor fortune in the last two and a half decades seeking to have the case reviewed and stirring up other aspects of the Kreuger debacle, including the scandal in Paris which arose out of the bear attacks there toward the end. Torsten still insists that his brother's bitter financial enemies in France, whose influence extended to America, had him murdered, and he has sponsored considerable propaganda in support of his argument. Two Stockholm newspapers that he owned until 1956 were used as instruments to promote his cause, and until very recently he was engaged in an obsessive search for absolution. In 1960 he more or less retired from the fray and moved to Switzerland—still a wealthy man.

Much more difficult than the criminal snarls of the Kreuger case to unravel were the financial. To dispose of Kreuger's personal trappings was simple enough—auctions were held in Stockholm, Berlin, London, Paris, and Amsterdam, and such things as his two fast motorboats, originally worth thousands, were sold for less than two hundred dollars—but the disposition of his corporate assets was extremely complicated. It had to be determined, first, what was real and what was false; then, who owned what and how the assets that remained should be divided; and, finally, what should be done with the salvageable companies. This became a monumental task, and for a period of at least a year Stockholm was a primary financial capital of the world. The high priests of the investigation were the accountants, particularly those of Price, Waterhouse, who had to trace back Kreuger's manipulations over fifteen years. This involved delving into the affairs of most of the four hundred companies the financier owned, operated, or had an interest in around the globe, ranging from major industrial enterprises of which he personally held all or most of the stock to such out-of-the-way holdings as two shares of a golf club in Chile.

In general, the accountants found his bookkeeping not only inadequate "but in some respects primitive" and "so childish that anybody with but a rudimentary knowledge of bookkeeping could see that the books were being falsified." There were, for example, a total of nearly seven hundred million dollars of entries under debits or credits in the books of Kreuger & Toll and its Dutch offspring, of Swedish Match, and of the Continental Investment Corporation which were not responded to—that is, items that appeared in one set of corporate books but were not listed where they should have been, as corresponding entries, in another set. Continental, for example, had one hundred and seventeen charges against Kreuger & Toll, but the latter had responded to only sixteen of them in its books. Most often, toward the end especially, a company's principal asset would be a claim on Ivar Kreuger himself; by simply debiting huge items in this fashion Kreuger had been able to create, kite, or dispose of values at will, and his balance sheets had ultimately become mere playthings.

Summing up in a final report, Price, Waterhouse wrote: "The perpetration of frauds on so large a scale and over so long a period would have been impossible but for (1) the confidence which Kreuger succeeded in inspiring, (2) the acceptance of his claim that complete secrecy in relation to vitally important transactions was essential to the success of the projects, (3) the autocratic powers which were conferred upon him, and (4) the loyalty or unquestioning obedience of officials, who were evidently selected with great care (some for their ability and honesty, others for their weaknesses), having regard to the parts which Kreuger intended them to take in the execution of his plans."

Special investigating accountants for the various companies in the Kreuger empire, and for other concerns that had dealt with the financier, were busily engaged in the unraveling process too. So were lawyers by the dozen, whose fees for representing the key firms and such outsiders as International Telephone & Telegraph, as well as a number of stockholders' protective committees, each seeking to obtain as many scraps as possible from the carcass, ran to many hundreds of thousands of dollars (among the top legal talents representing American investors were a former Secretary of State, Bainbridge Colby, and a future one, John Foster Dulles). Both Kreuger & Toll and IMCO in New York were immediately thrown into bankruptcy, and some of the lawyers involved in the ensuing litigation and negotiation spent the best part of five years traveling from country to country in the effort to track down assets and ascertain the nature of contracts and agreements Kreuger had made. Governments themselves frequently became involved, and the State Department had to intervene on several occasions in attempts to move frozen funds out of places and to re-negotiate Kreuger bond deals and sales affecting Americans.

The essential financial facts, as summarized in Chapter One, were eye-opening, and in addition to the fact that the net assets of his companies were only about half what he was claiming at the end—two hundred million dollars instead of four hundred million—Kreuger's personal liabilities at the time of the suicide amounted to about two hundred and sixty-five million dollars.

Individual investors everywhere were the greatest sufferers. In the case of the International Match Corporation, into which stockholders in America had poured a hundred and fifty million dollars—ninety per cent of it supposedly invested in profitable match monopolies abroad—the American trustee in bankruptcy, the Irving Trust

Company, began with only one hundred and seventy thousand dollars in cash in March 1932. In 1945, when the trustee finally wound up its affairs, it had managed to collect, through settlement of claims and division of leftover assets, a gross sum of thirty-seven million dollars, the bulk of which was paid out in liquidating dividends to investors at the rate of about twenty-one cents on each dollar originally invested.

The trustee's representatives, notably the law firm of Rosenberg, Goldmark & Colin, found themselves operating for several years a match business that extended from Norway to Turkey and from Spain to Syria and reached all the way out to the Philippines. The theory held and gradually put into practice by James N. Rosenberg, the senior counsel, however, was that there was no sound basis for Kreuger's match concessions once the depression started and the economic apple cart was everywhere upset. Rosenberg insisted on liquidating the foreign companies as quickly as possible, and also disposing of foreign government bonds, and his approach was vindicated in the light of wartime disruption and post-war political developments.

Much of the litigation had to do with claims filed by individuals or individual firms against the estate and by various companies in the Kreuger group against one another —the total of intercompany claims reached the stupendous figure of $1,176,796,684, only eight and a half per cent of which was ultimately allowed by the courts. Of the thirteen match concessions IMCO was holding in its name, three of the biggest turned out to be purely fictitious, and at the time of Kreuger's death the corporation had actual possession of only two sets of bonds, those of Turkey and Guatemala. The legal difficulties were enhanced by the fact that Kreuger, who had been able to move the bonds around Europe at will, had made twenty-three substitutions of one set for another, invariably using valuable securities to raise cash or credit and replacing them with something of far less worth. The German-Italian switch was simply the most brazen. More typically, he took French bonds, for example, which were good as collateral and were marketable, and substituted Hungarian ones belonging to IMCO, which represented a frozen asset. Trying to determine what company had the right to what bonds caused great difficulties. After much wrangling, IMCO got back twenty-one million dollars' worth of German bonds from the Scandinaviska bank in Stockholm, and through the direct intervention of President Roosevelt and considerable diplomatic pressure, another two million dollars in interest from the German government was collected. IMCO then sold its recovered share to a Norwegian company for $6,300,000, considered a good price because of the depressed market.

While the directors of IMCO in New York had certainly been as negligent as their Swedish counterparts in failing to carry out their responsibilities, there were no criminal prosecutions here, but the gullibility and blind faith of Kreuger's American supporters were thoroughly publicized as a result of bankruptcy hearings and of inquiries conducted by the Senate and the Securities & Exchange Commission. Furthermore, the partners of Lee, Higginson & Co. and their families lost nine million dollars in the Kreuger crash, and the esteemed company, which had sold a billion dollars' worth of securities to the American public in almost a hundred years, was broken up and later reorganized on a smaller scale. During the IMCO bankruptcy hearing here, the bankers freely admitted how Kreuger had hoodwinked them. Frederic Allen, in relating how completely they had taken Kreuger's word for everything and accepted his financial statements without question, said: "As years went by, we came to have even greater confidence in him. I recall no case where his statements did not come true . . . and up to the time he committed suicide I personally had no doubt of the integrity of the man." Donald Durant, whose life, like Littorin's, was undoubtedly shortened by the emotional impact of the scandal—he died in his early fifties ten years later, of a heart attack—testified as follows:

> Q: Well, in the conduct of practical affairs, was he [Kreuger] or was he not the one single dominating person in the whole thing?
> A: Absolutely.
> Q: What he said went?
> A: Well, not always, I would not say that.
> Q: Can you name one case where it didn't so happen?
> A: Well, I will be glad to refresh my memory.
> Q: You search your memory and give me a single instance in which the will of Ivar Kreuger did not prevail and control.
> A: Well, he usually convinced . . . His opinion prevailed.

Despite the fact that they were offering millions' worth of Kreuger issues to American investors, the Lee, Higginson directors knew little or nothing about IMCO's biggest subsidiary abroad, the Continental Investment Corporation, which owed it seventy-five million dollars at the end, very little of which was recovered. The directors, furthermore, admitted they had never even seen the match contracts Kreuger had made with foreign countries. Samuel Pryor, one of the directors who testified, said: "There would be so many languages to speak, and I speak only one."

When the Kreuger crash occurred and it was quickly decided that Kreuger & Toll and IMCO were insolvent, it was felt that the Swedish Match Company, alone of the major concerns, was salvageable. It had more bona-fide assets and fewer obligations, and its earning capacities seemed greater. Although toward the end, when he became desperate, Kreuger had passed a number of fictitious and padded entries through its books, it had always been regarded by him as the most legitimate part of his business, and he had kept its affairs pretty well apart from the inflations and fictions with which he had riddled his other concerns. Under the careful, penny-pinching guidance of a group of hardheaded independent Swedish bankers and businessmen who had had nothing to do with the match business before and who were selected for just that reason, Swedish Match began by declaring a moratorium on its own debts. It then reduced its share capital from just under a hundred million dollars to about twenty-five million, and set up a large reserve fund that was used to offset the writing down of assets.

The major bankrupt Kreuger firms displayed considerable jealousy of Swedish Match's survival, and there was a lot of backbiting at first over its right to match properties and concessions that had been divided and shifted about by Kreuger according to his own whim and to expediency, but with the help of an international committee consisting of the American Norman Davis, Wallenberg in Sweden, and a British banker, Sir Hugh Kindersley, claims and counterclaims were finally disposed of after three years of negotiations. For cash of about ten million dollars and shares of its own worth another five million, Swedish Match bought the match concessions that had been owned by IMCO and Kreuger & Toll; the bulk of them, IMCO's, were formally transferred in a transatlantic phone conversation in July 1936 that lasted six minutes and cost fifty-one dollars and served as fitting climax in the light of Kreuger's habit of negotiating fabulous deals in the same way.

Since its reorganization, Swedish Match has slowly

grown again, and today it has majority or partial interests in about fifty foreign match companies, though it controls only about a quarter of the world's match business as compared to the three-quarters control Kreuger had. The concern is no longer considered one of Sweden's biggest, though it might have been had not Hitler and the war come along, followed by the post-war sweep of the Russians into the Baltic area and into eastern Europe, as a result of which many valuable concessions were lost.

Kreuger's other companies, including some that have grown to be far bigger than Swedish Match, have long since become separate and independent. They were all involved in the Kreuger & Toll bankruptcy proceedings and were also the cause of much dissension, as their ownership was often obscure as a result of Kreuger's having pledged and re-pledged his securities in so many ways. The Kreuger & Toll bankruptcies in Sweden and America advanced slowly—the trustee here started with eighty-four thousand dollars and ended with three million—but, ultimately, the holders of secured Kreuger & Toll debentures received about two thirds of their claims in liquidation dividends, and the non-priority holders got about forty-three per cent of theirs.

Because of the heavy liabilities, it was decided very early in the liquidation proceedings that the individual components of the Kreuger group had to be disposed of as soon as possible in order to settle Kreuger's many debts and release funds to pay off the thousands of creditors and claimants. The first to go was the valuable L. M. Ericsson Telephone Company. The International Telephone & Telegraph Company renounced its eleven-million-dollar claim against Kreuger arising out of the abortive merger, in return for permission to keep the six hundred thousand shares of Ericsson stock it had received; this constituted a majority, but the Swedish courts later reduced the voting rights on those shares to one third. Other Ericsson shares, in Sweden, were pledged with banks for long-term credit to tide the company over. The Boliden mine went to the Scandinaviska bank to pay off part of Kreuger's debt there, and Kreuger's pulp trust went to the Handelsbanken which had been its main creditor—another well-known Swede, Axel Wenner-Gren, later bought a lot of these securities cheaply and made a fine profit out of them.

All of the banks that had given credit to Kreuger, especially the Scandinaviska bank, eventually got their money back when the collateral securities they were holding rose in value; the only losses they suffered were on loans they had given to individuals who had put up Kreuger stock as collateral. These people, mostly middle-class investors, were the Swedes who suffered most from the crash, and many of them lost all their savings. These losses were reflected in a ten-per-cent drop in taxable income in 1933. As most of Kreuger's business was done abroad, Sweden as a whole, however, did not suffer as much materially as morally from his demise.

Because the various Kreuger companies, such as Boliden and Ericsson, did well in the years after his death, his staunch defenders claimed that if the concerns had all been kept together under one roof, Kreuger & Toll would have weathered the storm, and that therefore it should not have been declared bankrupt. At least one writer, whose work was sponsored by Torsten Kreuger, described the dissolution of Kreuger's empire as "a jackal's feast" and "the greatest swindle of modern times," and declared that if the individual components "had been given a little breathing space they would have overcome their temporary liquidity difficulties without anybody needing to have lost a single cent." These partisans of Kreuger went further and maintained that Kreuger & Toll assets as a whole were improperly calculated and, in some cases, insufficiently traced. The argument included the claim that the Italian bonds represented a real value because Kreuger almost surely had made some sort of secret deal with Mussolini, that many of Kreuger's securities vanished at the end and were allegedly stolen by unknown henchmen to whom he had entrusted them in his efforts to raise more cash, and that many of the so-called fictitious entries on Kreuger's books were written off too hastily, without thorough investigation.

Whatever validity this point of view may have, it still seems unlikely that the break-up could have been delayed in the light of the obvious fabrications Kreuger had perpetrated, his squandering of capital through speculation and high dividends, and the mountain of claims against him. In the circumstances, everyone involved in dissecting Kreuger's financial corpse was justified in wanting to get what he could out of it as soon as possible. It was scarcely a time to be either patient or generous; and if it is true that other assets might have been found, or some false ones proved real, it was surely due to Kreuger's obsessive secrecy, and to his never letting his left hand know what his right was doing, that no other course but the one taken was feasible.

The mess Kreuger left after his death created some lasting ramifications. A protective committee for part of the gold debentures sold in America, and for which certificates of deposit are still, in 1960, being traded occasionally on the Stock Exchange, has for years been trying to sell some of the Hungarian bonds Kreuger owned—the bonds ostensibly retain some value, though the Communist government in Hungary refuses to recognize them. "We're stuck, we've been looking for a way to go out of business for fifteen years," says Tristan Antell, the broker who began guiding the committee's fortunes back in 1932. Until the bonds are disposed of somehow, Antell remains obligated to keep the committee alive. There are other continuing manifestations of Kreuger, not only in the match companies that still exist but also in small, scattered examples of the sway he once held over an entire industry. Travelers passing through parts of the Azores, for example, are warned by customs officials to declare any lighters they are carrying. An old Kreuger match-monopoly clause forbidding their importation is still in effect, and anyone caught using one in public is liable to a stiff fine.

Despite the eventful years since Ivar Kreuger shot himself, he is still one of the most vividly recalled and widely debated figures in the annals of high, and low, finance. Undoubtedly, in lending millions to European nations in the mid-twenties, he accomplished a positive good for which his sympathizers would chiefly like to remember him, but his greater contribution would seem to be his negative though salutary function in exposing an era of unbridled profligacy. His historical role was a dual one of victim and victimizer. It has been said of him that he was dishonest from the start and had bad luck at the end, but there was more to him and his case than that. When he rode high, he was the incarnate personality of his time, the symbol of wealth run rampant, but there was always the other aspect, the controlled and aloof individual, above the battle. Though he was less greedy for money than hungry for the sort of power that thrives on achieving the difficult and then strives for the impossible, his contempt for others and his cynical carelessness rooted in amorality blurred his role as a practical idealist who was also, ultimately, an impractical crook.

In the line of financial wizards, he followed naturally in the footsteps of such contradictory figures as the early eighteenth-century adventurer John Law, who developed the idea of government-supported stock companies and whose progressive scheme for French colonial development in Mississippi caused him to overreach himself and led him to disgrace. A more immediate mentor was Camille Castiglione, the Austro-Italian financier who masterminded the ascension of a single group to control over all the important Austrian industries after the First World War and who was the direct inspiration for the economic pyramids built first by Stinnes in Germany and then, on an even grander scale, by Kreuger.

In an economically healthy world Kreuger could not have achieved his startling success, at least not so easily. It must be emphasized again that he gained it because of the dislocation in post-war Europe and the availability of immobilized capital in America, to which he so early staked out a unique claim. He used to boast that the secret of his match loans was a twelve-per-cent return—the lending of capital at six-per-cent interest and a six-per-cent profit on the concessions he obtained—but the real secret was his robust dividends, which enabled him to go on raising all the capital he wanted through his vast stock issues. As a financial irrigator, he dreamed of creating a sort of international monetary superstate to collect all the savings of investors and apply them to worth-while projects that would also pay permanently good returns. The depression may have kept him from extending his hegemony over the pulp and telephone industries and moving further toward the aim he sought, but long before the slump began he had already succumbed to the speculative urge that increasingly made him more of a stock-market gambler than anything else, a vender and a buyer of pieces of paper whose value was purely arbitrary and ultimately illusory.

Indeed, Kreuger became the chief financial fantasist in the period when, in America especially, the mere smell of money lured multitudes down the primrose path. Kreuger's success, in these circumstances, depended on his being a self-perpetuating myth. Power equaled expansion, and

withdrawal equaled powerlessness, and he had to maintain
the appearance of organic growth in his companies,
whether they were real or false, and at the same time promote his private image as a modern alchemist. It is at this
point that his own personality must be carefully appraised.
Actually, beyond his inordinate ability to project figures
and schemes, he had little imagination and not much intuition. His essential gravity and reticence served to em-
phasize his isolation. Yet, without seeming to care about
people, he had an almost occult ability to make them respond to him and to feel in touch with his plans. It was
other-worldly, and so Kreuger often seemed.

Beyond the fact that Sweden was too small for him, he
was the sort of man who was bound to conquer in a foreign land, and the United States was of course made to order for him. Americans believed in him more than others
because they had so much more to start with, and wanted
still more. Kreuger offered it to them, and no questions
were asked. Lee, Higginson & Co., in fact, was no different
from most other major banking and investment houses of
the day. Anything that "worked" was "good business," and
it included mysterious foreign subsidiaries that were set up
in quaint pocketbook countries to avoid taxes, which
everyone was trying to do, and managerial secretiveness
and loose company laws, and lax accounting practices at
home and especially abroad. It would seem that the bankers
here should at least have been aware of the extent to which
Kreuger was weakening his organization by buying up his
own unsold securities, but even that was fairly common
practice. None of this is an excuse for what happened; it
simply serves to place Kreuger in time, and because his
turned out to be the greatest swindle, he became the greatest object lesson and was largely responsible for the subsequent reforms in accountancy and company direction
both here and in Sweden.

If the depression was the chief cause of Kreuger's disaster, there remains considerable doubt that, had he weathered it, he could have gone on indefinitely without detection. He might have reduced his falsifications and even made some dramatic pseudo-confession of his inflations; yet, beyond his ingrained habit of falsifying, he was shackled to the very system he pretended to outstrip. As he himself said, he did not believe in regular balance statements, in liabilities being set off against assets at stated intervals, but he had to put up a semblance of doing so; and while he thought about future fields to conquer, he was no reformer or even innovator at heart. Using standard crooked or shadowy methods, he dwelled completely in the present. It was not so much that, at the end, he exaggerated the importance of matches, or overestimated the stability of government bonds, or became too impressed with his talent for fooling all of the bankers all of the time, as that he really lacked the imaginative capacity to restrain himself and withdraw when he should have. One of his early biographers, Manfred Georg, wrote: "A man who believed in nothing except his own brain was bound some day to make a mistake in his calculations." Kreuger was a Raskolnikov of finance: he believed that superior men were not restricted by ordinary laws, and that the end justifies the means. Unlike Raskolnikov, who did not have the courage to go through with his plans, Kreuger did, but he was finally unable to face the consequences of what he had done, and others had to face them for him.

Index

A Note about the Author

EVER SINCE Robert Shaplen was a young crime reporter on the New York *Herald Tribune*, he has been fascinated by swindlers. His remarkable series for *The New Yorker* in 1955, "The Metamorphosis of Philip Musica"—the story of the McKesson and Robbins case—prompted him to look into the story of that greatest of all swindlers, Ivar Kreuger. In 1956 he spent a number of months in Kreuger's native Sweden and did research in England, France, and Germany, as well as in America, in preparation for this biography.

Shaplen was born in Philadelphia (1917), attended high school in Brooklyn, received his B.A. from the University of Wisconsin (1937) and an M.S. from the School of Journalism at Columbia University (1938). He was a Nieman Fellow at Harvard (1947-8). He lived abroad as a child when his newspaperman father, after covering the Russian Revolution for the United Press, was sent to post-World War I Germany by the New York *Tribune*. Following in his father's footsteps, Shaplen was a reporter and rewrite man for the *Herald Tribune* for six years until, in 1943, *Newsweek* sent him as a war correspondent to the Pacific. He followed MacArthur to Japan, and from 1945 to 1947 was chief of *Newsweek*'s Far East bureau, working out of Shanghai. During and after the war he did many broadcasts for NBC from Japan, the Philippines, and China. He now lives in New York with his wife and son. His previous books are *A Corner of the World* (1949), *Free Love and Heavenly Sinners* (1954), and *A Forest of Tigers* (1956). Shaplen is a regular contributor to *The New Yorker* and other magazines.

July 1960

A Note on the Type

THE TEXT of this book was set on the Linotype in Janson, a recutting made direct from the type cast from matrices long thought to have been made by Anton Janson, a Dutchman who was a practicing type-founder in Leipzig during the years 1668-1687. However, it has been conclusively demonstrated that these types are actually the work of Nicholas Kis (1650-1702), a Hungarian who learned his trade most probably from the master Dutch type-founder Dirk Voskens.

The type is an excellent example of the influential and sturdy Dutch types that prevailed in England prior to the development by William Caslon (1692-1766) of his own incomparable designs, which he evolved from these Dutch faces. The Dutch in their turn had been influenced by Claude Garamond (1510-1561) in France. The general tone of the Janson, however, is darker than Garamond and has a sturdiness and substance quite different from its predecessors.

This book was composed, printed, and bound by H. Wolff, New York. Paper manufactured by P. H. Glatfelter Company, Spring Grove, Pa. Typography and binding design by Vincent Torre.

Accounting Books Published by Garland

New Books

Ashton, Robert H., ed. *The Evolution of Behavioral Accounting Research: An Overview*. New York, 1984.

Ashton, Robert H., ed. *Some Early Contributions to the Study of Audit Judgment*. New York, 1984.

*Brief, Richard P., ed. *Corporate Financial Reporting and Analysis in the Early 1900s*. New York, 1986.

Brief, Richard P., ed. *Depreciation and Capital Maintenance*. New York, 1984.

Brief, Richard P., ed. *Four Classics on the Theory of Double-Entry Bookkeeping*. New York, 1982.

*Brief, Richard P., ed. *Estimating the Economic Rate of Return from Accounting Data*. New York, 1986

*Chambers, R. J., and G. W. Dean, eds. *Chambers on Accounting*. New York, 1986.
Volume I: Accounting, Management and Finance.
Volume II: Accounting Practice and Education.
Volume III: Accounting Theory and Research.
Volume IV: Price Variation Accounting.
Volume V: Continuously Contemporary Accounting.

Clarke, F. L. *The Tangled Web of Price Variation Accounting: The Development of Ideas Underlying Professional Prescriptions in Six Countries*. New York, 1982.

*Included in the Garland series Accounting Thought and Practice Through the Years.

Coopers & Lybrand. *The Early History of Coopers & Lybrand.* New York, 1984.

*Craswell, Allen. *Audit Qualifications in Australia 1950 to 1979.* New York, 1986.

Dean, G. W., and M. C. Wells, eds. *The Case for Continuously Contemporary Accounting.* New York, 1984.

Dean, G. W., and M. C. Wells, eds. *Forerunners of Realizable Values Accounting in Financial Reporting.* New York, 1982.

Edey, Harold C. *Accounting Queries.* New York, 1982.

*Edwards, J. R., ed. *Legal Regulation of British Company Accounts 1836–1900.* New York, 1986.

*Edwards, J. R., ed. *Reporting Fixed Assets in Nineteenth-Century Company Accounts.* New York, 1986.

Edwards, J. R., ed. *Studies of Company Records: 1830–1974.* New York, 1984.

Fabricant, Solomon. *Studies in Social and Private Accounting.* New York, 1982.

Gaffikin, Michael, and Michael Aitken, eds. *The Development of Accounting Theory: Significant Contributors to Accounting Thought in the 20th Century.* New York, 1982.

Hawawini, Gabriel A., ed. *Bond Duration and Immunization: Early Developments and Recent Contributions.* New York, 1982.

Hawawini, Gabriel, and Pierre Michel, eds. *European Equity Markets: Risk, Return, and Efficiency.* New York, 1984.

*Hawawini, Gabriel, and Pierre A. Michel. *Mandatory Financial Information and Capital Market Equilibrium in Belgium.* New York, 1986.

*Hawkins, David F. *Corporate Financial Disclosure, 1900–1933: A Study of Management Inertia within a Rapidly Changing Environment.* New York, 1986.

*Johnson, H. Thomas. *A New Approach to Management Accounting History.* New York, 1986.

*Kinney, William R., Jr., ed. *Fifty Years of Statistical Auditing.* New York, 1986.

Klemstine, Charles E., and Michael W. Maher. *Management Accounting Research: A Review and Annotated Bibliography.* New York, 1984.

*Lee, T. A., ed. *A Scottish Contribution to Accounting History.* New York, 1986.

*Lee, T. A. *Towards a Theory and Practice of Cash Flow Accounting.* New York, 1986.

Lee, Thomas A., ed. *Transactions of the Chartered Accountants Students' Societies of Edinburgh and Glasgow: A Selection of Writings, 1886–1958.* New York, 1984.

*McKinnon, Jill L. *The Historical Development and Operational Form of Corporate Reporting Regulation in Japan.* New York, 1986.

Nobes, Christopher, ed. *The Development of Double Entry: Selected Essays.* New York, 1984.

*Nobes, Christopher. *Issues in International Accounting.* New York, 1986.

*Parker, Lee D. *Developing Control Concepts in the 20th Century.* New York, 1986.

Parker, R. H. *Papers on Accounting History.* New York, 1984.

*Previts, Gary John, and Alfred R. Roberts, eds. *Federal Securities Law and Accounting 1933–1970; Selected Addresses.* New York, 1986.

*Reid, Jean Margo, ed. *Law and Accounting: Pre-1889 British Legal Cases.* New York, 1986.

Sheldahl, Terry K. *Beta Alpha Psi, from Alpha to Omega: Pursuing a Vision of Professional Education for Accountants, 1919–1945.* New York, 1982.

*Sheldahl, Terry K. *Beta Alpha Psi, from Omega to Zeta Omega: The Making of a Comprehensive Accounting Fraternity, 1946–1984.* New York, 1986.

Solomons, David. *Collected Papers on Accounting and Accounting Education*. New York, 1984.

Sprague, Charles F. *The General Principles of the Science of Accounts and the Accountancy of Investment*. New York, 1984.

Stamp, Edward. *Selected Papers on Accounting, Auditing, and Professional Problems*. New York, 1984.

*Storrar, Colin, ed. *The Accountant's Magazine—An Anthology*. New York, 1986.

Tantral, Panadda. *Accounting Literature in Non-Accounting Journals: An Annotated Bibliography*. New York, 1984.

*Vangermeersch, Richard, ed. *The Contributions of Alexander Hamilton Church to Accounting and Management*. New York, 1986.

*Vangermeersch, Richard, ed. *Financial Accounting Milestones in the Annual Reports of United States Steel Corporation—The First Seven Decades*. New York, 1986.

Whitmore, John. *Factory Accounts*. New York, 1984.

Yamey, Basil S. *Further Essays on the History of Accounting*. New York, 1982.

Zeff, Stephen A., ed. *The Accounting Postulates and Principles Controversy of the 1960s*. New York, 1982.

Zeff, Stephen A., ed. *Accounting Principles Through the Years: The Views of Professional and Academic Leaders 1938–1954*. New York, 1982.

Zeff, Stephen A., and Maurice Moonitz, eds. *Sourcebook on Accounting Principles and Auditing Procedures: 1917–1953 (in two volumes)*. New York, 1984.

Reprinted Titles

American Institute of Accountants. *Fiftieth Anniversary Celebration*. Chicago, 1963 (Garland reprint, 1982).

American Institute of Accountants. *Library Catalogue*. New York, 1937 (Garland reprint, 1982).

Arthur Andersen Company. *The First Fifty Years 1913–1963*. Chicago, 1963 (Garland reprint, 1984).

*Bevis, Heman W. *Corporate Financial Reporting in a Competitive Economy*. New York, 1965 (Garland reprint, 1986).

*Bonini, Charles P., Robert K. Jaedicke, and Harvey M. Wagner, eds. *Management Controls: New Directions in Basic Research*. New York, 1964 (Garland reprint, 1986).

Bray, F. Sewell. *Four Essays in Accounting Theory*. London, 1953. *Bound with* Institute of Chartered Accountants in England and Wales and the National Institute of Economic and Social Research. *Some Accounting Terms and Concepts*. Cambridge, 1951 (Garland reprint, 1982).

Brown, R. Gene, and Kenneth S. Johnston. *Paciolo on Accounting*. New York, 1963 (Garland reprint, 1984).

*Carey, John L., and William O. Doherty, eds. *Ethical Standards of the Accounting Profession*. New York, 1966 (Garland reprint, 1986).

Chambers, R. J. *Accounting in Disarray*. Melbourne, 1973 (Garland reprint, 1982).

Cooper, Ernest. *Fifty-seven Years in an Accountant's Office*. *See* Sir Russell Kettle.

Couchman, Charles B. *The Balance-Sheet*. New York, 1924 (Garland reprint, 1982).

Couper, Charles Tennant. *Report of the Trial... Against the Directors and Manager of the City of Glasgow Bank*. Edinburgh, 1879 (Garland reprint, 1984).

Cutforth, Arthur E. *Audits*. London, 1906 (Garland reprint, 1982).

Cutforth, Arthur E. *Methods of Amalgamation*. London, 1926 (Garland reprint, 1982).

Deinzer, Harvey T. *Development of Accounting Thought*. New York, 1965 (Garland reprint, 1984).

De Paula, F.R.M. *The Principles of Auditing*. London, 1915 (Garland reprint, 1984).

Dickerson, R. W. *Accountants and the Law of Negligence.* Toronto, 1966 (Garland reprint, 1982).

Dodson, James. *The Accountant, or, the Method of Bookkeeping Deduced from Clear Principles, and Illustrated by a Variety of Examples.* London, 1750 (Garland reprint, 1984).

Dyer, S. *A Common Sense Method of Double Entry Bookkeeping, on First Principles, as Suggested by De Morgan. Part I, Theoretical.* London, 1897 (Garland reprint, 1984).

*The Fifth International Congress on Accounting, 1938 [Kongress-Archiv 1938 des V. Internationalen Prüfungs- und Treuhand-Kongresses]. Berlin, 1938 (Garland reprint, 1986).

Finney, H. A. *Consolidated Statements.* New York, 1922 (Garland reprint, 1982).

Fisher, Irving. *The Rate of Interest.* New York, 1907 (Garland reprint, 1982).

Florence, P. Sargant. *Economics of Fatigue of Unrest and the Efficiency of Labour in English and American Industry.* London, 1923 (Garland reprint, 1984).

Fourth International Congress on Accounting 1933. London, 1933 (Garland reprint, 1982).

Foye, Arthur B. *Haskins & Sells: Our First Seventy-Five Years.* New York, 1970 (Garland reprint, 1984).

Garnsey, Sir Gilbert. *Holding Companies and Their Published Accounts.* London, 1923. *Bound with* Sir Gilbert Garnsey. *Limitations of a Balance Sheet.* London, 1928 (Garland reprint, 1982).

Garrett, A. A. *The History of the Society of Incorporated Accountants, 1885–1957.* Oxford, 1961 (Garland reprint, 1984).

Gilman, Stephen. *Accounting Concepts of Profit.* New York, 1939 (Garland reprint, 1982).

*Gordon, William. *The Universal Accountant, and Complete Merchant...[Volume II].* Edinburgh, 1765 (Garland reprint, 1986).

*Green, Wilmer. *History and Survey of Accountancy*. Brooklyn, 1930 (Garland reprint, 1986).

Hamilton, Robert. *An Introduction to Merchandise, Parts IV and V (Italian Bookkeeping and Practical Bookkeeping)*. Edinburgh, 1788 (Garland reprint, 1982).

Hatton, Edward. *The Merchant's Magazine: or, Trades-man's Treasury*. London, 1695 (Garland reprint, 1982).

Hills, George S. *The Law of Accounting and Financial Statements*. Boston, 1957 (Garland reprint, 1982).

A History of Cooper Brothers & Co. 1854 to 1954. London, 1954 (Garland reprint, 1986).

Hofstede, Geert. *The Game of Budget Control*. Assen, 1967 (Garland reprint, 1984).

Howitt, Sir Harold. *The History of The Institute of Chartered Accountants in England and Wales 1880–1965, and of Its Founder Accountancy Bodies 1870–1880*. London, 1966 (Garland reprint, 1984).

Institute of Chartered Accountants in England and Wales and The National Institute of Economic and Social Research. *Some Accounting Terms and Concepts. See* F. Sewell Bray.

Institute of Chartered Accountants of Scotland. *History of the Chartered Accountants of Scotland from the Earliest Times to 1954*. Edinburgh, 1954 (Garland reprint, 1984).

International Congress on Accounting 1929. New York, 1930 (Garland reprint, 1982).

*Jaedicke, Robert K., Yuji Ijiri, and Oswald Nielsen, eds. *Research in Accounting Measurement*. American Accounting Association, 1966 (Garland reprint, 1986).

Keats, Charles. *Magnificent Masquerade*. New York, 1964 (Garland reprint, 1982).

Kettle, Sir Russell. *Deloitte & Co. 1845–1956*. Oxford, 1958. *Bound with* Ernest Cooper *Fifty-seven Years in an Accountant's Office*. London, 1921 (Garland reprint, 1982).

Kitchen, J., and R. H. Parker. *Accounting Thought and Education: Six English Pioneers*. London, 1980 (Garland reprint, 1984).

Lacey, Kenneth. *Profit Measurement and Price Changes*. London, 1952 (Garland reprint, 1982).

Lee, Chauncey. *The American Accomptant*. Lansingburgh, 1797 (Garland reprint, 1982).

Lee, T. A., and R. H. Parker. *The Evolution of Corporate Financial Reporting*. Middlesex, 1979 (Garland reprint, 1984).

*Malcolm, Alexander. *A Treatise of Book-Keeping, or, Merchants Accounts; In the Italian Method of Debtor and Creditor; Wherein the Fundamental Principles of That Curious and Approved Method Are Clearly and Fully Explained and Demonstrated...To Which Are Added, Instructions for Gentlemen of Land Estates, and Their Stewards or Factors: With Directions Also for Retailers, and Other More Private Persons*. London, 1731 (Garland reprint, 1986).

*Meij, J. L., ed. *Depreciation and Replacement Policy*. Chicago, 1961 (Garland reprint, 1986).

Newlove, George Hills. *Consolidated Balance Sheets*. New York, 1926 (Garland reprint, 1982).

*North, Roger. *The Gentleman Accomptant; or, An Essay to Unfold the Mystery of Accompts; By Way of Debtor and Creditor, Commonly Called Merchants Accompts, and Applying the Same to the Concerns of the Nobility and Gentry of England*. London, 1714 (Garland reprint, 1986).

Pryce-Jones, Janet E., and R. H. Parker. *Accounting in Scotland: A Historical Bibliography*. Edinburgh, 1976 (Garland reprint, 1984).

Robinson, H. W. *A History of Accountants in Ireland*. Dublin, 1964 (Garland reprint, 1984).

Robson, T. B. *Consolidated and Other Group Accounts*. London, 1950 (Garland reprint, 1982).

Rorem, C. Rufus. *Accounting Method*. Chicago, 1928 (Garland reprint, 1982).

*Saliers, Earl A., ed. *Accountants' Handbook.* New York, 1923 (Garland reprint, 1986).

Samuel, Horace B. *Shareholder's Money.* London, 1933 (Garland reprint, 1982).

The Securities and Exchange Commission in the Matter of McKesson & Robbins, Inc. Report on Investigation. Washington, D.C., 1940 (Garland reprint, 1982).

The Securities and Exchange Commission in the Matter of McKesson & Robbins, Inc. Testimony of Expert Witnesses. Washington, D.C., 1939 (Garland reprint, 1982).

*Shaplen, Robert. *Kreuger: Genius and Swindler.* New York, 1960 (Garland reprint, 1986).

Singer, H.W. *Standardized Accountancy in Germany.* (With a new appendix.) Cambridge, 1943 (Garland reprint, 1982).

The Sixth International Congress on Accounting. London, 1952 (Garland reprint, 1984).

*Stewart, Jas. C. (with a new introductory note by T. A. Lee). *Pioneers of a Profession: Chartered Accountants to 1879.* Edinburgh, 1977 (Garland reprint, 1986).

Thompson, Wardbaugh. *The Accomptant's Oracle: or, Key to Science, Being a Compleat Practical System of Book-keeping.* York, 1777 (Garland reprint, 1984).

*Vatter, William J. *Managerial Accounting.* New York, 1950 (Garland reprint, 1986).

*Woolf, Arthur H. *A Short History of Accountants and Accountancy.* London, 1912 (Garland reprint, 1986).

Yamey, B. S., H. C. Edey, and Hugh W. Thomson. *Accounting in England and Scotland: 1543–1800.* London, 1963 (Garland reprint, 1982).